1/94

FEB 11

94   95   96   99   +uo9
          111   96   99   1
                    7
11   10
      7
09
7

ILL JAN 86

ERIC CLAPTON

THE COMPLETE
RECORDING SESSIONS

1963–1992

ERIC CLAPTON

THE COMPLETE RECORDING SESSIONS

1963–1992

Marc Roberty

ST. MARTIN'S PRESS
NEW YORK

For Verushka, Aslan and Chyna

ISBN 0–312–09798-0

First published in Great Britain by Blandford
(a Cassell imprint)
First U.S. Edition: October 1993
10 9 8 7 6 5 4 3 2 1

CONTENTS

You can't make music lie. It's either in tune or not.
It's either appealing to you or it isn't.
ERIC CLAPTON

ACKNOWLEDGEMENTS

I have followed Eric's musical career from The Yardbirds right through to the present and have kept up-to-date information on all his recordings. However, this book would not have been as complete had it not been for the kind co-operation of Bill Levenson, of Polygram in New York. Bill provided me with access to Polygram's tape vault in New Jersey, where all of Eric's tapes from the RSO period reside. I was able to listen to material and photocopy tape boxes, which enabled me to verify information, as well as to unearth long-forgotten and sometimes unknown sessions.

I would like to thank Eric's manager, Roger Forrester, as well as his personal assistant, Di Puplett, who have always been kind enough to provide me with information over the years.

A very special thank you goes to photographer John Peck for use of his pictorial work.

And lastly, thanks must also be given to Roger Gibbons and John Bauldie for use of certain passages from their Eric Clapton interview, printed in the excellent Bob Dylan Quarterly, *The Telegraph*.

Finally, 'Hello' to Guy and Mady Roberty, Karen Daws, Rose Clapp, Pat McDonald and Heather Sorensen.

Marc Roberty

Eric live at Royal Albert Hall, London, 1987

PREFACE

In the following pages, I have attempted to list all of Eric Clapton's officially recorded sessions – studio and live – and the material recorded at the sessions, whether released or unreleased.

I have also compiled and listed, within the same overall chronological order, all of the sessions on which Eric guested over the years. In so doing, his considerable musical contribution to the recorded output of other artists may well come as something of a surprise to readers whose initial interest is Eric's recording career as the featured artist. Many of the quotes from Eric and other participating musicians were obtained first hand and add to the fascination of the sessions.

As may be inferred from my Acknowledgements to this book, the work of research and compilation has been immense. One of the main problems in such a mammoth task has been to identify (hopefully) all of the many rumours about Eric's career which have appeared and gathered momentum over the years. In so doing, I have felt it a duty either to quash or to confirm such rumours as accurately as possible in light of my research. It has not always been a straightforward matter, given the length of the man's recording career and the near-legendary status of his music and of many of the associated stories. Nevertheless, I can confirm with certainty that Eric did *not* play on the following albums: The Beatles' ABBEY ROAD, George Harrison's DARK HORSE, Delaney Bramlett's CLASSIC REUNION and The Rolling Stones' BEGGARS BANQUET; nor did he play on Screaming Lord Sutch's 'Hand of Jack the Ripper' or Chas and Dave's 'Don't Give a Monkey's'.

Thereafter, I can state that Eric has appeared on every session listed in the book.

Wherever possible, and to avoid confusion about where tracks have appeared or been released over the years – original singles, album tracks, repackaged albums, 'Best of' releases, all manner of CDs, etc. – I have given the current availability of each session track (which is increasingly on CD only). However, the 'full story' of release patterns is presented as a total picture in the Discography on page 171.

One thing that did emerge during my research is the immense wealth of unreleased material. I consider that much of this is certainly worthy of release for musical as well as historical reasons. The fact that the CROSSROADS boxed set has eventually seen the light of day represents the tip of the iceberg. Possible projects could include a 'live-through-the-years' blues set, as well as a multi-boxed set comprising out-takes similar to the hugely popular 1991 release of the BOOTLEG SERIES from Bob Dylan. Let us live in hope and continue to enjoy the past, present and future work of a truly great musician. Whatever else, I hope that you will find the book as enjoyable to read and use as I did to research and write.

USING THE BOOK

The chapters run in chronological order of the dates of the sessions, etc. In addition to the accompanying descriptive texts and quotations from the musicians, details of the sessions themselves present the following information in sequence:

Identification of the session
  Type, or for whom the session was recorded
  Date of recordings
  Location and venue

Recordings made
  Title of track
  (facing) Recording on which available or released

Listing of participants
  Instruments: musician
  Specific guitar model used by Eric Clapton
  Producer of session
  Engineer on session

Throughout, this information is included wherever known. However, a —— (dash) indicates the rare occasions when complete details have proved impossible to determine or confirm.

The availability of each song performed during every studio or live session is shown opposite the song's title. On page 33 'Strange Brew', for example, is shown as A side/DISRAELI GEARS, indicating that the song was released both as a single and on the album DISRAELI GEARS. When a song is available on CD only – 'Spending All My Days', for example – it is identified in the form BLIND FAITH CD; that is, it is available only on the CD version of the album BLIND FAITH.

The Discography on page 171–83 lists in chronological order all of Eric Clapton's recorded work, including the names of the recording companies and record numbers and whether CDs are available. A separate section gives the details of records on which Eric made guest appearances; this section is organized in alphabetical order by artist.

YARDBIRDS ALIVE

1963–1964

After periods in burgeoning blues groups The Roosters, and Casey Jones And The Engineers (with Tom McGuinness, among others), Eric's first *recordings* were with The Yardbirds, a group of ex-art college students and school dropouts who fell in love with R & B and whom Eric had joined in October 1963. Managed by Giorgio Gomelsky, who ran the Crawdaddy in Richmond, they played regular gigs there and built a strong and loyal following. Giorgio also promoted the American Negro Blues Festival which was held at the Fairfield Halls in Croydon and featured such giants as Muddy Waters, Otis Spann and Sonny Boy Williamson. The latter stayed on and toured Britain, including some dates with The Yardbirds.

ERIC CLAPTON: *When Sonny Boy came over we didn't know how to back him up. It was frightening, really, because this man was real and we weren't. He wasn't very tolerant, either. He did take a shine to us after a while, but before that he put us through some bloody hard paces. In the first place, he expected us to know his tunes. He'd say, 'We're going to do "Don't Start Me To Talkin'" or "Fattening Frogs For Snakes"' and then he'd kick it off, and of course, some of the members of this particular band had never heard these songs.*

The Sonny Boy session came out in 1966 on the Fontana label as SONNY BOY WILLIAMSON AND THE YARDBIRDS. The Yardbirds' set was not released until 1982 on the Spanish Edigsa label. Both of these are currently available on Charly's excellent SHAPES OF THINGS 4-CD set. It's easy to hear why it took so long for them to be released – although the performances were spirited, they certainly were not good enough for a major label, and probably not intended for one either. However, it is fascinating to hear a little bit of history in the making.

Live Session
7–8 December 1963
Crawdaddy, Richmond, Surrey

Smokestack Lightning	SHAPES OF THINGS
Let It Rock	SHAPES OF THINGS
Honey In Your Hips	SHAPES OF THINGS
I Wish You Would	SHAPES OF THINGS
You Can't Judge A Book By The Cover	SHAPES OF THINGS
Who Do You Love	SHAPES OF THINGS

Guitar: Eric Clapton
Vocals/Harp: Keith Relf
Bass: Paul Samwell-Smith
Guitar: Chris Dreja
Drums: Jim McCarty

Bye Bye Bird	SHAPES OF THINGS
Mr Downchild	SHAPES OF THINGS
The River Rhine	SHAPES OF THINGS
23 Hours Too Long	SHAPES OF THINGS
A Lost Care	SHAPES OF THINGS
Pontiac Blues	SHAPES OF THINGS
Take It Easy Baby	SHAPES OF THINGS
Out On The Water Coast	SHAPES OF THINGS
I Don't Care No More	SHAPES OF THINGS
Western Arizona	SHAPES OF THINGS

Guitar: Eric Clapton
Vocals/harmonica: Sonny Boy Williamson
Bass: Paul Samwell-Smith
Guitar: Chris Dreja
Drums: Jim McCarty

Guitars used: Fender Telecaster, Gibson ES335

Producer: Giorgio Gomelsky
Engineer: ——
Recorded on 2-track reel-to-reel

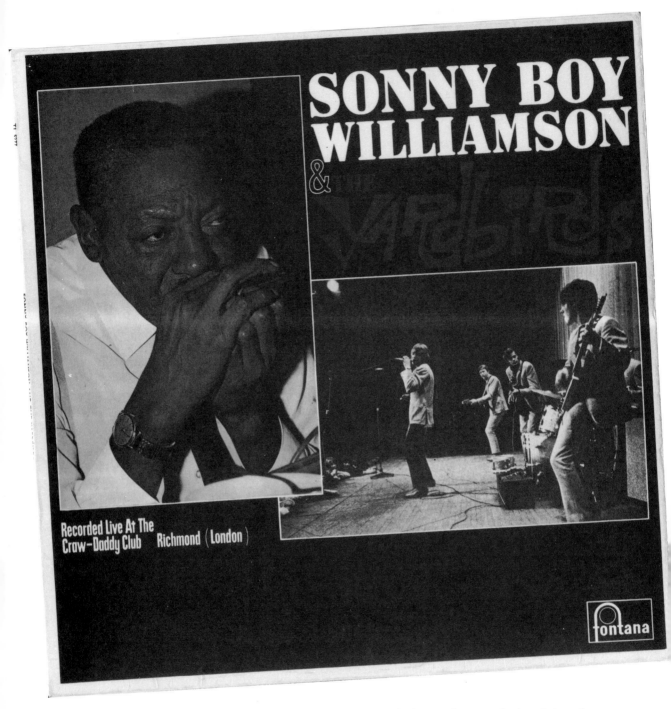

The original released album cover, the design of which has never been used subsequently

The Yardbirds' first studio session took place in a small recording studio in Morden, Surrey, called R.G. Jones. Giorgio had organized this session for them to record some demos to take round various labels in the hope of getting the band signed up.

The demos 'Boom Boom', 'Honey In Your Hips', 'Baby What's Wrong', 'I'm Talking About You', 'I Wish You Would', 'A Certain Girl' and 'You Can't Judge A Book By The Cover' were good enough for EMI as well as being representative of their live set at that time.

Studio Session
February 1964
R.G. Jones Studios, Morden, Surrey

Boom Boom	SHAPES OF THINGS/CROSSROADS
Honey In Your Hips	SHAPES OF THINGS/CROSSROADS
Baby What's Wrong	SHAPES OF THINGS/CROSSROADS
I'm Talking About You	SHAPES OF THINGS
I Wish You Would	REMEMBER . . . THE YARDBIRDS
A Certain Girl	*Unissued*
You Can't Judge A Book By The Cover	*Unissued*

Guitar: Eric Clapton
Vocals/harmonica: Keith Relf
Bass: Paul Samwell-Smith
Guitar: Chris Dreja
Drums: Jim McCarty

Guitar used: probably Fender Telecaster

Producer: Giorgio Gomelsky
Engineer: ———

Live Session
March 1964
Marquee Club, London

Too Much Monkey Business	FIVE LIVE YARDBIRDS
Got Love If You Want It	FIVE LIVE YARDBIRDS
Smokestack Lightning	FIVE LIVE YARDBIRDS
Good Morning Little Schoolgirl	FIVE LIVE YARDBIRDS
Respectable	FIVE LIVE YARDBIRDS
Five Long Years	FIVE LIVE YARDBIRDS
Pretty Girl	FIVE LIVE YARDBIRDS
Louise	FIVE LIVE YARDBIRDS
I'm A Man	FIVE LIVE YARDBIRDS
Here 'Tis	FIVE LIVE YARDBIRDS
I Wish You Would	*Unissued*

Guitar: Eric Clapton
Vocals/harmonica: Keith Relf
Bass: Paul Samwell-Smith
Guitar: Chris Dreja
Drums: Jim McCarty

Guitar used: Fender Telecaster

Producer: Giorgio Gomelsky
Engineer: Philip Wood
Recorded on Ampex 2-track reel-to-reel

ERIC CLAPTON: *We were building to musical climaxes, trying to develop crowd frenzy. Paul would start it on the bass, going up the fretboard, and everyone else would go up and up and up, and then you'd get to the leading pitch and come back down again. If you do that on just about every number, there's very little time for reflective or serious playing.*

After signing with EMI in February 1964, it was decided to record one of their legendary Marquee shows where they regularly played a residency. The resulting live album, FIVE LIVE YARDBIRDS, was representative of their shows at this time and still makes for enjoyable listening today.

It is unfortunate that a lot of the show was erased in error by Paul Samwell-Smith when he accidentally pressed the erase button while listening to a playback of the night's show. So don't expect any out-takes to materialize!

◆

Before releasing the live album, EMI wanted that all-important hit single. To that end, a session was set up by Giorgio at Olympic Sound Studios in Barnes to record their first single. 'I Wish You Would' was to be the A side.

Studio Session
April 1964
Olympic Sound Studios, Barnes, London

I Wish You Would	A side
A Certain Girl	B side

Guitar: Eric Clapton
Vocals/harmonica: Chris Dreja
Bass: Paul Samwell-Smith
Guitar: Chris Dreja
Drums: Jim McCarty

Guitar used: probably Fender Telecaster

Producer: Giorgio Gomelsky
Engineer: ———

The single did not do particularly well chartwise, but it did get them their first television appearance as well as music press articles.

◆

Eric's next studio session was his first as a guest guitarist. It was to be a memorable one as it featured Otis Spann and his half-brother Muddy Waters, who later became a father-figure to Eric as well as a main source of inspiration.

Live Session
1964
Go Tell It on the Mountain TV Show
Studio not known

Louise	*The Cream Of Eric Clapton* video
I Wish You Would	Part is available on *Yardbirds* video

Guitar: Eric Clapton
Vocals/harmonica: Keith Relf
Bass: Paul Samwell-Smith
Guitar: Chris Dreja
Drums: Jim McCarty

Studio Session for Otis Spann
4 May 1964
Decca Studios, West Hampstead, London

Pretty Girls Everywhere	CRACKED SPANNER HEAD
Stirs Me Up	B side

Guitar: Eric Clapton
Piano/vocals: Otis Spann
Guitar: Muddy Waters
Bass: Ransome Knowling
Drums: Willie Smith

Guitar used: probably Gibson ES335

Producer: Mike Vernon
Engineers: Roy Baker, Gus Dudgeon

ERIC CLAPTON: *I've got a copy of that record somewhere. Muddy was playing rhythm guitar and I played lead, which was strange, and it was two sides we did with Mike Vernon. And it was great, actually – they were both very friendly, you know, very encouraging. And they had these beautiful shiny silk suits, with big trousers. I was knocked out by the way they looked.*

The Yardbirds continued to tour the club circuit up and down the country and slotted a few more studio sessions for their next single.

Studio Session
August 1964
Olympic Sound Studios, Barnes, London

Good Morning Little Schoolgirl (take 1)	SHAPES OF THINGS
Good Morning Little Schoolgirl (take 2)	SHAPES OF THINGS
Good Morning Little Schoolgirl (master)	A side

Guitar: Eric Clapton
Vocals/harmonica: Keith Relf
Bass: Paul Samwell-Smith
Guitar: Chris Dreja
Drums: Jim McCarty

Guitar used: probably Gibson ES335

Producer: Giorgio Gomelsky
Engineer: ——

The first session for 'Good Morning Little School-girl' took place without Keith Relf, who had suffered a collapsed lung during the Richmond R & B Festival. As a result his vocal was added later.

Studio Session
September 1964
Olympic Sound Studios, Barnes, London

I Ain't Got You	B side

Guitar: Eric Clapton
Vocals/harmonica: Keith Relf
Bass: Paul Samwell-Smith
Guitar: Chris Dreja
Drums: Jim McCarty

Guitar used: probably Gibson ES335

Producer: Giorgio Gomelsky
Engineer: ——

'Good Morning Little Schoolgirl' was recorded at Eric's suggestion. Although it was Eric who sang it in concert, Keith performed the vocals on the studio version. It did not chart, mainly because there were already several versions of the song out at the same time.

The Yardbirds continued touring as well as joining various package tours with artists as diverse as Billy J. Kramer, Cliff Bennett and Jerry Lee Lewis, to name but a few. They would be required to perform four or five numbers, including their latest single, before the next act came on.

The highlight of the year, though, was appearing on The Beatles' Christmas Shows for a two-week period at London's Hammersmith Odeon. During December they also recorded their third and last single to feature Eric.

**Studio Session
November 1964
Olympic Sound Studios, Barnes, London**

Putty In Her Hands   SHAPES OF THINGS
Got To Hurry (take 1)   SHAPES OF THINGS
Got To Hurry (take 2)   SHAPES OF THINGS
Got To Hurry (master)   B side

Guitar: Eric Clapton
Bass: Paul Samwell-Smith
Guitar: Chris Dreja
Drums: Jim McCarty

Guitar used: probably Gibson ES335

Producer: Giorgio Gomelsky
Engineer: ——

**Studio Session
November 1964
IBC Studios, London**

Sweet Music   SHAPES OF THINGS

Guitar: Eric Clapton
Vocals: Keith Relf
Bass: Paul Samwell-Smith
Guitar: Chris Dreja
Drums: Jim McCarty
Backing vocals: Paul Jones

Guitar used: probably Gibson ES335

Producer: Manfred Mann
Engineer: ——

'Sweet Music' remained unreleased for many years, due to their lack of conviction at the sessions. In using the talents of producer Manfred Mann and his colleague Paul Jones it does show, however, a deliberate move to a more commercial approach.

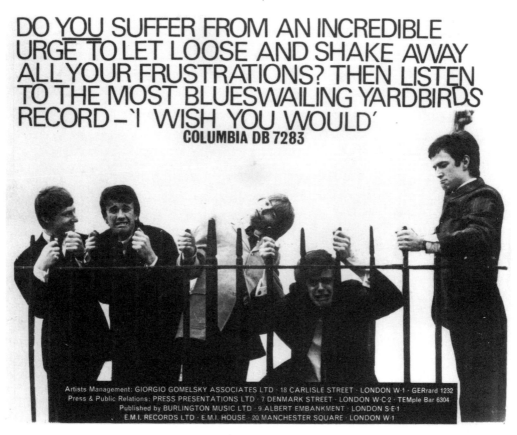

Left to right: Paul Samwell-Smith, Chris Dreja, Keith Relf, Jim McCarty and Eric

**Studio Session
December 1964
IBC Studios, London**

For Your Love   A side

Guitar: Eric Clapton
Vocals: Keith Relf
Bass: Paul Samwell-Smith
Guitar: Chris Dreja
Drums: Jim McCarty
Harpsichord: Brian Auger
Bongos: Denny Piercey

Guitar used: probably Gibson ES335

Producer: Giorgio Gomelsky
Engineer: ———

KEITH RELF: *Eric did not get on well with the business. He does not like commercialization. Eric did not like our new record, 'For Your Love'. He should have featured, but he did not want to sing or anything and he only did that boogie bit in the middle. His leaving is bound to be a blow to the group's image at first, because Eric was very popular.*

ERIC CLAPTON: *Giorgio came up with a song by Otis Redding. I thought that would make a great single because it was still R & B and soul, and we could do it really funky. Then Paul got the 'For Your Love' demo, and he heard it with harpsichord! Where does that leave me? Twelve-string guitar, I suppose. So we went in the studio to do both songs, but we did* 'For Your Love' *first. Everyone was so bowled over by the obvious commerciality of it that we didn't do the Otis Redding song, and I was very disappointed, disillusioned by that. So my attitude within the group got really sour, and it was kind of hinted that it would be better for me to leave. I left, and felt a lot better for it.*

'For Your Love', written by Graham Gouldman, was a big hit for them, reaching number 3 in the UK charts on its release in March 1965. This commercial number also proved to be the main reason for Eric's departure after his growing dissatisfaction with the 'pop' direction in which the group were heading. In fact, Eric only plays on the bridge of the song.

The B side, 'Got To Hurry', on the other hand, showed Eric's real direction, and was a showcase for his amazing solo guitar playing. The group went on to America with both Jeff Beck and later Jimmy Page, where their popularity became greater than at home. The Yardbirds are sadly mainly remembered for their lead guitarists and not as one of the most innovative groups of their time. Their only failing was lack of good legal advice, as their huge success did not reflect itself in financial terms.

BLUES BREAKER

1965–1966

Eric joined John Mayall's Blues Breakers in April 1965. He recorded a BBC session with them only a few days after joining.

Live Session for *Saturday Club*
24 April 1965
BBC Studios, London

Crawling Up A Hill	Radio broadcast
Crocodile Walk	Radio broadcast
Bye Bye Bird	Radio broadcast

Guitar: Eric Clapton
Vocals/harmonica: John Mayall
Bass: John McVie
Drums: Hughie Flint

Guitar played: Fender Telecaster

Producer: ——
Engineer: ——

Eric's first studio recording with them took place at Levy's Recording Studio for an informal jam with Bob Dylan, who was in town on his UK tour.

Studio Session with Bob Dylan
12 May 1965
Levy's Recording Studio, London

If You Gotta Go Go Now	*Unissued*

Guitar: Eric Clapton
Piano/vocals: Bob Dylan
Organ: John Mayall
Bass: John McVie
Drums: Hughie Flint

Producer: Tom Wilson
Engineer: ——

By all accounts the session was a shambles, with Dylan and producer Tom Wilson getting drunk and leaving early. It is possible that various instrumental jams were recorded.

ERIC CLAPTON: *It was just a jam session. He was interested in John Mayall. John had recorded a song called 'Life Is Like A Slow Train Going Up A Hill' [the song was actually called 'Crawling Up A Hill'] and that interested Bob. Bob came in, looked for John Mayall. I was just the guitar player on the session. He had a friend called Bobby Neuwirth who was a fantastic player. Bobby Neuwirth was his kind of court jester at the time. Bobby Neuwirth kept coming up to me and saying, 'You're playing too much blues, man. He needs to be more country!' I didn't actually speak to Bob at this time. He never actually came and spoke. I just watched him. We played for about two hours. Tom Wilson was behind the desk. The next thing I knew, he was gone. We did a lot of his blues songs which he . . . was making up. He was sitting at the piano and we just joined in.*

Shortly after, Eric recorded his first real session with the Blues Breakers for the Immediate label as well as doing some informal recording with Jimmy Page.

Studio Session
June 1965
Studio not known

I'm Your Witchdoctor	A side
Telephone Blues	B side
On Top Of The World	ANTHOLOGY OF BRITISH BLUES

Guitar: Eric Clapton
Keyboards/vocals: John Mayall
Bass: John McVie
Drums: Hughie Flint

Guitar used: Gibson Les Paul

Producer: Jimmy Page
Engineer: ———
Recorded on Simon 2-track reel-on-reel

Studio Session
June 1965
Jimmy Page's house

Miles Road	BLUES ANYTIME
Tribute To Elmore	BLUES ANYTIME
Freight Loader	BLUES ANYTIME

Guitar: Eric Clapton
       Jimmy Page

Guitar used: Gibson Les Paul

Producer: Jimmy Page
Engineer: ———
Recorded on Simon 2-track reel-to-reel

Studio Session
June 1965
Jimmy Page's house

Snake Drive	BLUES ANYTIME

Guitar: Eric Clapton
       Jimmy Page
Bass: Bill Wyman
Drums: Chris Winters

West Coast Idea	BLUES ANYTIME

Guitar: Eric Clapton
Piano: Ian Stewart
Bass: Bill Wyman
Harmonica: Mick Jagger

Draggin' My Tail	BLUES ANYTIME

Guitar: Eric Clapton
       Jimmy Page
Piano: Ian Stewart
Bass: Bill Wyman
Harmonica: Mick Jagger
Drums: Chris Winters

Chocker	BLUES ANYTIME

Guitar: Eric Clapton
       Jimmy Page
Bass: Bill Wyman
Drums: Chris Winters

Guitar used: Gibson Les Paul

Producer: Jimmy Page
Engineer: ———
Eric's and Jimmy's guitar tracks were recorded on Simon 2-track reel-to-reel. All other instruments were overdubbed in August 1965 at Olympic Sound Studios, Barnes.

The original reels to these sessions were sold at Sotheby's in 1988 after having been thrown out of Olympic Sound Studios' vaults when Richard Branson bought the studio. Longer versions and out-takes were on them, and unfortunately all CDs with these tracks have been mastered from vinyl copies. Particularly bad is the version of 'Miles Road', where cracks and pops are very audible.

◆

Eric and John Mayall next recorded a limited edition single for Mike Vernon's Purdah label, soon to become Blue Horizon. 'Lonely Years' and 'Bernard Jenkins' were truly Chicago blues-sounding numbers, made by blues purists for like-minded fans. It was to be another eight months before Eric's next session.

Studio Session
June 1965
Wessex Studios, Soho, London

Lonely Years	A side
Bernard Jenkins	B side

Guitar: Eric Clapton
Piano/vocals: John Mayall

Guitar used: Gibson Les Paul

Producer: Mike Vernon
Engineer: ———

Mike Vernon had brought bluesman Champion Jack Dupree over from Copenhagen, where he was living, to record a series of albums for Decca. The first session took place in February 1966, featuring members of The Artwoods and The Blues Breakers.

Studio Session for Champion Jack Dupree
February 1966
Decca Studios, West Hampstead, London

Third Degree	FROM NEW ORLEANS TO CHICAGO
Shim-Sham-Shimmy	FROM NEW ORLEANS TO CHICAGO
Calcutta Blues	RAW BLUES

Guitar: Eric Clapton
Piano/vocals: Champion Jack Dupree
Bass: Malcolm Pool
Drums: Keef Hartley
Guitar: Tony McPhee
Harmonica: John Mayall

Guitar used: Gibson Les Paul

Producer: Mike Vernon
Engineer: Vic Smith

One of The Blues Breakers' regular venues was the Flamingo in Wardour Street in London's Soho (which later became the Whiskey A GoGo and is today known as the Wag Club). John Mayall would regularly tape gigs at the so-called 'all-nighter' sessions on his 2-track reel-to-reel, and his collection would have been of great historical value today had it not been sadly destroyed in a fire back in the seventies at his Laurel Canyon home.

However, about 30 minutes of a live Flamingo show survived from March 1966; it included Jack Bruce on bass, temporarily replacing John McVie. Another five numbers from this line-up also exist from a BBC live session recorded two days later and which features some fiery guitar from Eric.

Live Session
17 March 1966
Flamingo Club, Soho, London

Maudie	PRIMAL SOLOS
It Hurts To Be In Love	PRIMAL SOLOS
Have You Ever Loved A Woman	PRIMAL SOLOS
Bye Bye Bird	PRIMAL SOLOS
Hoochie Coochie Man	PRIMAL SOLOS
Stormy Monday	LOOKING BACK

Guitar: Eric Clapton
Keyboards/vocals: John Mayall
Bass: Jack Bruce
Drums: Hughie Flint

Guitar used: Gibson Les Paul

Producer: John Mayall
Engineer: ——
Recorded on 2-track reel-to-reel

JOHN MAYALL: PRIMAL SOLOS *was done from my tapes that I'd done on my tape recorder, and on some of the things, the speed was a little off, but it's music, and I thought it should be out. The record company wasn't too thrilled with the quality. Music is the important thing, and I can hear through all that stuff. It's the only thing left now since all my tapes got burned in the big fire of '79. It's the only thing that I have, but at least I've got those things on it. There was so much stuff lost that I can't narrow it down. But the* PRIMAL SOLOS *stuff was the best Clapton stuff that I had, and there are records out there that represent every period.*

Live Session for *Saturday Club*
19 March 1966
BBC Studios, London

Little Girl	Radio broadcast
Hideaway	Radio broadcast
Steppin' Out	Radio broadcast
On Top Of The World	Radio broadcast
Key To Love	Radio broadcast

Guitar: Eric Clapton
Vocals/keyboards/harmonica: John Mayall
Bass: Jack Bruce
Drums: Hughie Flint

Guitar played: Gibson Les Paul

Producer: ——
Engineer: ——

Eric's next session also took place in March, under the guidance of Joe Boyd for Elektra Records. The resultant one-off compilation album featured the best of contemporary English and American blues artists. Eric's popularity and reputation as a great blues soloist were such that the tracks produced for this project were performed by Eric Clapton And The Powerhouse. This one-off group featured members of Manfred Mann, The Spencer Davis Group and The Blues Breakers.

Studio Session for The Powerhouse
March 1966
Studio not known

I Want To Know	WHAT'S SHAKIN'
Crossroads	WHAT'S SHAKIN'
Steppin' Out	WHAT'S SHAKIN'

Guitar: Eric Clapton
Keyboards/vocals: Stevie Winwood (Steve Anglo on LP cover)
Drums: Pete York
Bass: Jack Bruce
Harmonica: Paul Jones
Piano: Ben Palmer

Guitar used: Gibson Les Paul

Producer: Joe Boyd
Engineer: ——

John Mayall's Blues Breakers finally went into the studio to record their first album after signing with Decca. Their LP BLUES BREAKERS WITH ERIC CLAPTON is now regarded as the classic white blues album of the sixties, and perfectly reflects the mood of the day. Mike Vernon was once again producing, and decided to augment certain tracks with brass.

Studio Session for Blues Breakers album
April 1966
Decca Studio No.2, West Hampstead, London

All Your Love	BLUES BREAKERS WITH ERIC CLAPTON
Hideaway	BLUES BREAKERS WITH ERIC CLAPTON
Little Girl	BLUES BREAKERS WITH ERIC CLAPTON
Another Man	BLUES BREAKERS WITH ERIC CLAPTON
Double Crossing Time	BLUES BREAKERS WITH ERIC CLAPTON
What'd I Say	BLUES BREAKERS WITH ERIC CLAPTON
Key To Love	B side/
	BLUES BREAKERS WITH ERIC CLAPTON
Parchment Farm	A side/
	BLUES BREAKERS WITH ERIC CLAPTON
Have You Heard	BLUES BREAKERS WITH ERIC CLAPTON
Steppin' Out	BLUES BREAKERS WITH ERIC CLAPTON
It Ain't Right	BLUES BREAKERS WITH ERIC CLAPTON

Guitar/vocals: Eric Clapton
Piano/organ/harmonica/vocals: John Mayall
Bass: John McVie
Drums: Hughie Flint
Baritone sax: John Almond (Double Crossing Time, Key To Love, Have You Heard, Steppin' Out)

Eric at the BLUES BREAKERS session

Tenor sax: Alan Skidmore (Key To Love, Have You Heard, Steppin' Out)

Trumpet: Dennis Healey (Key To Love, Have You Heard, Steppin' Out)

Guitar used: Gibson Les Paul

Producer: Mike Vernon
Engineer: Gus Dudgeon

JOHN MAYALL: *We just went in there. I think it was either one day or two days, it didn't take much more than that. Basically, we were just playing the stuff that we were doing in the clubs, so the material was totally familiar to us. It felt pretty natural. The only difference was that we had to play a little quieter than we might have done in the clubs.*

JOHN MAYALL *(on Eric's first lead vocal in a studio):* 'Ramblin' On My Mind' *was a song that he wanted to do and, as I remember it, it was just that he didn't want anybody in the room, so it was one that we did as a separate session after the others had gone home. He was a bit shy about singing for the first time on record, but it worked out after a couple of takes. He just didn't want anybody listening in case it didn't work out.*

ERIC CLAPTON: *It was just a record of what we were doing every night in the clubs, with a few contrived riffs we made up kind of as afterthoughts, to fill out some of the things. It isn't any great achievement. It wasn't until I realized that the album was actually turning people on that I began to look at it differently.*

Eric on one of his rare nights off from The Blues Breakers, playing with the Jeff Beck period Yardbirds at the Marquee, London in 1966

1st

recording

"WRAPPING PAPER"

reaction

591 007

FRESH CREAM

1966–1967

By the time the BLUES BREAKERS album was released in July 1966, Eric had already been rehearsing with Jack Bruce and Ginger Baker. This was to take him on an extraordinary journey for the next two years with the world's first supergroup, Cream. Tired of simply copying his Chicago blues heroes, Eric wanted to expand his abilities into the field of improvisation. Sessions for their first single and album took place over a three-month period, during which they cut their teeth on the club circuit. Throughout their lifespan Cream also recorded several radio sessions for the BBC *Rhythm And Blues* show, broadcast on the World Service, as well as several *Saturday Club* shows.

Studio Session
July, August, September 1966
Chalk Farm Studios and Mayfair Studios, London

Wrapping Paper (take 1)	*Unissued*
Wrapping Paper (master)	A side/FRESH CREAM CD
Cat's Squirrel (take 1)	*Unissued*
Cat's Squirrel (master)	B side/FRESH CREAM
I Feel Free (basic track)	*Unissued*
I Feel Free (rehearsal)	*Unissued*
I Feel Free (rehearsal 2)	*Unissued*
I Feel Free (master)	A side/FRESH CREAM CD
N.S.U.	FRESH CREAM
Sleepy Time Time	FRESH CREAM
Dreaming	FRESH CREAM
Sweet Wine (take 1 with feedback solo)	*Unissued*
Sweet Wine (master)	FRESH CREAM
Spoonful	FRESH CREAM
Four Until Late	FRESH CREAM
Rollin' And Tumblin'	FRESH CREAM
I'm So Glad	FRESH CREAM
Toad (take 1)	*Unissued*
Toad (master)	FRESH CREAM
Coffee Song (take 1)	*Unissued*
Coffee Song (master)	FRESH CREAM
Beauty Queen	*Unissued*
You Make Me Feel (take 1)	*Unissued*
You Make Me Feel (take 2)	*Unissued*

Guitar/vocals: Eric Clapton
Bass/vocals/harmonica/piano: Jack Bruce
Drums: Ginger Baker

Guitar used: Gibson Les Paul

Producer: Robert Stigwood
Engineer: ——

The group had not had a chance to know itself musically on the live circuit, so the first recordings consisted of blues standards and pop songs. Several takes of the above exist, some of which are better than the released material; an example is 'Sweet Wine', which features a great feedback solo. The only two unreleased numbers are not essential listening: 'Beauty Queen' is basically a pop instrumental, and 'You Make Me Feel' is a song that would not be out of place on an early Who release, with the lyrics: 'You make me feel like a hat stand, tall, grim and brown, you make me feel like a deserted house, dark and empty in the dusk.'

Jack Bruce was the main influence, due to his varied experience taking in jazz, R & B and pop. Together with his partner, lyricist Pete Brown, he wrote some of Cream's best songs. Their first single was a strange choice, however – one could go so far as saying commercial suicide! 'Wrapping Paper' was about as far away as you'd imagine their sound to be. Where were Eric and his legendary guitar solos? It was basically a laid-back twelve-bar blues that reached no further than number 34 in the charts and was no doubt a contributory factor to their slow commercial success in the UK.

MONO
SPOT PRODUCTIONS LIMITED
(CUSTOM DIVISION)

64 SOUTH MOLTON STREET
MAYFAIR LONDON W.1
TELEPHONE: GROSVENOR 7173-4-5

REEL II OF II

Date | Client: ROBERT STIGWOOD
Job No. | Programme: CREAM L.P. SIDE II

1 CAT SQUIRREL
4 TILL LATE
5 THE COFFEE SONG
6 ROLLIN & TUMBLIN
5 I'M SO GLAD
6 TOAD
7
Remarks

Producer: ROBERT STIGWOOD | Engineer: MR. J. TIMPERLEY
MONO | MASTER | 15 I.P.S | CCIR

JACK BRUCE: *You shouldn't be limited by only recording material that you can play on stage. People who come to see us in clubs may not buy records and record-buyers may not only go to clubs, so we please them both.*

ERIC CLAPTON: *I don't think it's a betrayal of the fans because I don't think it's a bad pop record. If people have enough intelligence they can accept pop records if they're good.*

Their second single, 'I Feel Free', was an altogether better number – still commercial, however. Featuring a guitar solo by Eric, it reached number 11 in the charts on its release in December 1966.

Live Session for BBC Radio
8 November 1966
BBC Studios, London

Wrapping Paper	Radio broadcast
Sweet Wine	Radio broadcast
Steppin' Out	Radio broadcast

Guitar: Eric Clapton
Bass/piano/vocals: Jack Bruce
Drums: Ginger Baker

Guitar used: Gibson Les Paul

Producer: ——
Engineer: ——

THE **CREAM'S** L.P. IS RELEASED ON DECEMBER 9TH. THE TITLE IS **'FRESH CREAM'**
THEIR SECOND SINGLE IS ALSO RELEASED ON THE SAME DAY– IT IS CALLED **'I FEEL FREE'**
THE FLIP: **'N.S.U.'**–BOTH ON

reaction

SINGLE: 591 011/ THE L.P.: 593 001 (MONO) & 594 001 (STEREO)
MANAGED & DISTRIBUTED BY POLYDOR RECORDS LTD. FOR THE ROBERT STIGWOOD ORGANISATION.

**Live Session for BBC Radio
9 December 1966
BBC Studios, London**

Cat's Squirrel	Radio broadcast
Traintime	Radio broadcast
Lawdy Mama	CROSSROADS/Radio broadcast
I'm So Glad	Radio broadcast

Guitar/vocals: Eric Clapton
Bass/vocals/harmonica: Jack Bruce
Drums: Ginger Baker

Guitar used: Gibson Les Paul

Producer: ——
Engineer: ——

The above session features a unique recording of 'I'm So Glad', with Eric playing part of Tchaikovsky's '1812 Overture' during his solo!

REAL CREAM

1967–1968

Live Session for BBC Radio
10 January 1967
BBC Studios, London

Four Until Late	Radio broadcast
I Feel Free	Radio broadcast
N.S.U.	Radio broadcast

Guitar/vocals: Eric Clapton
Bass/vocals: Jack Bruce
Drums: Ginger Baker

Guitar used: Gibson SG

Producer: ———
Engineer: ———

In February 1967, Cream started their first overseas tour of Europe and Scandinavia. Swedish Radio recorded and broadcast the show from Stockholm.

Live Session
March 1967
Konserthuset, Stockholm, Sweden

N.S.U.	Radio broadcast
Steppin' Out	Radio broadcast
Traintime	Radio broadcast
Toad	Radio broadcast
I'm So Glad	Radio broadcast

Guitar/vocals: Eric Clapton
Bass/vocals/harmonica: Jack Bruce
Drums: Ginger Baker

Guitar used: Gibson SG

Producer: Swedish Radio
Engineer: ———

By now Cream were musically very tight, and as the prospect of America loomed closer, the group were on the verge of a major breakthrough. The purpose of their first visit to the USA was to record their next single and album at New York's Atlantic Studios.

Studio Session
8–19 May 1967
Atlantic Studios, New York

Strange Brew	A side/DISRAELI GEARS
Tales Of Brave Ulysses	B side/DISRAELI GEARS
Lawdy Mama (version 1)	LIVE CREAM
Lawdy Mama (version 2)	*Unissued*
Sunshine Of Your Love	A side/DISRAELI GEARS
Swlabr	B side/DISRAELI GEARS
World Of Pain	DISRAELI GEARS
Dance The Night Away	DISRAELI GEARS
Blue Condition	DISRAELI GEARS
We're Going Wrong	DISRAELI GEARS
Outside Woman Blues	DISRAELI GEARS
Take It Back	DISRAELI GEARS
Mother's Lament	DISRAELI GEARS

Guitar/vocals: Eric Clapton
Bass/vocals: Jack Bruce
Drums: Ginger Baker

Guitar used: Gibson SG

Producer: Felix Pappalardi
Engineer: Tom Dowd

The unissued version of 'Lawdy Mama' is a real gem, with multi-tracked guitars and sung by Eric and Jack. It is totally different from version 1, which is basically 'Strange Brew' with alternative lyrics. On its release in November 1967 DISRAELI GEARS was a huge success, reaching the top five in both the UK and US charts.

'Strange Brew', backed with 'Tales Of Brave Ulysses', was released as a taster to the album in June 1967, but only reached number 17 in the charts.

TOM DOWD: *It was a three-day album, because they were on the end of a visitor's visa, and had to leave the country. Ahmet Ertegun [head of Atlantic Records] called me up one day in the studio, and told me he wanted me to record this English group, who were arriving that afternoon, over the next three days, because they had to be on a plane on the Sunday evening, which was when their visas would expire [for actual dates see session heading].*

On their return to the UK, Cream recorded another BBC session as well as some work on a new number called 'White Room'. The basic track was recorded at IBC in London. Around this time they also recorded two takes for a Falstaff beer commercial, which were never released.

Live Session for BBC Radio
30 May 1967
BBC Studios, London

Strange Brew	Radio broadcast
Tales Of Brave Ulysses	Radio broadcast
We're Going Wrong	Radio broadcast
Take It Back	Radio broadcast

Guitar/vocals: Eric Clapton
Bass/vocals: Jack Bruce
Drums: Ginger Baker

Guitar used: Gibson SG

Producer: ——
Engineer: ——

Studio Session
July–August 1967
IBC Studios, London

White Room (basic track)	WHEELS OF FIRE
Sitting On Top Of The World (basic track)	WHEELS OF FIRE
Born Under A Bad Sign (basic track)	WHEELS OF FIRE
Falstaff beer commercial (two takes)	*Unissued*

Guitar: Eric Clapton
Bass/vocals: Jack Bruce
Drums: Ginger Baker

Guitar used: Gibson SG

Producer: Felix Pappalardi
Engineer: Tom Dowd

At the end of August, Cream returned to the USA for their first American tour and booked time at Atlantic Studios in New York for some more recording. Overdubs were spread over two separate sessions at the studios in New York.

Studio Session
September–October 1967
Atlantic Studios, New York

White Room (overdubs)	WHEELS OF FIRE
Sitting On Top Of The World (finish)	WHEELS OF FIRE
Born Under A Bad Sign (finish)	WHEELS OF FIRE
Politician (basic track)	WHEELS OF FIRE
Pressed Rat And Warthog (basic track)	WHEELS OF FIRE
Anyone For Tennis (basic track)	WHEELS OF FIRE

Guitar/vocals: Eric Clapton
Bass/vocals: Jack Bruce
Drums/timpani: Ginger Baker
Viola: Felix Pappalardi

Guitar used: Gibson SG

Producer: Felix Pappalardi
Engineer: Tom Dowd

ERIC CLAPTON: *We used Atlantic's New York studios. It's done quicker there – we get a better sound.*

Cream were comfortable in these legendary studios, as well as finding a very like-minded producer and engineer. The sound was better than those of British studios at the time, and both DISRAELI GEARS and WHEELS OF FIRE are proof of this. At Tom Dowd's suggestion, Eric also contributed a guitar solo on an Aretha Franklin session being held at the same time.

Studio Session
September 1967
Atlantic Studios, New York

Good To Me As I Am To You   LADY SOUL

Guitar: Eric Clapton
Vocals/piano: Aretha Franklin
Electric piano/organ: Spooner Oldham
Guitar: Bobby Womack
        Joe South
        Jimmy Johnson
Trumpet: Mel Lastie
        Joe Newman
        Bernie Glow
Tenor sax: King Curtis
        Selden Powell
        Frank Wess
Baritone sax: Haywood Henry
Bass trombone: Tony Studd
Bass: Tom Cogbill
Drums: Roger Hawkins

Guitar used: Gibson SG

Producer: Jerry Wexler
Engineer: Tom Dowd

Eric plays a wonderfully expressive blues solo on this one track from the great LADY SOUL album that should be in everybody's collection.

It is interesting to note that two of the musicians were to cross paths with Eric in later years. King Curtis figured in a memorable session in 1970, while Roger Hawkins played with Eric during the recording of the MONEY AND CIGARETTES album sessions in 1983, as well as on a few live dates in the USA to promote the LP.

Cream returned to England in October for another BBC session and more club dates that would take them through to January 1968. Then they once again flew out to America to record more tracks for their forthcoming album before embarking on another US tour. However, before leaving, Eric participated on a session for George Harrison's WONDERWALL MUSIC soundtrack, which features him soloing alongside various sitars. It's not essential by any means, but interesting for completists. It is interesting to note that George did not play on the session.

Live Session for BBC Radio
24 October 1967
BBC Studios, London

Outside Woman Blues   Radio broadcast
Born Under A Bad Sign   Radio broadcast
Sunshine Of Your Love   Radio broadcast

Guitar/vocals: Eric Clapton
Bass/vocals: Jack Bruce
Drums: Ginger Baker

Guitar used: Gibson SG

Producer: ——
Engineer: ——

Studio Session for George Harrison
December 1967 – January 1968
Abbey Road Studios, London

Ski-ing   WONDERWALL MUSIC

Guitar: Eric Clapton
Drums: Roy Dyke
Piano/organ: Tony Ashton
Bass: Philip Rogers
Sitar: Shambu-Das
        Indril Bhattacharya
        Shankar Ghosh
Harmonium/tabla-tarang: Rij Ram Desad

Guitar used: Gibson Les Paul

Producer: George Harrison
Engineer: ——

Live Session for BBC Radio
9 January 1968
BBC Studios, London

Politician   Radio broadcast
Steppin' Out   CROSSROADS/Radio broadcast
Swalbr   Radio broadcast
Blue Condition   Radio broadcast

Guitar: Eric Clapton
Bass/vocals: Jack Bruce
Drums: Ginger Baker

Guitar used: Gibson Firebird

Producer: ——
Engineer: ——

Studio Session
January–February 1968
Atlantic Studios, New York

Pressed Rat And Warthog (finish)	B side/WHEELS OF FIRE
Anyone For Tennis (finish)	A side/GOODBYE CREAM CD
Politician (finish)	WHEELS OF FIRE
Passing The Time (basic track)	WHEELS OF FIRE
White Room (wah-wah overdub)	A side/WHEELS OF FIRE
Deserted Cities Of The Heart (basic track)	WHEELS OF FIRE
Those Were The Days (basic track)	B side/WHEELS OF FIRE
As You Said (basic track)	WHEELS OF FIRE

Guitar/vocals: Eric Clapton
Bass/vocals: Jack Bruce
Drums/percussion/timpani: Ginger Baker
Viola: Felix Pappalardi

Guitar used: Gibson SG

Producer: Felix Pappalardi
Engineers: Tom Dowd, Adrian Barber

TOM DOWD: *When it came to the time for* WHEELS OF FIRE, *they were a smash, the supergroup of the century.*

The version of 'Passing The Time' that came out had a 90-second jam edited out. The original version is far superior, with some great interplay between all three members.

As soon as the studio sessions were finished Cream embarked on their US tour, which started in San Francisco at the Winterland on 29 February 1968. It was decided to record several shows for possible release.

Live Session
7 March 1968
Fillmore West, San Francisco

First show

N.S.U.	*Unissued*
Spoonful	*Unissued*
Sunshine Of Your Love	AFTER MIDNIGHT single CD
Crossroads	*Unissued*
Rollin' And Tumblin'	LIVE CREAM
Sweet Wine	*Unissued*

Live Session
7 March 1968
Fillmore West, San Francisco

Second show

Tales Of Brave Ulysses	*Unissued*
Toad	WHEELS OF FIRE
I'm So Glad	*Unissued*

Although more songs were played and recorded, these are the only tapes for this show left in the tape vault.

Live Session
8 March 1968
Winterland, San Francisco

First show

Cat's Squirrel	*Unissued*
Sunshine Of Your Love	*Unissued*
Spoonful	*Unissued*
Traintime	WHEELS OF FIRE
I'm So Glad	*Unissued*
Toad	*Unissued*

Live Session
9 March 1968
Winterland, San Francisco

First show

Tales Of Brave Ulysses	*Unissued*
N.S.U.	*Unissued*
Sleepy Time Time	LIVE CREAM
Crossroads	*Unissued*
Sweet Wine	*Unissued*
Toad	*Unissued*

Live Session
9 March 1968
Winterland, San Francisco

Second show

Spoonful	*Unissued*
Sunshine Of Your Love	LIVE CREAM VOL. 2
Sitting On Top Of The World	*Unissued*

N.S.U.	*Unissued*
I'm So Glad	*Unissued*
Toad	*Unissued*

Live Session
10 March 1968
Winterland, San Francisco

First show

Tales Of Brave Ulysses	LIVE CREAM VOL. 2
Spoonful	WHEELS OF FIRE
Crossroads	WHEELS OF FIRE
We're Going Wrong	*Unissued*
Sweet Wine	LIVE CREAM
Toad	*Unissued*

Live Session
10 March 1968
Winterland, San Francisco

Second show

Sunshine Of Your Love	*Unissued*
N.S.U.	LIVE CREAM
Hideaway	LIVE CREAM VOL. 2
I'm So Glad	*Unissued*
Toad	*Unissued*

Guitar/vocals: Eric Clapton
Bass/vocals: Jack Bruce
Drums: Ginger Baker

Guitar used: Gibson SG

Producer: Felix Pappalardi
Engineer: Bill Halverson

Cream's new album was a double set. The first consisted of new studio material featuring songs by Jack Bruce and Pete Brown, as well as some written by Ginger Baker. Eric decided to cover a couple of his favourite blues numbers but did not contribute to the writing of any material. The second album was a live one, recorded on their huge American tour of 1968.

It is interesting to note that, although the live album of the WHEELS OF FIRE set was called LIVE AT THE FILLMORE, the majority of the set came from the Winterland shows. Another interesting point is that the long-rumoured shortened version of 'Crossroads' is in fact the correct length. There is nothing

to indicate an edit and, after hearing other versions recorded in concert during the tour, they all run for approximately the same length of time.

ERIC CLAPTON: *The idea is to get so far away from the original line that you're playing something that's never been heard before.*

When WHEELS OF FIRE was released in August it became their biggest-selling album, reaching number 1 in America and number 3 in the UK. They all received a platinum disc on stage at New York's Madison Square Arena on 2 November 1968, for selling over two million dollars' worth of WHEELS OF FIRE albums.

In May 1968 Cream appeared on the popular *Smothers Brothers* TV show, miming to their new single 'Anyone For Tennis' and performing an explosive version of 'Sunshine Of Your Love'. 'Anyone For Tennis' was originally recorded for the *Savage Seven* soundtrack. When released as a single in May 1968 it only reached number 40 in the UK chart, and did not even make it into the US top sixty.

Television Session
May 1968
CBS Studios, Los Angeles

Anyone For Tennis	A side/GOODBYE CREAM CD
Sunshine Of Your Love	*Unissued*

Guitar/vocals: Eric Clapton
Bass/vocals: Jack Bruce
Drums: Ginger Baker

Guitars used: Gibson Firebird, Guild 12-string acoustic

Producer: CBS TV
Engineer: ——

Studio Session
June 1968
Atlantic Studios, New York

White Room (finish)	WHEELS OF FIRE
Passing The Time (finish)	WHEELS OF FIRE
As You Said (finish)	WHEELS OF FIRE
Deserted Cities Of The Heart (finish)	WHEELS OF FIRE
Those Were The Days (finish)	WHEELS OF FIRE

Guitar/vocals: Eric Clapton (Eric does not play on As You Said)
Bass/vocals: Jack Bruce
Drums: Ginger Baker
Viola/organ pedals/Swiss hand bells: Felix Pappalardi

Guitars used: Gibson Les Paul, Gibson Firebird
Producer: Felix Pappalardi
Engineers: Tom Dowd, Adrian Barber

Cream's huge US tour continued into mid-June, by which time the rot had set in due to personality clashes and musical differences and the band had decided to split, although not before a farewell tour had been organized. During his three months off, Eric kept himself busy by playing on various sessions for his friend George Harrison as well as a memorable session for Martha Velez.

Studio Session for Jackie Lomax
June 1968
Trident Studios, London

Sour Milk Sea	IS THIS WHAT YOU WANT?
The Eagle Laughs At You	IS THIS WHAT YOU WANT?
You've Got Me Thinking	IS THIS WHAT YOU WANT?
New Day	IS THIS WHAT YOU WANT? CD version

Guitar: Eric Clapton
Vocals: Jackie Lomax
Guitar: George Harrison
Drums: Ringo Starr
Bass: Klaus Voorman
Piano: Nicky Hopkins

Guitars used: probably Gibson Firebird

Producer: ——
Engineer: ——

Collector's Note: Eric had given his prized Gibson SG/Les Paul with psychedelic paint job, as used on both DISRAELI GEARS and WHEELS OF FIRE, to George Harrison, who in turn gave it to Jackie after the session. Later, in 1974, he sold it to Todd Rundgren, who still uses it to this day.

JACKIE LOMAX *told* Goldmine *magazine about the session: Clapton did like five tracks with us. Which was, to me, incredibly generous. I knew Eric quite well, but I could not have used my influence to get him into the studio to record with me. George*

could, of course. Eric was great, he worked for hours. We had Ringo on drums.

Studio Session for Martha Velez
June–July 1968
Decca Studios, West Hampstead, London

It Takes A Lot To Laugh, It Takes A Train To Cry	FIENDS AND ANGELS
I'm Gonna Leave You	FIENDS AND ANGELS
Feel So Bad	FIENDS AND ANGELS
In My Girlish Days	FIENDS AND ANGELS

Guitar: Eric Clapton
Vocals: Martha Velez
Bass: Jack Bruce
Drums: Mitch Mitchell
          Jim Capaldi
Piano: Christine McVie
Organ: Brian Auger
Brass: ——

Guitar used: probably Gibson Les Paul or Firebird

Producer: Mike Vernon
Engineer: Derek Varnals

MARTHA VELEZ: *Mike Vernon had lined up all the English blues players. We did the* FIENDS AND ANGELS *album in London. It was a very raw record, but it's got a real uninhibited energy. It was a large studio with all these levels. I was on the top level and all the musicians were down at the lower levels, looking up at me. I remember thinking it was a dream.*

The next session Eric did was certainly one of the most historic, laying down a guitar solo on a Beatles track at George's invitation.

Studio Session for The Beatles
6 September 1968
Abbey Road Studios, Studio No. 2, London

While My Guitar Gently Weeps	THE BEATLES

Guitar: Eric Clapton
Guitar/vocals: George Harrison
Guitar: John Lennon
Bass/piano: Paul McCartney
Drums: Ringo Starr

MARTHA VELEZ

it takes a
lot to laugh,
it takes a
train to cry
HLK 10266
45 rpm

fiends and
angels
LP soon
⑤ SHK 8395
Ⓜ HAK 8395

LONDON

Decca Record a division of
the Decca Record Company Limited Decca House Albert Embankment London S.E.1

Guitar used: Gibson Les Paul

Producer: George Martin
Engineer: Ken Scott

Eric was also rumoured to have played on 'Not Guilty', which was recorded in August during the same sessions, although no documented proof of this exists. Certainly, the versions of this track which I have heard do not appear to feature Eric. George had to push hard for 'While My Guitar Gently Weeps' to be accepted by the other Beatles.

GEORGE HARRISON: *I worked on that song with John, Paul and Ringo one day, and they were not interested in it at all. And I knew inside of me that it was a nice song. The next day I was with Eric, and I was going into the session, and I said, 'We're going to do this song. Come on and play on it.' He said, 'Oh, no. I can't do that. Nobody ever plays on the Beatles records.' I said, 'Look, it's my song, and I want you to play on it.' So Eric came in, and the other guys were as good as gold, because he was there. Also, it left me free to do the vocal and play rhythm. Then we listened to it back, and he said, 'Ah, there's a problem, though; it's not Beatley enough.' So we put it through the ADT [automatic double-tracker], to wobble it a bit. The drums would be all on one track, bass on another, the acoustic on another, piano on another, Eric on another, and the vocal on another, and then whatever else. I sang it with the acoustic guitar with Paul on piano, and Eric and Ringo. Later Paul overdubbed bass on it.*

'Sunshine Of Your Love' was released as a single in September and did extremely well in America, where it reached number 5 in the charts.

Cream started their farewell tour in October 1968, and several dates were recorded for a farewell album.

Live Session
4 October 1968
Oakland Coliseum Arena, California

White Room	LIVE CREAM VOL. 2
Politician	LIVE CREAM VOL. 2
Crossroads	*Unissued*
Sunshine Of Your Love	*Unissued*
Spoonful	*Unissued*
Deserted Cities Of The Heart	LIVE CREAM VOL. 2
Passing The Time/drum solo (aka Scatafaragus)	*Unissued*
I'm So Glad	*Unissued*

Guitar/vocals: Eric Clapton
Bass/vocals: Jack Bruce
Drums: Ginger Baker

Recorded by: Bill Halverson

Live Session
18 October 1968
The Forum, Los Angeles

White Room	*Unissued*
Politician	*Unissued*
I'm So Glad	*Unissued*
Sitting On Top Of The World	*Unissued*
Sunshine Of Your Love	*Unissued*
Crossroads	*Unissued*
Traintime	*Unissued*
Toad	*Unissued*
Spoonful	*Unissued*

Live Session
19 October 1968
The Forum, Los Angeles

White Room	*Unissued*
Politician	GOODBYE CREAM
I'm So Glad	GOODBYE CREAM
Sitting On Top Of The World	GOODBYE CREAM
Crossroads	*Unissued*
Sunshine Of Your Love	*Unissued*
Traintime	*Unissued*
Toad	*Unissued*
Spoonful	*Unissued*

Guitar/vocals: Eric Clapton
Bass/vocals: Jack Bruce
Drums: Ginger Baker

Recorded by: Bill Halverson

Live Session
20 October 1968
Sports Arena, San Diego, California

White Room	*Unissued*
Politician	*Unissued*
I'm So Glad	*Unissued*
Sitting On Top Of The World	*Unissued*
Sunshine Of Your Love	*Unissued*
Crossroads	*Unissued*
Traintime	*Unissued*
Toad	*Unissued*
Spoonful	*Unissued*

Guitar/vocals: Eric Clapton
Bass/vocals: Jack Bruce
Drums: Ginger Baker

Guitars used: Gibson Firebird, Gibson ES335

Producer: Felix Pappalardi
Engineer: Bill Halverson

The Forum shows in LA were well reviewed and the crowds gave the band a warm reception. They were not the best shows on this farewell tour, but it was decided to include three numbers from them on their GOODBYE CREAM album.

Cream returned to London's Royal Albert Hall for their final two concerts, which were filmed by Tony Palmer for the BBC. The shows were incredible – so much so that the band almost had second thoughts about splitting up.

Live Session
26 November 1968
Royal Albert Hall, London

First show

White Room	*Farewell Cream* film
Politician	*Unissued*
I'm So Glad	*Unissued*
Sitting On Top Of The World	*Unissued*
Crossroads	*Unissued*
Toad	*Unissued*
Spoonful	*Unissued*
Sunshine Of Your Love	*Unissued*
Steppin' Out	*Unissued*

Guitar/vocals: Eric Clapton
Bass/vocals: Jack Bruce
Drums: Ginger Baker

Producer: BBC
Engineer: ———

Live Session
26 November 1968
Royal Albert Hall, London

Second show

White Room	*Unissued*
Politician	*Farewell Cream* film
I'm So Glad	*Farewell Cream* film

THEIR FAREWELL APPEARANCE

SPECIAL GUEST STAR

DEEP PURPLE

TWO NIGHTS ONLY

Fri., OCT 18 & Sat., OCT. 19

AT THE FABULOUS **FORUM**

MANCHESTER & PRAIRIE IN INGLEWOOD

ALL SEATS RESERVED

PRICES: $6.50 • $5.50 • $4.50 • $3.50

Tickets on sale at the Forum Box Office, So. Calif. Music & Mutual Agencies (MA 7 1248), Wallichs (466 3553), Buffums Long Beach & La Habra, The Groove Co., TRS Outlets. Mail orders accepted.

FOR RESERVATIONS OR INFORMATION 24 HRS. A DAY CALL OR 3 1100

PRODUCED BY CONCERT ASSOCIATES

SPECIAL PRIORITY SEAT COUPON

THE CREAM THE FORUM

PLEASE SEND ME   TICKETS @ $

FRI [ ] SAT [ ]   Enclosed is [ ] Check or [ ] Money Order

MAKE CHECK PAYABLE TO THE CREAM THE FORUM

(PLEASE PRINT)

NAME

ADDRESS

CITY   STATE   ZIP

Sitting On Top Of The World	*Farewell Cream* film
Crossroads	*Farewell Cream* film
Toad	*Farewell Cream* film
Spoonful	*Farewell Cream* film
Sunshine Of Your Love	*Farewell Cream* film
Steppin' Out	*Farewell Cream* film

Guitar/vocals: Eric Clapton
Bass/vocals: Jack Bruce
Drums: Ginger Baker

Guitars used: Gibson Firebird, Gibson ES335

Producer: BBC
Engineer: ———

Cream did record a few last tracks in the studio for a proposed farewell album. The plan had been to do another double, with one album of new studio material and the other containing live material recorded on their farewell tour. However, the idea was shelved and a single album was released.

Studio Session
October 1968
IBC Studios, London

Badge	A side/GOODBYE CREAM
What A Bringdown	B side/GOODBYE CREAM
Doing That Scrapyard Thing	GOODBYE CREAM

Guitar/vocals: Eric Clapton
Bass/vocals: Jack Bruce
Drums/vocals: Ginger Baker
Piano/mellotron/bass: Felix Pappalardi
Guitar: George Harrison (Badge)

Guitars used: Gibson ES335, Gibson Firebird

Producer: Felix Pappalardi
Engineer: Damon Lyon-Shaw

For contractual reasons, George Harrison's name could not be used on the cover and he went under the pseudonym of L'Angelo Misterioso. 'Badge' was co-written with George and is still performed in concert today, being a firm favourite with the fans and Eric.

On its release in March 1969, GOODBYE CREAM reached the top ten in both America and England.

GEORGE HARRISON: *On 'Badge' Eric doesn't play guitar up until that bridge. He sat through it with his guitar in the Leslie [rotating speaker], and Felix Pappalardi was the piano player. So there was Felix, Jack Bruce, Ginger Baker and me. I played the rhythm chops right up to the bridge, at which point Eric came in on the guitar with the Leslie. And he overdubbed the solo later. I wrote most of the words, Eric had the bridge and he had the first couple of chord changes. I was writing the words down, and when we came to the middle bit I wrote 'Bridge'. And from where he was sitting, opposite me, he looked and said, 'What's that – Badge?' So he called it 'Badge' because it made him laugh.*

Eric made no more public appearances this year, but did participate in the filming of The Rolling Stones' *Rock And Roll Circus* under the direction of *Ready, Steady, Go*'s Michael Lindsay Hogg. The cast was impressive, featuring Jethro Tull, Taj Mahal, The Who, John and Yoko Lennon, Mitch Mitchell, Marianne Faithfull, Eric Clapton and, of course, The Rolling Stones. It was an entertainment extravaganza that was intended to be shown to television audiences worldwide, but it was never broadcast due to Mick Jagger's dissatisfaction with the Stones' performance. However, at the time of going to press it would seem likely that both the video and soundtrack will be released.

In between filming and rehearsals, Eric jammed with Taj Mahal and his guitarist, Jesse Ed Davis. Eric struck up a friendship with Jesse and played on sessions with him for his solo album in 1970.

Eric was also to play in a one-off supergroup alongside John Lennon, Keith Richards and Mitch Mitchell. During rehearsals on the first day, Mick Jagger joined them for a Buddy Holly tune! This group was known as Winston Legthigh And The Dirty Macs.

Studio Session for *Rock And Roll Circus*
10 December 1968
Intertel Studios, Wembley, London

Peggy Sue	*Unissued*
Jam 1	*Unissued*
Jam 2	*Unissued*
It's Now Or Never	*Unissued*
Yer Blues (several takes)	*Unissued*

Guitar: Eric Clapton
Guitar/vocals: John Lennon
Bass: Keith Richards
Drums: Mitch Mitchell
Vocals: Mick Jagger (Peggy Sue)

Producer: ——
Engineer: ——

Studio Session for *Rock And Roll Circus*
11 December 1968
Intertel Studios, Wembley, London

Yer Blues	*Unissued*
Yoko Ono Jam	*Unissued*

Guitar: Eric Clapton
Guitar/vocals: John Lennon
Bass: Keith Richards
Drums: Mitch Mitchell
Vocals: Yoko Ono
Violin: Ivry Gitlis

Guitar used: Gibson ES335

Producer: ——
Engineer: ——

The rehearsal jams feature some masterful soloing from Eric on his Gibson ES335. However, on 'Yer Blues' he stays faithful to the original version.

(CONTINUED FROM REEL (4).

Olympic Sound Studios

01-748 7961

ENGINEER ALAN / KEITH-H
Date 24/6/69 Location 1
Speed 15 Reel 5

CLIENT "ISLAND"
SUBJECT "BLIND FAITH"

PRODUCER "JIMMY MILLER"

TITLE

TITLE	TAKE	TIME	REMARKS	Master
2) "I HAD TO CRY TO-DAY"	6.		B/D.	
	7		B/D.	
	8.		B/D.	
	9		COMP (F.M. BLUE) (GOOD)	
	10.			
			(CONTINUED ON)	
			REEL (6).	
"SPACE AT END OF REEL"				
(SLEEPING IN THE GROUND)	4.		COMP.	
	5.		F.M. F/S	
	6.		F.M. COMP (V.GOOD) PB.	
(CONTINUED FROM REEL 8.)				

53

N.A.B.

8-TRACK

JS. No.

FAITH AND FRIENDS

1969-1970

1969 was the year of the supergroup. They consisted of established stars formed from the ashes of fragmented groups, much to the delight of record company execs. Crosby, Stills and Nash were the first, with backgrounds from The Byrds, The Hollies and Buffalo Springfield.

Stevie Winwood and Eric were rumoured to be forming such a group together, after weeks of informal jamming at each other's houses. They'd known each other since the early R & B days of The Yardbirds and Spencer Davis Group, and frequently played together in the clubs, as well as recording for The Powerhouse project in 1966. As both were now free of commitments, Stevie having left Traffic in December, it seemed logical to form a band.

Ginger Baker joined the line-up on drums, mainly at Stevie's request, despite Eric's reservations. They went to London's Morgan Studios for their initial recording sessions in February 1969, calling themselves simply Clapton, Baker, Winwood. The first few weeks were spent running through various instrumentals of different styles such as jazz, blues, pop and rock in the hope of finding some ideas for songs. Listening to these reveals some inspired soloing from all three members, including several takes of Billy Roberts 'Hey Joe', which had been Jimi Hendrix's first hit single.

STEVIE WINWOOD: *It's all coming together . . . blues, jazz, folk, pop, rock, everything. A great blend in music.*

ERIC CLAPTON: *The songs stand up themselves, and what we're playing just complements the songs.*

One of the instrumentals was released as a very limited edition single by Island Records to advise their clients of a change of address. There was no indication on the label as to who the band was, and it featured the same instrumental on both sides. It is now a highly sought after item among collectors. Family's bassist, Rick Grech, augmented the line-up in late April, when sessions moved on to Olympic Studios. Press reporters at the time suggested that there were enough tracks for a double album, but this is incorrect. The tape boxes reveal that all the usable material was released. The group called themselves Blind Faith, as the world's press was already praising this combo before hearing a single note!

Studio Session
February–June 1969
Morgan Recording Studios, Studio No. 2, London, and Olympic Sound Studios, Barnes, London

How's Your Father, How's Your Mother Alright Backwards (34 takes)	*Unissued*
Instrumental blues in E	*Unissued*
Instrumental (untitled – several takes)	*Island promo*
Instrumental (untitled – several takes)	*Unissued*
Hey Joe (eight takes)	*Unissued*
Instrumental (early version of Presence Of The Lord)	*Unissued*
Presence Of The Lord (master)	BLIND FAITH
Instrumental (early version of Do What You Like)	*Unissued*
Have You Ever Loved A Woman (instrumental)	*Unissued*
Well All Right (various instrumental takes)	*Unissued*
Well All Right (master)	BLIND FAITH
Instrumental (untitled – several takes)	*Unissued*
Sleeping In The Ground	CROSSROADS
Can't Find My Way Home (acoustic)	BLIND FAITH

Can't Find My Way Home
  (electric)   UP CLOSE radio show CD
Do What You Like   BLIND FAITH
Sea Of Joy   BLIND FAITH
Had To Cry Today   BLIND FAITH

Guitar/vocals: Eric Clapton
Keyboards/guitar/bass/vocals: Stevie Winwood
Drums: Ginger Baker
Bass/electric violin: Rick Grech

Guitars used: Gibson Firebird, Fender Telecaster, Gibson ES335

Producer: Jimmy Miller
Engineer: ——

Sessions were interrupted so Eric could participate in a massive jam session which was to be filmed and recorded for either television or cinema. The idea of the project was to fuse the best of contemporary pop, blues and jazz music over a two-day period, with different line-ups for each jam. Musicians such as Stephen Stills, Buddy Miles, Roland Kirk, John Hiseman, Buddy Guy and Jack Bruce all played together to make uncommercial sounds. As a concept, it was superb. As a film, it left a lot to be desired due to technical difficulties, such as picture–sound synchronization, off about two seconds, and bad splicing. However the film, called

Supershow, is worth having in your collection as one of the last truly great happenings of the sixties. It was thought to have disappeared over the years, but Virgin released it on home video in 1986. The two highlights are Eric exchanging guitar solos with Buddy Guy, and Jack Bruce playing on the same stage as Eric only months after the end of Cream.

Live Session
18 March 1969
Staines Television Studios, Middlesex

Slate 27   *Supershow* film

Guitar: Eric Clapton
Electric bass: Jack Bruce
Upright bass: Vernon Martin
Organ: Ron Burton
Sax: Roland Kirk
        Dick Heckstall-Smith
Drums: Jon Hiseman

Everything's Gonna Be Alright   *Supershow* film

Guitar: Eric Clapton
Guitar/vocals: Buddy Guy
Bass: Stephen Stills
Drums: Buddy Miles
        Dallas Taylor
Harp: Duster Bennett
Sax: Chris Mercer
Organ: Jack Bruce

Guitar used: Gibson Firebird

Producer: Tom Parkinson
Engineer: ——

During the BLIND FAITH recording Eric also played on Billy Preston's 'That's The Way God Planned It' single, which was his first recording for Apple Records.

Studio Session for Billy Preston
April 1969
Trident Studios, Soho, London

That's The Way God Planned It   A side/
                    THAT'S THE WAY GOD PLANNED IT
Do What You Want To   B side/
                    THAT'S THE WAY GOD PLANNED IT

Guitar: Eric Clapton
        George Harrison
Bass: Keith Richards
Drums: Ginger Baker
Keyboards/vocals: Billy Preston

Guitar used: Gibson Firebird

Producer: George Harrison
Engineer: ——

Blind Faith played their first gig in London's Hyde Park at a free concert in front of an estimated crowd of 100,000 fans. The group were understandably nervous at having to live up to the world's expectations. The concert was not particularly good, but the highlights were the unexpected version of 'Under My Thumb' and Eric's amazing solo in Sam Myers' 'Sleeping In The Ground'.

Live Session
7 June 1969
Hyde Park, London

Well All Right   *Unissued*
Sea Of Joy   *Unissued*
Sleeping In The Ground   *Unissued*
Under My Thumb   *Unissued*
Can't Find My Way Home   *Unissued*
Do What You Like   *Unissued*
Presence Of The Lord   *Unissued*
Means To An End   *Unissued*
Had To Cry Today   *Unissued*

Guitar/vocals: Eric Clapton
Keyboards/vocals: Stevie Winwood
Drums: Ginger Baker
Bass: Rick Grech

Guitar used: Fender Telecaster with Stratocaster neck

Producer: ——
Engineer: ——

The show was filmed and recorded by Island Records, but the tapes were thought to have been subsequently lost. However, when Polygram bought Island in 1990 a search of the London vaults was instigated; the tapes were found, and may be partly used in a future live compilation retrospective.

Controversy followed Blind Faith, from the riots at their concerts in America to the release of their album whose cover featured a nude young girl holding a silver spaceship. It was inevitable that all this, plus the pressure of having to perform past hits from Cream and Traffic, would cause a split.

The Blind Faith tour ended at the end of August 1969. One of the support groups was Delaney And Bonnie; they greatly impressed Eric, who had a musical affinity with them. He stayed on in Los Angeles to record some tracks with them and discuss plans for his solo album, with Delaney producing. While there, Delaney also introduced him to Leon Russell. In fact, the first time Eric met Leon was at a session for Joe Cocker's version of 'Delta Lady'. Although Eric was at the session, he did not play. The guitar solo at the end of the track is actually Leon on Fender Stratocaster, and not Eric, as many of us had thought before.

Studio Session for Delaney And Bonnie
27 September–10 October 1969
A&M Studios, Los Angeles

Coming Home	A side
Groupie (Superstar)	B side

Guitar: Eric Clapton
Guitar/vocals: Delaney Bramlett
Vocals: Bonnie Bramlett
Guitar: Dave Mason
Keyboards: Bobby Whitlock
Bass: Carl Radle
Drums: Jim Gordon
Trumpet: Jim Price
Sax: Bobby Keys
Percussion: Tex Johnson
Vocals: Rita Coolidge

Guitar used: Fender Stratocaster

Producer: Delaney Bramlett
Engineer: ——

On his return to England, Eric received a call from John Lennon asking him if he would participate in a live concert the next night in Toronto, Canada. Eric, of course, accepted and flew out with the Plastic Ono Band. Rehearsals took place on the plane!

Live Session
13 October 1969
Varsity Stadium, Toronto, Canada

Blue Suede Shoes	LIVE PEACE IN TORONTO
Money	LIVE PEACE IN TORONTO
Dizzy Miss Lizzie	LIVE PEACE IN TORONTO
Yer Blues	LIVE PEACE IN TORONTO
Cold Turkey	LIVE PEACE IN TORONTO
Give Peace A Chance	LIVE PEACE IN TORONTO
Don't Worry Kyoko	LIVE PEACE IN TORONTO
John John	LIVE PEACE IN TORONTO

Guitar: Eric Clapton
Guitar/vocals: John Lennon
Bass: Klaus Voorman
Drums: Alan White
Vocals: Yoko Ono

Guitar used: Gibson Les Paul Black Top

Producers: John and Yoko
Engineer: ——

Considering they had not properly rehearsed, they performed well to an appreciative audience who were thrilled to see a Beatle in concert with Eric Clapton. Listen out for Eric's cutting guitar during the tuning-up at the start of side one. The album is as raw as the concert, and was made available on home video in 1989.

Eric also joined the Plastic Ono Band for the recording of their first single.

Studio Session for Plastic Ono Band
25–28 September 1969
Abbey Road Studios, London

Cold Turkey (26 takes)	A side

KLAUS VOORMAN: *The first time we did it, it started with John playing very straight rhythm guitar. Then we did tracks with drums and bass. In the end we had loads of incredible guitar pieces, and when we finally finished we scrapped nearly all the original ideas and got back to a very hard, tight sound which everyone was pleased with.*

Studio Session
3–6 October 1969
Abbey Road Studios, London

Don't Worry Kyoko   B side

Guitar: Eric Clapton
Guitar/vocals: John Lennon
Bass: Klaus Voorman
Drums: Ringo Starr
Vocals: Yoko Ono

Guitar used: Gibson Les Paul

Producers: John and Yoko
Engineer: Tony Clark

'Cold Turkey' was probably one of the most intense records ever released. John's anguished lyrics were rendered even more harrowing by his and Eric's guitars, providing a powerful, screaming, tortured landscape.

◆

The day after this session, Eric participated in a recording for a proposed Rick Grech solo album, which never materialized. Two tracks, however, did show up as bonus cuts on the European issue of the BLIND FAITH CD, incorrectly naming these as unreleased numbers by Blind Faith.

Studio Session for Rick Grech
7 October 1969
Morgan Studios, London

Exchange And Mart   BLIND FAITH CD
Spending All My Days   BLIND FAITH CD

Guitar: Eric Clapton
         George Harrison
Bass/violin/vocals: Rick Grech
Drums: Alan White

Other musicians known to have participated at the sessions include: Ginger Baker, Trevor Burton, Jim Capaldi, Stevie Winwood, Chris Wood and Graham Bond

Guitar used: Gibson Les Paul Black Top

Producer: ——
Engineer: ——

Eric brought over Delaney And Bonnie And Friends for a European tour at the end of October. Before this, however, Eric played on a Leon Russell session, as did many other top English musicians such as George Harrison, Stevie Winwood, Ringo Starr, Charlie Watts, Bill Wyman, Klaus Voorman, Jon Hiseman and Chris Stainton. When Delaney And Bonnie And Friends arrived in late October they joined in Leon's sessions, as well as recording numbers with Eric for his solo album.

Studio Session for Doris Troy
October 1969
Apple Studios and Trident Studios, London

Ain't That Cute   A side/DORIS TROY

Guitar: Eric Clapton
Vocals: Doris Troy
Guitar: George Harrison
Drums: Ringo Starr
Bass: Klaus Voorman
Sax: Bobby Keys
Trumpet: Jim Price
Keyboards: Gary Wright
Keyboards/backing vocals: Billy Preston

Give Me Back My Dynamite   DORIS TROY

Guitar: Eric Clapton
Vocals: Doris Troy
Guitar: George Harrison
Organ/backing vocals: Billy Preston
Drums: Ringo Starr
Bass: Klaus Voorman

I've Got To Be Strong   DORIS TROY

Guitar: Eric Clapton
Vocals: Doris Troy
Guitar: George Harrison
Organ/backing vocals: Billy Preston
Keyboards: Gary Wright
Drums: Ringo Starr

You Give Me Joy Joy   DORIS TROY

Guitar: Eric Clapton
Vocals: Doris Troy
Guitar: George Harrison
         Stephen Stills (first solo)
         Peter Frampton (second solo)
Sax: Bobby Keys

Apple Records Present
DORIS TROY

Ain't that cute
Produced by George Harrison
Apple 24 Released 13th February

Trumpet: Jim Price
Organ/backing vocals: Billy Preston
Bass: Klaus Voorman
Drums: Ringo Starr

Don't Call Me No More   DORIS TROY

Guitar: Eric Clapton
Vocals: Doris Troy
Guitar: George Harrison
Organ/backing vocals: Billy Preston
Drums: Ringo Starr
Bass: Klaus Voorman

Get Back   B side/DORIS TROY CD

Guitar: Eric Clapton
Vocals: Doris Troy
Guitar: George Harrison
Organ/backing vocals: Billy Preston
Drums: Ringo Starr
Bass: Klaus Voorman
Sax: Bobby Keys
Trumpet: Jim Price

Guitar used: probably Gibson Firebird

Producer: George Harrison
Engineer: ———

Studio Session for Leon Russell
October–November 1969
Olympic Sound Studios, Barnes, London

Prince Of Peace   LEON RUSSELL
Sweet Home Chicago   *Unissued*
Blues jam   *Unissued*

Guitar: Eric Clapton
Piano/vocals/guitar: Leon Russell
Bass: Klaus Voorman
Drums: Jon Hiseman

Alcatraz   LEON RUSSELL AND THE SHELTER PEOPLE
Beware Of Darkness   LEON RUSSELL AND THE SHELTER PEOPLE

Guitar: Eric Clapton
Piano/vocals/guitar: Leon Russell
Bass: Carl Radle
Drums: Jim Gordon

Guitar used: Fender Stratocaster

Producer: Denny Cordell and Leon Russell
Engineer: Glyn Johns

Studio Session for Shawn Phillips
October 1969
Trident Studios, Soho, London

Man Hole Covered Wagon   CONTRIBUTION

Guitar: Eric Clapton
Guitar/vocals: Shawn Phillips
Organ: Stevie Winwood
Piano: Mick Weaver
Conga: John Carr

Guitar used: Gibson Les Paul

Producer: Jonathan Weston
Engineer: Robin Cable

This session is defintely not essential for fans of Eric's guitar work, as it is so well buried in the mix that you can hardly hear him!

Studio Session for start of solo album
November 1969
Olympic Sound Studios, Barnes and
Trident Studios, Soho, London

Told You For The Last Time (8 takes)	*Unissued*
Lovin' You, Lovin' Me	ERIC CLAPTON
I Don't Know Why	*Unissued*
Where There's A Will There's A Way	*Unissued*
She Rides	*Unissued*

Guitar/vocals: Eric Clapton
                        Delaney Bramlett
Vocals: Bonnie Bramlett
Drums: Jim Gordon
Bass: Carl Radle
Organ/vocals: Bobby Whitlock
Trumpet: Jim Price
Sax: Bobby Keys
Vocals: Rita Coolidge
Percussion: Tex Johnson

Guitars used: Fender Stratocaster, Gibson Les Paul

Producer: Delaney Bramlett
Engineer: ———

After rehearsing at Eric's home, Delaney And Bonnie And Friends went on tour. They started in Germany, which included a television appearance on *Beat Club*, and went on to the UK, Scandinavia and, later, the USA. George Harrison joined them for most of the UK dates as well as three shows in Copenhagen. One of these Danish shows was televised and may even see release on home video at some time in the future.

The first and last UK concerts were recorded for a live album, released as ON TOUR.

Live Session for *Beat Club* TV programme
November 1969
Studio not known

Coming Home	TV broadcast
Poor Elijah (Tribute to Robert Johnson)	TV broadcast
Where There's A Will There's A Way	TV broadcast

Musicians as listed for Royal Albert Hall shows

Live Session
1 December 1969
Royal Albert Hall, London

Two shows

Tracks not known and have not been issued

Guitar/vocals: Eric Clapton
                        Delaney Bramlett
Vocals: Bonnie Bramlett
Guitar: Dave Mason
Drums: Jim Gordon
Bass: Carl Radle
Organ/vocals: Bobby Whitlock
Trumpet: Jim Price
Sax: Bobby Keys
Vocals: Rita Coolidge
Percussion: Tex Johnson

Guitar used: Gibson Les Paul

Producers: Jimmy Miller, Delaney Bramlett
Engineers: Andy Johns, Glyn Johns

Live Session
7 December 1969
Fairfield Halls, Croydon

Two shows

Things Get Better	ON TOUR
Poor Elijah (Tribute to Robert Johnson)	ON TOUR
Only You Know And I Know	ON TOUR
I Don't Want To Discuss It	ON TOUR
That's What My Man Is For	ON TOUR
Where There's A Will There's A Way	ON TOUR
Coming Home	ON TOUR
Little Richard Medley	ON TOUR

Musicians same as Royal Albert Hall plus:
Guitar: George Harrison

Guitar used: Gibson Les Paul

Producers: Jimmy Miller, Delaney Bramlett
Engineers: Andy Johns, Glyn Johns

52

Live Session
13 December 1969
Falkoner Theatre, Copenhagen

Tracks not known but were similar to the Croydon shows and the show was televised in Denmark

Musicians same as Fairfield Halls, Croydon

As soon as the tour finished, plans were already in motion for more recording, including the completion of Eric's solo album, a session with sax ace King Curtis and some Buddy Holly tunes with The Crickets, all to be done early in 1970 at Village Recorders and Sunset Sound in Los Angeles.

ERIC CLAPTON: *We've worked out a few things we are going to do together … like we are going to do some recording – we've already cut a 'live one' at the Royal Albert Hall and Fairfield Halls in Croydon. At the same time as we do studio recording, we can go out and play a few concerts.*

Before heading off to Los Angeles, however, Eric joined The Plastic Ono Band in a special UNICEF charity *Peace For Christmas* concert at the Lyceum in London, alongside a cast of thousands, and played on a session for his friend Vivian Stanshall.

Live Session for Plastic Ono Band
15 December 1969
Lyceum Ballroom, London

Cold Turkey	SOMETIME IN NEW YORK CITY
Don't Worry Kyoko	SOMETIME IN NEW YORK CITY

Guitar: Eric Clapton
Guitar/vocals: John Lennon
Vocals: Yoko Ono
Drums: Jim Gordon
      Alan White
Bass: Klaus Voorman
Guitar: George Harrison
      Delaney Bramlett
Keyboards: Billy Preston
Percussion: Bonnie Bramlett
      Keith Moon
Trumpet: Jim Price
Sax: Bobby Keys
Tambourine: Legs Larry Smith
      Tony Ashton

Guitar used: early sixties Fender Stratocaster painted in day-glo colours, loaned to Eric by George Harrison

Producers: John and Yoko
Engineer: ——

This amazing one-off band only played two numbers, which were basically the A and B side of the new Plastic Ono Band single. The press were not too kind in their reviews, but the show remained one of John's favourite musical evenings and he even went on to say, in an interview in 1980, that the show may have been an inspiration to the punk bands of the late seventies. The music was indeed chaotic and could not be ignored, whether you liked it or not.

Studio Session for Vivian Stanshall
December 1969
Studio not known

Labio-Dental Fricative	A side
Paper Round	B side

Guitar: Eric Clapton
Vocals: Vivian Stanshall
Bass: Denis Cowan
Percussion: Rema Kabaka

Guitar used: probably Gibson Les Paul

Producer: ——
Engineer: ——

Eric spent most of January recording his first solo album, with Delaney Bramlett producing and the Friends providing the backing. One of the first things Eric did on arrival in Los Angeles was to participate in a session for King Curtis.

Studio Session for King Curtis
January 1970
Sunset Sound Studios, Los Angeles

Teasin'	A side

Guitar: Eric Clapton
Soprano sax: King Curtis
Acoustic guitar/rhythm guitar: Delaney Bramlett
Bass: Carl Radle
Drums: Jim Gordon

Guitar used: Sunburst Fender Stratocaster

Producer: Delaney Bramlett
Engineer: Bill Halverson

Studio Session
January 1970
Village Recorders, Los Angeles

Slunky   ERIC CLAPTON

ERIC CLAPTON: *The first track on side one will be the instrumental we did, which was just a good day of recording in Los Angeles, when Leon Russell came along. It was just a jam. Sounds nice, I'm really pleased with it. It's also matched to another track called 'Blues Power', which is a song that Leon wrote. The words are really applicable to me.*

Blues Power   ERIC CLAPTON
Lonesome And A Long Way From Home   ERIC CLAPTON

ERIC CLAPTON: *It's a song Delaney wrote a long time ago. Originally he did it acoustically, and the Hertz people were trying to buy it from him for a commercial. He was doing it when I arrived in Los Angeles and King Curtis didn't like his voice on it. Curtis doesn't sing much but he's a great singer. So I said I'd like to do a version of it.*

After Midnight   ERIC CLAPTON

ERIC CLAPTON: *It's a song that J.J. Cale wrote. He's one of those people from Tulsa and I think he's an engineer now. He made a record of it and I dug the record a lot so we did our version of that.*

Lovin' You, Lovin' Me   ERIC CLAPTON

ERIC CLAPTON: *It started out as a song that Delaney and Leon wrote for Blind Faith to do. I liked it very much. I don't know if the others ever heard it. I said I wanted to do it if I ever did a solo album, so we changed it around a bit to suit the way I could sing it and cut it in England.*

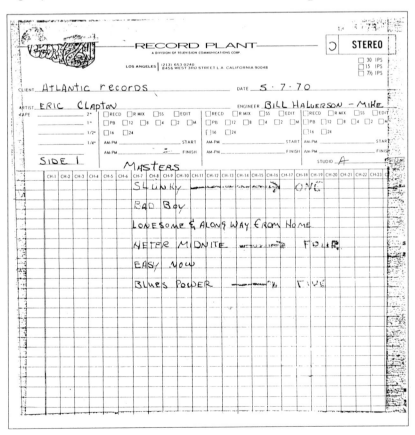

Don't Know Why   ERIC CLAPTON

ERIC CLAPTON: *It's a love ballad, a love song kind of thing. It was an idea that Delaney had when he came to England, and we finished it while he was staying at my house. We recorded it again in Los Angeles.*

Bottle Of Red Wine   ERIC CLAPTON

ERIC CLAPTON: *It's a ballad too. We were going to the studio one day in LA and we had no songs, nothing at all to do. We were getting panicky on the way and we just thought up the song and did it when we got there. It's just a shuffle.*

I Told You For The Last Time   ERIC CLAPTON

ERIC CLAPTON: *It's a song Delaney played on acoustic guitar. One of his motel shot numbers I think. We changed that around and arranged it for a big band sort of feel and it came out like a country number really.*

She Rides   *Unissued*

ERIC CLAPTON: 'She Rides' *just came from the lyrics of the original song we wrote. But when we went into the studio, the track came off so well that we abandoned the original song and since then I've been trying to think up a set of lyrics to go with the track.*

Let It Rain (was She Rides)   ERIC CLAPTON
Bad Boy   ERIC CLAPTON
Easy Now   ERIC CLAPTON

Guitar/vocals: Eric Clapton
                Delaney Bramlett
Vocals: Bonnie Bramlett
         Rita Coolidge
         Sonny Curtis
         Jerry Allison
Piano: Leon Russell
Organ: Bobby Whitlock
Bass: Carl Radle
Drums: Jim Gordon
Trumpet: Jim Price
Sax: Bobby Keys
Guitar/vocals: Stephen Stills (on Let It Rain)

Guitar used: Sunburst Fender Stratocaster

Producer: Delaney Bramlett
Engineer: Bill Halverson

Three mixes of the album exist and all are remarkably different. The finished product that was released was mixed by Atlantic's Tom Dowd.

ERIC CLAPTON: *I left the tapes in LA for Delaney to mix them, and he was waiting on me to finish one of the tracks! And he didn't realize that I was waiting on him to mix the tracks and send them over. Finally, my manager got kind of impatient and told Atlantic to send the tapes to me, and I mixed them very badly. Atlantic heard them, didn't like 'em. Then they sent them to Tom Dowd, who mixed them again. So they were mixed three times in all. Naturally, I never heard Delaney's mixes until it was too late – the record was already out.*

Having heard all three, I would say Delaney's was the best, giving Eric's guitar a more prominent sound.

◆

Eric also recorded a couple of tracks with Buddy Holly's backing band, The Crickets, for their album ROCKIN' 50's ROCK 'N' ROLL.

Studio Session for The Crickets
January 1970
Village Recorders, Los Angeles

Rockin' 50's Rock 'N' Roll   ROCKIN' 50's ROCK 'N' ROLL
That'll Be The Day   ROCKIN' 50's ROCK 'N' ROLL

Guitar: Eric Clapton
Vocals: Jerry Allison
         Sonny Curtis
Guitar/vocals: Delaney Bramlett
Drums: Jim Gordon
Bass: Carl Radle
Organ: Bobby Whitlock
Piano: Leon Russell
Trumpet: Jim Price
Sax: Bobby Keys

Guitar used: Sunburst Fender Stratocaster

Producer: Delaney Bramlett
Engineer: ———

After the solo album sessions, Eric joined Delaney And Bonnie for a short American tour which included an appearance on ABC's *Dick Cavett Show*. During a three-day break in the touring schedule Eric also participated in a huge jam session at the Record Plant in New York. It was organized by Earle Doud, who normally produced big-selling American satire albums. Other musicians involved included Jeff Beck, Keith Emerson, Delaney Bramlett, Mitch Mitchell, Dr John, Harvey Mandel, Todd Rundgren and Linda Ronstadt.

The resultant album was to be called SUMMIT MEETING and released on Ahmet Ertegun's Atlantic label. However, due to severe contractual difficulties he dropped the project, as Eric Clapton's and Jeff Beck's managers refused permission for their artists to be named. A double album was eventually released two years later on the Charisma label, with Eric appearing as King Cool.

Studio Session for SUMMIT MEETING project
3–5 February 1970
Record Plant, New York

Road Song   MUSIC FROM FREE CREEK

Guitar: Eric Clapton
Piano: Dr John
Organ: Moogy Klingman (Vagrants)
Drums: Richard Crooks (Dr John)
Bass: Stu Woods (Congregation)
Rhythm guitar: Delaney Bramlett (Delaney And Bonnie)
Vocals: Tommy Cosgrove (Congregation)

Getting Back To Molly   MUSIC FROM FREE CREEK

Guitar: Eric Clapton
       Dr John
Harp: Moogy Klingman (Vagrants)
Vocal: Earle Doud
Bass: Stu Woods (Congregation)
Drums: Richard Crooks (Dr John)
Back-up vocals: Maretha Stewart (Motown singer)
               Hilda Harris (Motown singer)
Back-up singer: Valerie Simpson (Motown singer)

No One Knows   MUSIC FROM FREE CREEK

Guitar: Eric Clapton
Vocal: Eric Mercury
Organ: Dr John
Piano: Moogy Klingman (Vagrants)

Bass: Stu Woods (Congregation)
Trombone: Lou Delgatto (Buddy Rich Big Band)
               Bobby Keller (Buddy Rich Big Band)
               Meco Monardo
Trumpet: Bill Chase (Woody Herman Band)
            Lou Soloff (Blood Sweat And Tears)
            Alan Rubin (Blood Sweat And Tears)
Drums: Richard Crooks (Dr John)
Back-up vocals: same as Getting Back To Molly

Guitar used: Sunburst Fender Stratocaster

Producers: Earle Doud, Tom Flye
Engineers: Tony Bongiovi, Jack Hunt

When the Delaney And Bonnie tour ended, Eric returned to the UK to finish one of the songs for his solo album. Later he received the remainder of the tapes to supervise the mixing of the album by Bill Halverson, who was also working on Stephen Still's first solo album at Island Studios.

March and April were busy months for Eric. Not only was he busy mixing his first solo project, he also helped friends out on various sessions. These were Stephen Stills, Ashton Gardner And Dyke, Billy Preston, Jesse Ed Davis, Jonathan Kelly and Howlin' Wolf.

Live Session for Delaney And Bonnie
5 February 1970
ABC Television Studios, New York

Coming Home   TV broadcast
Poor Elijah   TV broadcast
Where There's A Will There's A Way   TV broadcast

Guitar: Eric Clapton
Rest: Delaney And Bonnie And Friends

Studio Session for Stephen Stills
March 1970
Island Studios, London

Go Back Home   STEPHEN STILLS
Fishes and Scorpions   STEPHEN STILLS 2

Guitar: Eric Clapton
Guitar/keyboards/vocals: Stephen Stills

Bass: Calvin Samuels
Drums: Dallas Taylor

Guitar used: Sunburst Fender Stratocaster

Producers: Stephen Stills, Bill Halverson
Engineer: Bill Halverson

STEPHEN STILLS: 'Go Back Home' *was done first take. Actually, that's Eric just warming up. You know, he said: 'Let me practise a little' and Bill [Halverson, co-producer and engineer] would say 'Sure' – click! And he'd take it. That's Eric Clapton warming up, folks.*

Studio Session for Ashton Gardner And Dyke
March 1970
De Lane Lea Sound Centre, Soho, London

I'm Your Spiritual Breadman   THE WORST OF A, G AND D

Guitar: Eric Clapton
        George Harrison
Piano/organ/vocals: Tony Ashton
Bass: Kim Gardner
Drums: Roy Dyke
Trumpet: Jim Price
Sax: Bobby Keys

Guitar used: Sunburst Fender Stratocaster

Producer: Ashton Gardner And Dyke
Engineer: John Stewart

Studio Session for Jonathan Kelly
March 1970
Studio unknown

Don't You Believe It   A side

Slide guitar: Eric Clapton
Guitar/vocals: Jonathan Kelly
Keyboards: Tony Ashton
Bass: Kim Gardner
Drums: Roy Dyke
Guitar used: Sunburst Fender Stratocaster

Producer: ——
Engineer: ——

JONATHAN KELLY: *Eric Clapton played slide on* 'Don't You Believe It'. *Colin Peterson [ex-drummer with the Bee Gees] used to work for Stigwood, and I*

guess he met the Cream guys when he was in the office, and asked Eric if he'd come and play on a twelve-bar, and he just turned up, which blew my mind. He listened to the backing tracks and bang, just played it.

Studio Session for Ringo Starr
March 1970
Apple Studios, London

It Don't Come Easy (three versions)   A side

Guitar: Eric Clapton
Drums/vocals: Ringo Starr
Guitar: George Harrison
Piano: Stephen Stills
Bass: Klaus Voorman

Guitar played: ——

Producer: George Harrison
Engineer: ——

Melody Maker reported Eric and Stephen Stills at Apple playing on a session for Ringo's 'It Don't Come Easy' single. However, I have not been able definitely to verify this fact, as all the above musicians were in and out of Apple sessions quite frequently at this time. Certainly the version that was released does not sound like Eric's playing, in which case he must be on one of the out-takes.

Studio Session for Howlin' Wolf
April 1970
Olympic Sound Studios, Barnes, London

I Ain't Superstitious	THE LONDON HOWLIN' WOLF SESSIONS
Poor Boy	THE LONDON HOWLIN' WOLF SESSIONS
The Red Rooster (rehearsal)	THE LONDON HOWLIN' WOLF SESSIONS
The Red Rooster	THE LONDON HOWLIN' WOLF SESSIONS
Worried About My Baby	THE LONDON HOWLIN' WOLF SESSIONS
Do The Do	THE LONDON HOWLIN' WOLF SESSIONS
Built For Comfort	THE LONDON HOWLIN' WOLF SESSIONS
Sitting On Top Of The World	THE LONDON HOWLIN' WOLF SESSIONS
Highway 49	THE LONDON HOWLIN' WOLF SESSIONS
What A Woman	THE LONDON HOWLIN' WOLF SESSIONS
Who's Been Talking	THE LONDON HOWLIN' WOLF SESSIONS
Rockin' Daddy	THE LONDON HOWLIN' WOLF SESSIONS

Wang Dang Doodle   THE LONDON HOWLIN' WOLF SESSIONS
Going Down Slow   LONDON REVISITED
Killing Floor   LONDON REVISITED
I Want To Have A Word With You   LONDON REVISITED

Guitar: Eric Clapton
Vocals: Howlin' Wolf (harmonica on Worried About My Baby,
    Who's Been Talking; acoustic guitar on Red Rooster)
Piano/organ: Stevie Winwood
Bass: Bill Wyman
Drums: Charlie Watts
Rhythm guitar: Hubert Sumlin
Harmonica: Jeffrey Carp
Piano: Ian Stewart (Rockin' Daddy, Built For Comfort, Do The
        Do, Wang Dang Doodle)
        John Simon (Who's Been Talking)
        Lafayette Leake (Sitting On Top Of The World, Worried
        About My Baby, Red Rooster)
Bass: Klaus Voorman (I Ain't Superstitious)
       Phil Upchurch (Rockin' Daddy)
Drums: Ringo Starr (I Ain't Superstitious)
Horns: Joe Miller
       Jordan Sandke
       Dennis Lansing (I Ain't Superstitious, Built For Comfort)

Guitar used: Sunburst Fender Stratocaster

Producer: Norman Dayron
Engineer: Glyn Johns

GLYN JOHNS: *I very much wanted to work with Howlin' Wolf, so whether I was producer or not meant very little, because it was a good opportunity to maybe learn something again, and from that point of view it was very well worth doing. Wolf was absolutely amazing, it was a fascinating experience from that point of view, and also watching the young English rock 'n' roll whiteys react with this man.*

ERIC CLAPTON: *Howlin' taught me how to play 'Red Rooster'. It was a hairy experience. He came over and got hold of my wrist and said, 'You move your hand up HERE!' He was very, very vehement about it being done right. Because he considered us to be English and foreigners, and therefore we wouldn't have heard the song, right? So he just got his guitar out and said, 'This is how it goes.' It's not on the album unfortunately, but he played it all the way through once on his own with us just sitting there and listening. He was playing slide dobro, and it was just bloody amazing! And he said, 'Okay, you try it.' So we all tried playing it like him, but it didn't sound right, so I said, 'Well, why don't you do it*

with us?' And that's the bit that got on the record.

The guy that organized the session wanted me to play lead instead of Hubert Sumlin [Howlin's guitar player]. Hubert ended up supplementing, playing rhythm, which I thought was all wrong, because he knew all the parts that were necessary and I didn't. For the first couple of days I was scared stiff of the 'Wolf', because he wasn't saying anything to anyone – he just sat there in a corner and let this young white kid kinda run the show and tell everyone what to do! It was a bit strange . . . and when he finally did open up he was great, but he was very intimidating to look at. We weren't sure what he was thinking. But with Charlie Watts and Bill Wyman playing and everything, it was great and – well, I think it turned out pretty well . . . that album.

Studio Session for Billy Preston
April 1970
Apple Studios and Trident Studios, London

Right Now   ENCOURAGING WORDS
Encouraging Words   ENCOURAGING WORDS

Guitar: Eric Clapton
Keyboards/vocals: Billy Preston
Guitar: George Harrison
Drums: Ringo Starr
Bass: Klaus Voorman
Backing vocals: Doris Troy

Guitar used: Sunburst Fender Stratocaster

Producer: George Harrison

Studio Session for Jesse Ed Davis
April 1970
Olympic Sound Studios, Barnes, London, and
Village Recorders, Los Angeles

Reno Street Incident   JESSE DAVIS
Tulsa County   JESSE DAVIS
Washita Love Child   JESSE DAVIS
Every Night Is Saturday Night   JESSE DAVIS
You Belladonna You   JESSE DAVIS
Rock And Roll Gypsies   JESSE DAVIS
Golden Sun Goddess   JESSE DAVIS
Crazy Love   JESSE DAVIS

Guitar: Eric Clapton
Guitar/keyboards/vocals: Jesse Ed Davis
Drums:Alan White
       Bruce Rowland
       Steve Mitchell
       Chuck Blackwell
Bass: Billy Rich
       Steve Thompson
Brass: James Gordon
       Jerry Jumonville
       Darrell Leonard
       Frank Mayes
Keyboards: Larry Knechtel
       Leon Russell
       Ben Sidran
       Larry Pierce
Percussion: Patt Daley
       Sandy Konikoff
       Jackie Lomax
       Pete Waddington
Backing vocals: Merry Clayton
       Vanetta Fields
       Gloria Jones
       Clydie King
       Gram Parsons

Guitar used: Sunburst Fender Stratocaster

Producer: Jesse Ed Davis
Engineer: Glyn Johns

Eric was spending most of his time in and out of recording studios, not really knowing what direction to head in.

ERIC CLAPTON: *I sat down in a state of confusion for some time after the Delaney And Bonnie tour, with no particular plans or whatever. Bobby Whitlock had left them and came to England as an instinctive move and it all started rolling from there.*

He was pleased with his solo album and wanted to tour to be able to play the new songs live. So when Bobby Whitlock arrived, it seemed obvious to bring in 'Friends' Carl Radle and Jim Gordon, who had just left Joe Cocker's Mad Dogs and Englishmen. They rehearsed at Eric's house, just as had Blind Faith and Delaney And Bonnie. The first session they did was for George Harrison's solo album, providing backing on the majority of the tracks. During the session they also recorded their first single with George.

Studio Session for George Harrison
May, June, July 1970
Apple Studios, Abbey Road Studios, Trident Studios, all London

Wah Wah	ALL THINGS MUST PASS
Isn't It A Pity	ALL THINGS MUST PASS
What Is Life	ALL THINGS MUST PASS
Run Of The Mill	ALL THINGS MUST PASS
Beware Of Darkness	ALL THINGS MUST PASS
Awaiting On You All	ALL THINGS MUST PASS
My Sweet Lord	ALL THINGS MUST PASS

Guitar: Eric Clapton
Guitar/vocals: George Harrison
Guitar: Dave Mason
Bass: Carl Radle
Drums: Jim Gordon
       Ringo Starr
Keyboards: Gary Wright
Trumpet: Jim Price
Sax: Bobby Keys
Keyboards: Gary Brooker (My Sweet Lord)
Backing vocals: Badfinger

Guitar used: Sunburst Fender Stratocaster

Out Of The Blue	ALL THINGS MUST PASS

Guitar: Eric Clapton
       George Harrison
Bass: Carl Radle
Drums: Jim Gordon
Keyboards: Bobby Whitlock
       Gary Wright
Trumpet: Jim Price
Sax: Bobby Keys

Plug Me In	ALL THINGS MUST PASS

Guitar: Eric Clapton
       George Harrison
       Dave Mason
Bass: Carl Radle
Drums: Jim Gordon
Keyboards: Bobby Whitlock

I Remember Jeep (jam)	ALL THINGS MUST PASS

Guitar: Eric Clapton
       George Harrison
Drums: Ginger Baker
Bass: Klaus Voorman
Keyboards: Billy Preston

Thanks For The Pepperoni (jam)   ALL THINGS MUST PASS

Guitar: Eric Clapton
          George Harrison
          Dave Mason
Bass: Carl Radle
Drums: Jim Gordon
Keyboards: Bobby Whitlock

Guitar used: Sunburst Fender Stratocaster

Producer: ——
Engineer: ——

Studio Session for first Derek And The Dominos single
18 June 1970
Apple Studios, London

Tell The Truth   A side
Roll It Over   B side

Guitar/vocals: Eric Clapton
Guitar: George Harrison
Bass: Carl Radle
Drums: Bobby Whitlock
Keyboards: Bobby Whitlock
Guitar: Dave Mason (Roll It Over)

Guitar used: Sunburst Fender Stratocaster

Producer: Phil Spector
Engineer: ——

Phil Spector's production was not sympathetic to their sound. So when the single came out in September it was almost immediately withdrawn at Eric and the band's request, as they had just recorded a new, superior version at Criteria Studios in Miami. Consequently, the single now fetches high prices on the collector's market although both tracks are readily available on the excellent CROSSROADS retrospective.

Derek And The Dominos played their first gig at the Lyceum in June, while still recording with George Harrison. They planned a large British tour of clubs and mid-size venues in August before going to Miami to record their historic LAYLA album.

◆

Eric still found time in July to play on a session for Dr John, who was planning a triple album called SUN MOON AND HERBS.

Studio Session for Dr John
July 1970
Trident Studios, Soho, London

Black John The Conqueror   SUN MOON AND HERBS

Basic personnel:
Slide guitar: Eric Clapton
Guitar/piano/organ/vibes/percussion: Dr John
Rhythm guitar: Tommy Feronne
Trumpet/organ: Vic Brox
Tuba/percussion/vocals: Ray Draper
Trap drums: Fred Staehle
Backing vocals: Mick Jagger
                 Shirley Goodman
                 Tammi Lynn
                 PP Arnold
                 Joni Jonz
Plus:
Flute: Ken Terroade
Sax: Chris Mercer
Alto sax: Graham Bond
Piano: Walter Davis
Backing vocals: Doris Troy
                 Bobby Whitlock
Horns: The Memphis Horns

Where Ya At Mule   SUN MOON AND HERBS

Basic personnel as Black John The Conqueror plus:
Tenor sax: Bobby Keys
Bass: Carl Radle
Congas: Jim Gordon
Backing vocals: Doris Troy
                 Bobby Whitlock
Horns: The Memphis Horns

Craney Crow   SUN MOON AND HERBS

Basic personnel as Black John The Conqueror plus:
Flute: Ken Terroade
Piano: Walter Davis
Bass: Jesse Boyce
Percussion: Freeman Brown

Pots On Fiyo/Who I Got To Fall On   SUN MOON AND HERBS

Basic personnel as Black John The Conqueror plus:
Trumpet: Jim Price
Alto sax: Graham Bond
Flute: Ken Terroade
Piano: Walter Davis
Acoustic bass: Steve York
Congas: Calvin Samuels
Percussion: Freeman Brown
Horns: The Memphis Horns

Zu Zu Mama
SUN MOON AND HERBS

Basic personnel as Black John The Conqueror plus:
Flute: Ken Terroade
Acoustic bass: Steve York
Percussion: Jesse Boyce
            Freeman Brown
Backing vocals: Doris Troy

Familiar Reality – reprise
SUN MOON AND HERBS

Basic personnel as Black John The Conqueror plus:
Tenor sax: Bobby Keys
Alto sax: Graham Bond
Sax: Chris Mercer
Trumpet: Jim Price
Bass: Carl Radle

Congas: Jim Gordon
Backing vocals: Doris Troy
                       Bobby Whitlock

Guitar used: Fender Telecaster

Producers: Malcolm Rebennack, Charles Greene
Engineer: Roy Baker

Although 12 sides of 16-track tape were filled, only the above tracks were released, many in edited form. So the original idea of a triple album was reduced to a single.

◆

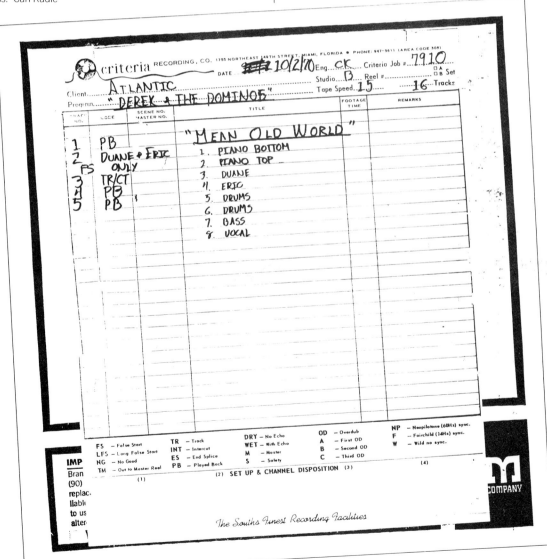

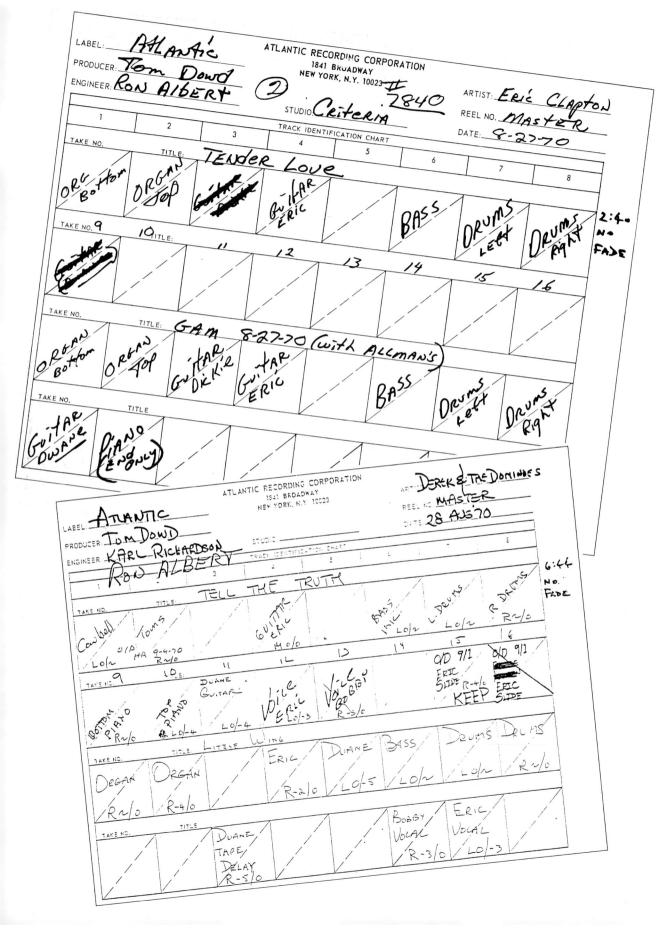

Derek And The Dominos flew out to Miami in late August to start recording their first album. They had played several gigs by now and were quite tight musically. Once at Miami's Criteria Studios, they started jamming and recording songs written during their early weeks together at Eric's house. Duane Allman joined in the sessions early on as second guitarist at the request of Eric, who had met him at an Allman Brothers Band show. Both Duane and Eric hit it off straightaway, having admired each other's guitar styles on different sessions and records. The Allman Brothers Band also jammed a few times with The Dominos at Criteria, whilst recording the historic LAYLA double album.

Studio Session for Derek And The Dominos
August–September 1970
Criteria Studios, Miami

Key of E jam	20TH ANNIVERSARY
Key of D jam (20 minutes)	*Unissued*

Guitar: Eric Clapton
        Duane Allman
        Dickey Betts
Organ: Bobby Whitlock
Piano: Gregg Allman
Bass: Berry Oakley
Drums: Butch Trucks

Key of D jam	20TH ANNIVERSARY

Guitar: Eric Clapton
Bass: Carl Radle
Organ: Bobby Whitlock
Drums: Jim Gordon

Key of A jam	20TH ANNIVERSARY

Guitar: Eric Clapton
        Duane Allman
Bass: Carl Radle
Organ: Bobby Whitlock
Drums: Jim Gordon

Key of B jam	20TH ANNIVERSARY
Key of E jam	20TH ANNIVERSARY

Guitar: Eric Clapton
Bass: Carl Radle
Organ: Bobby Whitlock
Drums: Jim Gordon

Tender Love (no vocals)	*Unissued*
Tender Love (key of A)	*Unissued*
Tender Love (alternative master)	20TH ANNIVERSARY
I Looked Away	20TH ANNIVERSARY
Bell Bottom Blues	20TH ANNIVERSARY
Have You Ever Loved A Woman (alternative 1)	20TH ANNIVERSARY
Have You Ever Loved A Woman (alternative 2)	20TH ANNIVERSARY
Tell The Truth jam 1	20TH ANNIVERSARY
Tell The Truth jam 2	20TH ANNIVERSARY

Guitar/vocals: Eric Clapton
Bass: Carl Radle
Organ/paino/vocals: Bobby Whitlock
Drums: Jim Gordon

It Hurts Me Too (jam)	20TH ANNIVERSARY

Guitar: Eric Clapton
        Duane Allman

Keep On Growing	20TH ANNIVERSARY
Nobody Knows You When You're Down And Out	20TH ANNIVERSARY
I Am Yours	20TH ANNIVERSARY
Anyday	20TH ANNIVERSARY
Key To The Highway	20TH ANNIVERSARY
Why Does Love Got To Be So Sad	20TH ANNIVERSARY
Have You Ever Loved A Woman	20TH ANNIVERSARY
Little Wing	20TH ANNIVERSARY
It's Too Late	20TH ANNIVERSARY
It's Too Late (alternative)	20TH ANNIVERSARY
Layla	20TH ANNIVERSARY
Thorn Tree In The Garden	20TH ANNIVERSARY
Mean Old World (several takes)	20TH ANNIVERSARY

Guitar/vocals: Eric Clapton
Guitar: Duane Allman
Bass: Carl Radle
Drums: Jim Gordon
Keyboards/vocals: Bobby Whitlock

Guitar used: Sunburst Fender Stratocaster

Mean Old World	20TH ANNIVERSARY

Guitar/vocals: Eric Clapton
Guitar: Duane Allman
Bass drum: Jim Gordon

Mean Old World   CROSSROADS

Guitar/vocals: Eric Clapton
Guitar: Duane Allman

Guitar used: dobro

Producers: Derek And The Dominos, Tom Dowd
Engineers: Ron Albert, Chuck Kirkpatrick, Howie Albert, Karl
   Richardson, Mac Emmerman

TOM DOWD: *After the Allman Brothers concert was over, they all came back to the studio and jammed until, like, six o'clock the next night. There was no control, you just kept the machines rolling. It was a wonderful experience.*

ERIC CLAPTON: *It didn't sell a fucking copy for about two years. Now it sells more each year than it has the previous year. It didn't even make the charts in Britain, although the single got in about three years after the album came out. You see, I just refused to have my name displayed across the album. The idea wasn't even to have a double album. It was the thing where you've got so many tracks that you can't decide what to use, so you decide that if you cut two or three more maybe you can make a double album.*

As soon as they had finished their sessions, they returned to the UK to play the remainder of their tour there before heading off to start a US tour. Two dates at the Fillmore East were recorded for possible release. Before this, however, Eric flew out to Paris to jam with Buddy Guy and Junior Wells.

Live Session
22 September 1970
Palais des Sports, Paris

It's My Life Baby   Radio broadcast

Guitar: Eric Clapton
       Buddy Guy
Vocals/Harmonica: Junior Wells
Rest: ———

Guitar used: Sunburst Fender Stratocaster

Producer: ———

Live Session
23 October 1970
Fillmore East, New York

Second Set

Got To Get Better In A Little While	IN CONCERT
Key To The Highway	CROSSROADS
Tell The Truth	*Unissued*
Why Does Love Got To Be So Sad	*Unissued*
Blues Power/Have You Ever Loved A Woman	*Unissued*
Bottle Of Red Wine	IN CONCERT
Presence Of The Lord	*Unissued*
Little Wing (with organ breakdown)	*Guitar Player Magazine*
Let It Rain	*Unissued*
Crossroads	CROSSROADS

Guitar/vocals: Eric Clapton
Bass: Carl Radle
Drums: Jim Gordon
Keyboards/vocals: Bobby Whitlock

Guitar used: Sunburst Fender Stratocaster

Producer: ———
Engineer: Eddie Kramer

Live Session
24 October 1970
Fillmore East, New York

Second Set

Got To Get Better In A Little While	*Unissued*
Blues Power/Have You Ever Loved A Woman	IN CONCERT
Key To The Highway	*Unissued*
Tell The Truth	IN CONCERT
Nobody Knows You When You're Down And Out	*Unissued*
Let It Rain	IN CONCERT
Why Does Love Got To Be So Sad	IN CONCERT
Presence Of The Lord	IN CONCERT
Bottle Of Red Wine	*Unissued*
Roll It Over	IN CONCERT
Little Wing	*Unissued*

Guitar/vocals: Eric Clapton
Bass: Carl Radle
Drums: Jim Gordon
Keyboards/vocals: Bobby Whitlock

Guitar used: Sunburst Fender Stratocaster

Producer: ——
Engineer: Eddie Kramer

Eric's playing in concert during this period was aggressive, almost Hendrix-like in some circumstances. Luckily, some of the shows were recorded.

◆

Eric went back to Criteria Studios in Miami during a break in the Dominos tour to record with and produce an album by Buddy Guy and Junior Wells. It was partly Buddy Guy's use of a Fender Stratocaster in the sixties that made Eric change over to one, replacing his Gibson Les Paul. The two of them had first played together at the *Supershow* filming back in Staines in March 1969.

Studio Session for Buddy Guy and Junior Wells
October 1970
Criteria Studios, Miami

A Man Of Many Words	PLAY THE BLUES
My Baby She Left Me	PLAY THE BLUES
Come On In This House	PLAY THE BLUES
Have Mercy Baby	PLAY THE BLUES
T-Bone Shuffle	PLAY THE BLUES
A Poor Man's Plea	PLAY THE BLUES
Messin' With The Kid	PLAY THE BLUES
I Don't Know	PLAY THE BLUES
Bad Bad Whiskey	PLAY THE BLUES

Rhythm guitar/bottleneck: Eric Clapton
Guitar/vocals: Buddy Guy

Harmonica/vocals: Junior Wells
Tenor sax: A.C. Reed
Piano/organ: Mike Utley
Bass: Leroy Stewart
Drums: Roosevelt Shaw
Piano: Dr John (A Man Of Many Words, T-Bone Shuffle, Messin' With The Kid)
Bass: Carl Radle (A Man Of Many Words)
Drums: Jim Gordon (A Man Of Many Words)

Guitar used: Sunburst Fender Stratocaster

Producers: Eric Clapton, Ahmet Ertegun, Tom Dowd
Engineer: Ron Albert

Studio Session for James Luther Dickinson
October 1970
Criteria Studios, Miami

The Judgement   DIXIE FRIED

Guitar: Eric Clapton
Vocals: Jim Dickinson
Piano: Dr John
Organ: Mike Utley
Bass: ——
Drums: ——
Guitar: ——

Guitar used: Fender Sunburst Stratocaster

Producers: Tom Dowd, Jim Dickinson
Engineer: Karl Richardson

Live Session
5 November 1970
Johnny Cash TV Show

It's Too Late   TV broadcast
Got To Get Better In A Little While   Unissued
Blues Power   Unissued

Guitar/vocals: Eric Clapton
Bass: Carl Radle
Drums: Jim Gordon
Keyboards/vocals: Bobby Whitlock

Matchbox (version 1)   Unissued
Matchbox (version 2)   Unissued
Matchbox (version 3)   TV broadcast

Guitar/vocals: Eric Clapton
               Johnny Cash
               Carl Perkins

Bass: Carl Radle
Drums: Jim Gordon
Keyboards/vocals: Bobby Whitlock

Guitar used: Sunburst Fender Stratocaster

Producer: ——
Engineer: ——

This very rare television appearance of Derek And The Dominos is a treat to see and hear. Eric is obviously nervous, particularly when talking to Johnny Cash, but his playing is quite superb. It is unlikely that this video will ever be released, but it is readily available in collectors' circles and is certainly worth the effort of obtaining a copy, as it is the only chance of seeing Eric as Derek.

Studio Session for The Rolling Stones
December 1970
Olympic Sound Studios, Barnes, London

Brown Sugar   *Unissued*

Guitar: Eric Clapton
Vocals: Mick Jagger
Guitar: Mick Taylor
        Keith Richards
Drums: Charlie Watts
Keyboards: Al Kooper
Sax: Bobby Keys
Bass: Bill Wyman

Guitar used: Sunburst Fender Stratocaster

Producer: ——
Engineer: ——

AL KOOPER: *I'd played with the Stones on 'You Can't Always Get What You Want' and 'Memo From Turner'. I played with them again a few years later at a birthday party for Keith Richards at Olympic Studios in London. They were working on the STICKY FINGERS album. After the party, they cleared away the debris and set up to record. They cajoled Eric Clapton, myself and Bobby Keys to join them in a previously unheard tune called 'Brown Sugar'. George Harrison, who was among the partygoers, was invited to play but declined. I read in an interview with Keith that it came out great and that they would release it someday, but the version on STICKY FINGERS is another one entirely.*

PYE RECORDING STUDIOS *Bcc*

A.T.V. HOUSE, BRYANSTON ST., LONDON, W.1.

13.3.73	CLIENT	R.S.O. Records Ltd	PRODUCER		MONO	4T.	
	ARTIST	Eric Clapton.	ENGINEER	Copy J. Chinnery	STEREO	8T.	D

1ST SHOW.

LAYLA
BADGE
BLUES POWER.
DOWN AND OUT
ROLL IT OVER
WHY DOES LOVE (PART 1)

TRACK ALLOCATION

TITLE	1	2	3	4	5	6	7	8	9	10	11	12	1
										S	T	E	k
										C	O		f

OUT OF TIME

1971–1973

The US tour ended in December, and they were never to play live again. Eric's next session was for Bobby Whitlock's solo album, which was basically The Dominos plus various friends such as George Harrison, Klaus Voorman, Jim Price and Bobby Keys.

Studio Session for Bobby Whitlock
January 1971
Olympic Sound Studios, Barnes, London

Where There's A Will There's A Way	BOBBY WHITLOCK
A Day Without Jesus	BOBBY WHITLOCK
Back In My Life Again	BOBBY WHITLOCK
The Scenery Has Slowly Changed	BOBBY WHITLOCK
The Dreams Of A Hobo	RAW VELVET
Hello LA Bye Bye Birmingham	RAW VELVET

Guitar: Eric Clapton
Guitar/keyboards/vocals: Bobby Whitlock
Bass: Carl Radle
Drums: Jim Gordon
Guitar: George Harrison
Trumpet: Jim Price
Sax: Bobby Keys

Guitar used: Sunburst Fender Stratocaster

Producers: Bobby Whitlock, Andy Johns
Engineer: Joe Zagarino

Note: 'The Dreams Of A Hobo' is on the US version of BOBBY WHITLOCK but can be found on RAW VELVET on the UK version. Also, Delaney Bramlett produced 'Hello LA Bye Bye Birmingham'.

◆

Eric's next session was one that would take him back to the days of The Blues Breakers. John Mayall was making a reunion album featuring some of the musicians who had played with him throughout the years and, of course Eric was asked to contribute. As he was touring with The Dominos at the time the album was being recorded, he overdubbed his parts in London at a later date.

The original mix of the aptly titled double album BACK TO THE ROOTS was pretty muddy, partly due to too many overdubs. John Mayall was in fact never happy with the final product, and a new version of the album appeared in 198o, ..titled ARCHIVES TO EIGHTIES. It had newly recorded drum and vocal parts, and certain guitar overdubs had been dropped.

JOHN MAYALL: *I was fortunate enough to have a second chance at making some better sense of the mixes that have most bothered me down through time. Months of diligent searching in distant warehouses finally unearthed the original 8-track master tapes. The tapes were brittle, the boxes faded and the reels beginning to rust. Back in Los Angeles, I began the renovation by transferring the contents to 24-track tape before starting my new efforts. I brought in Joe Yuele, my hard-driving drummer from the current Blues Breakers, and by the time he'd put down his tracks the music began to form some unity. With the selected eight songs now locked together, I felt justified in singing the old lyrics again and played anew most of my instrumental contributions.*

During the mix, I discovered some essential performances that I'd mysteriously left out before and in other cases found far too many overdubbed solos all playing at the same time!

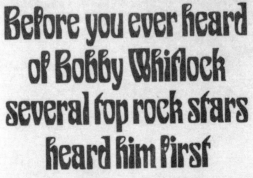

The new versions are indeed far better-sounding and Eric's solos are crystal-clear. Usually history should not be tampered with – the results can be disastrous, such as 'Crash Landing' by Jimi Hendrix. However, on this occasion it works brilliantly.

The details below are the ones for the original session.

Studio Session for John Mayall
January 1971
IBC Studios, London

Prisons On The Road — BACK TO THE ROOTS

Guitar: Eric Clapton
Piano/vocals: John Mayall
Violin: Sugarcane Harris
Drums: Paul Lagos
Bass: Larry Taylor

Accidental Suicide — BACK TO THE ROOTS

Guitar: Eric Clapton
Guitar/harmonica/vocals: John Mayall
Guitar: Mick Taylor
        Harvey Mandel
Violin: Sugarcane Harris
Bass: Larry Taylor

Home Again — BACK TO THE ROOTS

Guitar: Eric Clapton
Piano/harmonica/vocals: John Mayall
Bass: Larry Taylor

Looking At Tomorrow — BACK TO THE ROOTS

Guitar: Eric Clapton
Guitar/piano/vocals: John Mayall
Violin: Sugarcane Harris
Drums: Paul Lagos
Bass: Larry Taylor

Force Of Nature — BACK TO THE ROOTS

Guitar: Eric Clapton
Tambourine/drums/vocals: John Mayall
Slide guitar: Mick Taylor
Guitar: Harvey Mandel
Bass: Larry Taylor

70

Goodbye December

BACK TO THE ROOTS

Guitar: Eric Clapton
Guitar/harmonica/vocals: John Mayall
Guitar: Harvey Mandel
Drums: Keef Hartley
Bass: Larry Taylor

Guitar used: Sunburst Fender Stratocaster

Producer: John Mayall
Engineer: Damon Lyon-Shaw

Listed below are the revised songs:

Accidental Suicide

ARCHIVES TO EIGHTIES

Guitar: Eric Clapton
Guitar/harmonica/vocals: John Mayall
Violin: Sugarcane Harris
Bass: Larry Taylor
Drums: Joe Yuele

Force Of Nature

ARCHIVES TO EIGHTIES

Guitar: Eric Clapton
Vocals: John Mayall
Slide guitar: Mick Taylor
Guitar: Harvey Mandel
Bass: Larry Taylor
Drums: Joe Yuele

Prisons On The Road

ARCHIVES TO EIGHTIES

Guitar: Eric Clapton
Piano/vocals: John Mayall
Violin: Sugarcane Harris
Bass: Larry Taylor
Drums: Joe Yuele

Home Again

ARCHIVES TO EIGHTIES

Guitar: Eric Clapton
Piano: John Mayall
Bass: Larry Taylor
Drums: Joe Yuele

Looking At Tomorrow

ARCHIVES TO EIGHTIES

Guitar: Eric Clapton
Vocals/synthesized flute/juno I keyboard: John Mayall
Violin: Sugarcane Harris
Bass: Larry Taylor
Drums: Joe Yuele

'Goodbye December' did not make the revised edition, unfortunately.

Derek And The Dominos made their last recordings at Olympic Sound Studios in Barnes. Arguments created a totally different atmosphere from that of the magical LAYLA sessions. A row between Jim Gordon and Eric signalled the end of the band, as Eric went into hiding and his well-documented heroin addiction.

Two of the numbers were not lost forever as they were re-recorded for later albums: 'Mean Old Frisco' for SLOWHAND and 'High' for THERE'S ONE IN EVERY CROWD. The best numbers were finally released on the CROSSROADS retrospective.

Studio Session
April–May 1971
Olympic Sound Studios, Barnes, London

Moody Jam	*Unissued*
Jim's Song	*Unissued*
Chocolate	*Unissued*
Carl And Me	*Unissued*
Evil	CROSSROADS
Snake Lake Blues	CROSSROADS
Mean Old Frisco	CROSSROADS
High	*Unissued*
I've Been All Day	*Unissued*
It's Got To Get Better In A Little While	CROSSROADS
One More Chance	CROSSROADS
It's Hard To Find	*Unissued*
Till I See You Again	*Unissued*

Guitar/vocals: Eric Clapton
Bass: Carl Radle
Drums: Jim Gordon
Keyboards: Bobby Whitlock

Guitar used: Sunburst Fender Stratocaster

Producer: Derek And The Dominos
Engineer: Andy Johns

ERIC CLAPTON: *I remember it came to a crunch when one day Jim was playing the drums, and he heard that I'd made some remark about a drummer in another band. I don't remember making the remark, but he got up from behind the kit and said, 'Why don't you get so-and-so in here? He could play it better than I could!' and walked out. Or maybe I walked out. Somebody walked out. And we never went back into the studio again. It was that dramatic.*

There was a feeling of real sadness there, of futility. The tapes stayed in the studio. I never went back. Nor did the others. The fact that the tracks are out now is fine [on CROSSROADS]. But it is a closed book.

Eric came out of self-imposed exile to play at George Harrison's charity concert in aid of the people of Bangladesh. This concert was the Live Aid of its time and featured many stars such as Bob Dylan, Ringo Starr and Leon Russell. Both concerts were filmed and recorded for later release.

Live Session
August 1971
Madison Square Garden, New York

Two shows (afternoon and evening)

Wah Wah	THE CONCERT FOR BANGLADESH
My Sweet Lord	THE CONCERT FOR BANGLADESH
Awaiting On You All	THE CONCERT FOR BANGLADESH
That's The Way God Planned It	THE CONCERT FOR BANGLADESH
It Don't Come Easy	THE CONCERT FOR BANGLADESH
Beware Of Darkness	THE CONCERT FOR BANGLADESH
While My Guitar Gently Weeps	THE CONCERT FOR BANGLADESH
Jumpin' Jack Flash	THE CONCERT FOR BANGLADESH
Youngblood	THE CONCERT FOR BANGLADESH
Something	THE CONCERT FOR BANGLADESH
Bangla Desh	THE CONCERT FOR BANGLADESH

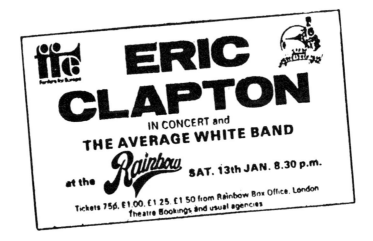

Guitar: Eric Clapton
Guitar/vocals: George Harrison
Guitar: Jesse Ed Davis
Guitar: Don Preston
Drums: Ringo Starr
      Jim Keltner
Bass: Klaus Voorman
      Carl Radle
Keyboards/vocals: Billy Preston
      Leon Russell
Horns: Jim Price
      Jim Horn
      Chuck Findley
Backing vocals: Badfinger
      Claudia Linnear, Jackie Kelso, Dolores Hall

Guitars used: Sunburst Fender Stratocaster (first show), Gibson Byrdland (second show)

Producers: George Harrison, Phil Spector
Engineer: ———
Recorded by: The Record Plant Recording Studio Mobile Unit

The only other person able to get Eric to play at this time was Stevie Wonder. Eric had long admired Stevie's music, and always went to see him at his London shows. It was at one of these shows at The Talk Of The Town that Stevie asked Eric to participate on a session he was doing at Air Studios.

Studio Session for Stevie Wonder
October 1972
Air Studios, London

I'm Free   *Unissued*

Guitar: Eric Clapton
Keyboards/drums/vocals: Stevie Wonder

Guitar used: Fender Stratocaster

Producer: Stevie Wonder
Engineer: ———

STEVIE WONDER: *We just had a mutual feeling for each other, I really admired his riffs. They were in the same bag as what Ralph Hammer and Ray Parker were doing.*

◆

Eric's next appearance was at The Rainbow in London as part of the *Fanfare For Europe* concerts. Pete Townshend assembled a band that would back Eric in his first concerts for two years. Rehearsals took place at Ronnie Wood's house on Richmond Hill and then moved on to the Civic Hall in Guildford.

PETE TOWNSHEND: *Most of the material we've been working on is drawn from songs that Eric wrote on his solo albums, and little classics like 'Let It Rain', 'Layla', and 'Little Wing'. Then we're doing things like 'Badge' and 'Crossroads' from the Cream period and 'Presence Of The Lord', which he wrote while with Blind Faith.*

PYE RECORDING STUDIOS
A.T.V. HOUSE, BRYANSTON ST., LONDON, W.1.

E	13.3.73	CLIENT	R.S.O. Records Ltd	PRODUCER			MONO		4T
:ATION		ARTIST	Eric Clapton etc	ENGINEER	Copy J. Chinnery		STEREO	X	8T

(2)

1ST SHOW.

Little Wing
Red Wine
After Midnight
Bell Bottom Blues
Presence of the Lord.

TITLE	1	2	3	4

PYE RECORDING STUDIOS
A.T.V. HOUSE, BRYANSTON ST., LONDON, W.1.   Tel. No.

ISICC OA

3.3.73	CLIENT	R.S.O. Limited	PRODUCER			MONO	4T	16T.
	ARTIST	Eric Clapton etc	ENGINEER	Copy J. Chinnery		STEREO	8T	DOLBY
						X		

2nd Show Part I

LAYLA
BADGE *
T6
B.H.L. BLUES POWER
NABODY LOVES YOU WHEN YOU'RE DOWN AND OUT *
ROLL IT OVER

TRACK ALLOCATION

ITLE	1	2	3	4	5	6	7	8	9	10	11	12	13	14
									S	T	E	R	E	O
									C	O	P	Y		

**Live Session
13 January 1973
Rainbow, London**

Two shows (18.30 and 20.30)

Show 1

Layla	*Unissued*
Badge	*Unissued*
Blues Power	*Unissued*
Nobody Knows You When You're Down And Out	*Unissued*
Roll It Over	*Unissued*
Why Does Love Got To Be So Sad	*Unissued*
Little Wing	RAINBOW CONCERT
Bottle Of Red Wine	*Unissued*
After Midnight	*Unissued*
Bell Bottom Blues	*Unissued*
Presence Of The Lord	RAINBOW CONCERT
Tell The Truth	*Unissued*
Pearly Queen	*Unissued*
Let It Rain	*Unissued*
Encore:	
Crossroads	*Unissued*

Show 2

Layla	*Unissued*
Badge	RAINBOW CONCERT
Blues Power	*Unissued*
Nobody Knows You When You're Down And Out	*Unissued*
Roll It Over	RAINBOW CONCERT
Why Does Love Got To Be So Sad	*Unissued*
Little Wing	*Unissued*
Bottle Of Red Wine	*Unissued*
Presence Of The Lord	RAINBOW CONCERT
Tell The Truth	*Unissued*
Pearly Queen	RAINBOW CONCERT
Key To The Highway	*Unissued*
Let It Rain	*Unissued*
Encore:	
Crossroads	*Unissued*
Layla	*Unissued*

Guitar/vocals: Eric Clapton
              Pete Townshend
              Ron Wood
Drums: Jim Capaldi
        Jimmy Karstein
Bass: Rich Grech
Keyboards/vocals: Stevie Winwood
Percussion: Rebop

Guitars used: 'Blackie' Fender Stratocaster (first show),
      Gibson Les Paul (second show)

Producer: Bob Pridden
Engineer: Phil Chapman
Recorded by: Ronnie Lane Mobile

ERIC CLAPTON
461 OCEAN BOULEVARD

811 697-2

BACK IN EVERY CROWD

1974

Before making his official comeback, Eric participated in his first soundtrack recording at the invitation of his friend Pete Townshend, for Ken Russell's version of the classic *Tommy*.

Studio Session for *Tommy* soundtrack
March 1974
Ramport Studios, Battersea, London

Eyesight To The Blind	TOMMY

Guitar/vocals: Eric Clapton
Drums: Kenny Jones
Bass: John Entwistle
Vocals: Arthur Brown (on film version only)

Sally Simpson	TOMMY

Guitar: Eric Clapton
Drums: Graham Deacon
Bass: Phil Chen
Piano: Nicky Hopkins
Vocals: Pete Townshend
        Roger Daltrey

Guitar used: 'Blackie' Fender Stratocaster

Producer: Pete Townshend
Engineer: Ron Nevison

Eric flew out to Miami to record his comeback studio album, which was followed by a huge stadium tour around North America and further shows in Europe and Japan.

The aborted Derek And The Dominos' second LP tapes were remixed for possible release with new material, but this idea was shelved when the wealth of great new songs recorded was revealed.

Studio Session
April–May 1974
Criteria Studios, Miami

B Minor jam	*Unissued*
Blues jam	*Unissued*
Old Vibs	*Unissued*
Something You Got	*Unissued*
It's Too Late	*Unissued*
Please Be With Me	461 OCEAN BOULEVARD
Motherless Children (key of A)	*Unissued*
Motherless Children (jam)	*Unissued*
Motherless Children	461 OCEAN BOULEVARD
Jam in E 1	*Unissued*
Jam in E 2	*Unissued*
Dobro jam 1	*Unissued*
Dobro jam 2	*Unissued*
Give Me Strength	461 OCEAN BOULEVARD
I Shot The Sheriff	461 OCEAN BOULEVARD
Eat The Cook	*Unissued*
Mainline Florida	461 OCEAN BOULEVARD
Ain't That Lovin' You	CROSSROADS
Blues In E	*Unissued*
Gypsy	*Unissued*
Steady Rollin' Man	461 OCEAN BOULEVARD
Meet Me (instrumental)	*Unissued*
Meet Me (with vocals)	*Unissued*
I Can't Hold Out	461 OCEAN BOULEVARD
Willie And The Hand Jive	461 OCEAN BOULEVARD
Get Ready	461 OCEAN BOULEVARD
Let It Grow	461 OCEAN BOULEVARD

Guitar/dobro/vocals: Eric Clapton
Guitar: George Terry
Bass: Carl Radle
Drums: Jamie Oldaker
Keyboards: Dick Sims
Backing vocals: Yvonne Elliman
Keyboards: Albhy Galuten (Motherless Children, Get Ready,
    I Shot The Sheriff, Let It Grow, Steady Rollin' Man, Mainline
    Florida)

TAILS

"MASTER"

criteria recording studios
1755 NE 149 ST/MIAMI FLORIDA 33161/305 947-5611

CLIENT RSO

ARTIST EC   DATE 4/18/74   CRI. JOB #

PRODUCER TD   ENGINEER KR   REEL # 2   TR'S 16

                STUDIO C   SPEED ☒ 30 ☐ 7½

TAKE #	MCI - LOG	TITLE	TIME	COMMENTS
1		DOBRO		ERIC ONLY
2		DOBRO W/BASS + GUIT		
3		BE JAM		

"OUTTAKES"

criteria recording studios
1755 NE 149 ST/MIAMI FLORIDA 33161/305 947-5611

CLIENT RSO

ARTIST EC

PRODUCER TD   DATE 4-26-74   CRI. JOB # 11448

                ENGINEER KR   REEL # 19 TR'S 16

                STUDIO C   SPEED ☒ 30 15 ☐ 7½

TAKE #	MCI - LOG	TITLE	TIME	COMMENTS
1	006	I SHOT THE SHERIFF		
2	476			TR PB 7:00
3	536			
4	1478			CON'T FROM #2
5	2137	BULLER! 4-30-74		TR OTM SK
	"	EAT THE COOK	5:15	TR SK
5	010			
6	560			4-30-74
7	1090	RE"0" AT SPLICE		TR OTM SK
		MAINLINE FLA.		TR OTM SK
1	000			
2	570			

"OUTTAKES"

78

30 IPS NAB +3 over 0

"MASTER"

criteria recording studios 1755 NE 149 ST/MIAMI FLORIDA 33161/305 947-5611

DATE MAY 10, 1974   CRI. JOB # 11448

REEL # M 1   TR'S 16

CLIENT __R.S.O.__   ENGINEER __KR__   SPEED ☒30 ☐7½

ARTIST __ERIC CLAPTON__   STUDIO __C__

PRODUCER __TOM DOWD__

TAKE #	MCI - LOG	TITLE	TIME	COMMENTS
				FADE AT 5:15
1.		STEADY ROLLIN' MAN	4:15	ENDS
2.		GIVE ME STRENGTH	2:51	ENDS
3.		MOTHERLESS CHILDREN	4:57	

---

30 IPS NAB +3 over 0

"MASTER"

criteria recording studios 1755 NE 149 ST/MIAMI FLORIDA 33161/305 947-5611

DATE MAY 10, 1974   CRI. JOB # 11448

REEL # M 2   TR'S 16

CLIENT __R.S.O.__   ENGINEER __KR__   SPEED ☒30 ☐7½

ARTIST __ERIC CLAPTON__   STUDIO __C__

PRODUCER __TOM DOWD__

TAKE #	MCI - LOG	TITLE	TIME	COMMENTS
				FADE @ 4:25
1.		I SHOT THE SHERIFF	6:55	FADE 4:25
2.		LET IT GROW	5:00	
3.		I CAN'T HOLD OUT MUCH LONGER	4:07	ENDS.

THIS TAPE MUST BE RETURNED TO
Polygram Tape Facility
10 Distribution Blvd.
Edison, N.J. 08817
IMMEDIATELY AFTER MASTERING

Drums: Jim Fox (Steady Rollin' Man)
　　　　 Al Jackson (Give Me Strength)
Guitar: Dave Mason (Ain't That Lovin' You)

Guitars used: 'Blackie' Fender Stratocaster, Gibson ES335

Producer: Tom Dowd
Engineer: Karl Richardson

The two dobro jams are basically instrumental versions of 'Give Me Strength', with just Eric on dobro and George Terry on electric guitar, and are quite stunning. They were to be included on Polygram's amazing CROSSROADS retrospective, but were left off when it came to the final track listing.

It is also interesting to note that the full version of 'I Shot The Sheriff' was actually 6.55 minutes long and included a guitar solo, but was shortened for the album release to 4.24 minutes.

Some of the out-takes are breathtaking, particularly the blues jams, which may one day see a release. They feature some particularly fine guitar solos and interplay between Eric and George Terry, and were left off the 461 OCEAN BOULEVARD album because Eric wanted to get away from the 'Guitar God' tag he'd been labelled with for so many years.

Studio Session for Ronnie Wood
18 May 1974
Ronnie Wood's home studio, The Wick, Richmond Hill

Various jams	*Unissued*

Guitar: Eric Clapton
　　　　 Ronnie Wood
　　　　 Keith Richards

Guitar used: ——

Producer: ——
Engineer: ——

RONNIE WOOD: *The last thing I wanted was a jam . . . everybody sitting around playing E for two days. It did happen sometimes, like if I had three drummers in and no drum kit or something, but usually once everybody got behind their instruments in the studio it was dead serious. I was really out of my head the night Eric turned up and he was really violent and boisterous. We had a long play but it wasn't very productive. Instead he was good in that*

I played him the album [I'VE GOT MY OWN ALBUM TO DO] and he made me sing all the words down his ear and he'd be making remarks like 'You can't play that' or something. We just had a good time. Also he's inspirational to play with anyway, like George Harrison or Keith Richards, because they've all got a lot of roots in the past and can connect immediately with an old number of something.

RSO decided to record several shows (four in 1974 and two in 1975) with the idea of releasing a live album at some future date. Eric's tour was a huge sell-out, hot on the heels of the hit album 461 OCEAN BOULEVARD. It therefore seemed logical to capture some of his live performances, if only to placate the shouts of 'Where are the guitar solos?' from fans who naturally expected his solo studio albums to be full of superlative guitar breaks.

The live shows were hit-and-miss affairs at first. However, a week into the tour things improved dramatically, as did the reviews. Eric was now playing some great solos, particularly during the blues numbers. In fact, his solo in 'Have You Ever Loved A Woman' on 19 July 1974 convinced him that a live album would be a worthwhile proposition.

Live Session
19 July 1974
Long Beach Arena, Long Beach, California

Smile	*Unissued*
Let It Grow	*Unissued*
Can't Find My Way Home	*Unissued*
I Shot The Sheriff	*Unissued*
Badge	*Unissued*
Willie And The Hand Jive	*Unissued*
Get Ready	*Unissued*
Crossroads	*Unissued*
Mainline Florida	*Unissued*
Layla	*Unissued*
Have You Ever Loved A Woman	EC WAS HERE
Tell The Truth	*Unissued*
Steady Rollin' Man	*Unissued*
Little Queenie	*Unissued*
Blues jam	*Unissued*

Guitar/vocals: Eric Clapton
Guitar: George Terry
Bass: Carl Radle

Keyboards: Dick Sims
Drums: Jamie Oldaker
Backing vocals: Yvonne Elliman
Guitar: John Mayall (Blues jam)

Guitars used: 'Blackie' Fender Stratocaster, Martin acoustic

Producer: Tom Dowd
Engineer: Ed Barton
Recorded by: Wally Heider Recording Studio Mobile Unit

Live Session
20 July 1974
Long Beach Arena, Long Beach, California

Smile	TIME PIECES VOL. 2
Easy Now	*Unissued*
Let It Grow	*Unissued*
I Shot The Sheriff	*Unissued*
Layla	*Unissued*
Little Wing	*Unissued*
Willie And The Hand Jive	*Unissued*
Get Ready	*Unissued*
Badge	*Unissued*
Can't Find My Way Home	EC WAS HERE
Driftin' Blues	EC WAS HERE
Let It Rain	*Unissued*
Presence Of The Lord	EC WAS HERE
Crossroads	*Unissued*
Steady Rollin' Man	*Unissued*
Little Queenie	*Unissued*
Blues Power	*Unissued*

Guitar/vocals: Eric Clapton
Guitar: George Terry
Bass: Carl Radle
Keyboards: Dick Sims
Drums: Jamie Oldaker
Backing vocals: Yvonne Elliman

Guitars used: 'Blackie' Fender Stratocaster, Martin acoustic

Producer: Tom Dowd
Engineer: Ed Barton
Recorded by: Wally Heider Recording Studio Mobile Unit

One of the live highlights was the rarely performed 'Easy Now' from his first solo album, which fitted well into the three-song acoustic introduction. The set would differ nightly, which kept things fresh as well as keeping everyone on their toes. The version of 'Have You Ever Loved A Woman' from the first Long Beach concert is probably more emotive than his studio version, recorded back in October 1970, and the interplay between George Terry and Eric was alone worth the price of admission. Other highlights include a powerful version of the Blind Faith classic 'Presence Of The Lord', featuring a demonic wah wah guitar solo, and the acoustic blues 'Driftin' Blues', which sadly faded out after a few minutes on the vinyl version of EC WAS HERE, but was thankfully restored to its full 11 minutes when re-released on CD. In fact it's a miracle that it survived, as most recordings during the mid-seventies were made on Ampex tape, which unfortunately started to stick together after some years. The only way of rescuing them involves an elaborate 24-hour baking system before transferring them to digital!

◆

At the end of the first part of the tour, Eric and his band went to Miami's Criteria Studios to guest on RSO's latest signing – who also happened to be one of his heroes – Freddie King. Freddie played the support slot on several dates during the tour, and would occasionally jam with Eric.

Studio Session for Freddie King
5 August 1974
Criteria Studios, Miami

Sugar Sweet	1934–1976/BURGLAR
TV Mama	1934–1976
Gambling Woman Blues	1934–1976
Blues jam	*Unissued*

Guitar: Eric Clapton
Guitar/vocals: Freddie King
Bass: Carl Radle
Keyboards: Dick Sims
Drums: Jamie Oldaker

Guitar used: 'Blackie' Fender Stratocaster

Producer: Bill Oakes
Engineer: Steve Klein

ERIC CLAPTON: *He [Freddie King] taught me just about everything I needed to know, when and when not to make a stand, when and when not to show your hand, and most important of all, how to make love to a guitar.*

Studio Session
29 August–18 September 1974
Dynamic Sounds Studios, Jamaica

Singing The Blues	THERE'S ONE IN EVERY CROWD
Little Rachel	THERE'S ONE IN EVERY CROWD
We've Been Told	THERE'S ONE IN EVERY CROWD
Fool Like Me	*Unissued*
I Found A Love	CROSSROADS
When Things Go Wrong	CROSSROADS
Burial	*Unissued*
Don't Blame Me	THERE'S ONE IN EVERY CROWD
Better Make It Through Today	THERE'S ONE IN EVERY CROWD
Whatcha Gonna Do	CROSSROADS
High	THERE'S ONE IN EVERY CROWD
Swing Low Sweet Chariot	A Side/THERE'S ONE IN EVERY CROWD
The Sky Is Crying	THERE'S ONE IN EVERY CROWD
Pretty Blue Eyes	B Side/THERE'S ONE IN EVERY CROWD

Guitar/vocals: Eric Clapton
Guitar: George Terry
Bass: Carl Radle
Keyboards: Dick Sims
Drums: Jamie Oldaker
Backing vocals: Yvonne Elliman
                Marcy Levy
Guitar/vocals: Peter Tosh (Burial, Whatcha Gonna Do)

Guitar used: 'Blackie' Fender Stratocaster

Producer: Tom Dowd
Engineer: ——

Studio Session
November 1974
Criteria Studios, Miami

Opposites	THERE'S ONE IN EVERY CROWD

Guitar/vocals: Eric Clapton
Guitar: George Terry
Bass: Carl Radle
Keyboards: Dick Sims
Drums: Jamie Oldaker
Backing vocals: Yvonne Elliman
                Marcy Levy

Guitar used: 'Blackie' Fender Stratocaster

Producer: Tom Dowd
Engineer: ——

YVONNE ELLIMAN: *We were doing this one song, 'Singing The Blues', and it just needed a bit more punch. So at six o'clock one morning, Eric asked Marcy to try it and she did it like that, in one take.*

Being in Jamaica, you get that reggae feeling in your bones just being there. And the minute you step in the studio it's just da-da-da. We recorded about five reggae tunes, the Wailers came down, and some steel drum players. And George Terry and Eric wrote the answer to 'I Shot The Sheriff – who shot the deputy, right? The song is called 'Don't Blame Me', about the poor guy stuck in jail saying, 'Don't blame me, I did not shoot the deputy.'

CARL RADLE: *The tracks were done in Jamaica and then we put a little polish on them, if you like, in Miami. In fact we recorded one of the tracks in Miami. They are not similar to 461 OCEAN BOULEVARD. You see, the band was a little more established as far as relationships between the musicians are concerned. We had 461 and two or three tours behind us and by the time we came to this one we were really together.*

ERIC CLAPTON: *We did it in Jamaica and had a fairly good time. It's the kind of record that if you didn't like it after maybe the third or fourth time, you wouldn't play it again, but if you did like it and you carried on listening to it, you'd hear things that were really fine, just little things in the background, little touches. My voice still sounds too young. I was very concerned during the first part of my career about whether I should sound young or old, or like so-and-so or so-and-so, and when I was making those records I was actually contriving a young voice, a sweet voice. But over the years, seeing as I smoke sixty cigarettes a day, that's no longer possible, so I just have to face the truth now and sing with the normal voice I've got.*

The reggae influence was evident on several numbers, including backing by Byron Lee's Ironmen on 'Swing Low Sweet Chariot' as well as Peter Tosh on two numbers. Eric's main influences at this time were Philly's Gamble and Huff team and anyone on the Shelter label. So it came as no surprise that he recorded two songs by artists signed to that label, Mary McCreary ('Singing The Blues') and Jim Byfield ('Little Rachel').

ARTIST ERIC CLAPTON
PRODUCER TOM DOWD
ATLANTIC
DATE 8/29/74-9/18/74
STUDIO DYNAMIC/JAMAICA

TAKE	MIX	TITLE	TIME	REMARKS
		BURIAL	4:28	must fade ending
		MAKE IT THROUGH THE DAY	4:20	has natural ending
		DON'T BLAME ME (I DIDN'T SHOOT NO DEPUTY)	7:40	must fade ending

ARTIST ERIC CLAPTON
PRODUCER TOM DOWD
ATLANTIC
DATE 8/29/74-9/18/74
STUDIO DYNAMIC/JAMAICA

TAKE	MIX	TITLE	TIME	REMARKS
		SWING LOW SWEET CHARIOT	4:30	has natural end, avoid
		TIL THE SKY IS CRYING	3:90	has natural ending
		PRETTY BLUE EYES	4:53	must fade end

ARTIST ERIC CLAPTON
PRODUCER TOM DOWD
ATLANTIC
DATE 8/29/74-9/18/74
STUDIO DYNAMIC/JAMAICA

TAKE	MIX	TITLE	TIME	REMARKS
		WHATCHA GONNA DO (OH MAMA)	9:10	must fade ending
		HIGH	4:00	has natural ending

THIS TAPE MUST BE RETURNED TO
Polygram Tape Facility
10 Distribution Blvd.
Edison, N.J. 08817
IMMEDIATELY AFTER MASTERING

MONO ☐
STEREO ☐
15 ☐
7½ ☐
3¾ ☐
ORIG. ☐
REMIX ☐
OVERDUB ☐

ENGINEER

The album THERE'S ONE IN EVERY CROWD also had its fair share of blues ('The Sky Is Crying') as well as gospel ('We've Been Told'), although some of the best numbers were left off, probably because they featured lengthy guitar solos. Eric was still trying to get away from his guitar hero tag, which he felt had become something of an albatross around his neck.

When the album was released, in April 1975, it did very little chartwise. Nor did the first single, 'Swing Low Sweet Chariot'. It just wasn't the sort of album people expected from him at the time. However, it does show many different styles performed by an impeccable band.

◆

RSO wasted no time in readying a live guitar album, EC WAS HERE, for release in August 1975 to restore the public's faith in Eric's guitar abilities.

Live Session
4 December 1974
Hammersmith Odeon, London

Smile	*Unissued*
Let It Grow	*Unissued*
Can't Find My Way Home	*Unissued*
I Shot The Sheriff	*Unissued*
Tell The Truth	*Unissued*
Ramblin' On My Mind	EC WAS HERE
Have You Ever Loved A Woman	*Unissued*
Willie And The Hand Jive	*Unissued*
Get Ready	*Unissued*
Opposites	*Unissued*
Blues Power	*Unissued*
Little Wing	*Unissued*
Singing The Blues	*Unissued*
Badge/All I Have To Do Is Dream	*Unissued*
Steady Rollin' Man	*Unissued*
Layla	*Unissued*
Let It Rain	*Unissued*

Guitar/vocals: Eric Clapton
Guitar: George Terry
Bass: Carl Radle
Keyboards: Dick Sims
Drums: Jamie Oldaker
Backing vocals: Yvonne Elliman
　　　　　　　　Marcy Levy

Guitars used: Martin acoustic, 'Blackie' Fender Stratocaster, Gibson Explorer

Producer: Tom Dowd
Engineer: ——
Recorded by: Ronnie Lane Mobile

Live Session
5 December 1974
Hammersmith Odeon, London

Smile	*Unissued*
Let It Grow	*Unissued*
Can't Find My Way Home	*Unissued*
Tell The Truth	*Unissued*
The Sky Is Crying	*Unissued*
Have You Ever Loved A Woman	*Unissued*
Ramblin' On My Mind	*Unissued*
Badge	*Unissued*
Little Rachel	*Unissued*
I Shot The Sheriff	*Unissued*
Better Make It Through Today	*Unissued*
Blues Power	*Unissued*
Key To The Highway	*Unissued*
Let It Rain	*Unissued*
Little Wing	*Unissued*
Singing The Blues	*Unissued*
Layla	*Unissued*
Steady Rollin' Man	*Unissued*
Little Queenie	*Unissued*

Guitar/vocals: Eric Clapton
Guitar: George Terry
　　　　　Ronnie Wood (Steady Rollin' Man and Little Queenie)
Bass: Carl Radle
Keyboards: Dick Sims
Drums: Jamie Oldaker
Backing vocals: Yvonne Elliman
　　　　　　　　Marcy Levy

Guitars used: Martin acoustic, 'Blackie' Fender Stratocaster, Gibson Explorer

Producer: Tom Dowd
Engineer: ——
Recorded by: Ronnie Lane Mobile

YVONNE ELLIMAN: *There's no strings now – it is a band. Before, it was just Eric getting together with some people who could help him get himself out there again. He relies on us now – it's a give-and-take thing now. And Eric can't believe it.*

Sometimes during the shows he'll stop playing, turn around and look at the band and just sigh. People have been sayings things like 'You're the best band in the world.' And to have come from being a good-time ensemble to that kind of notoriety is great. And to get that kind of respect from fellow musicians – I mean Led Zeppelin came on Wednesday night and they just all stood back there in amazement.

CARL RADLE: *They were two good gigs. It was a good place for sound. In fact for a small place it was an* incredible sound. Anyway, whatever it was like it's all down on tape. We had Tom Dowd there recording the shows.

These two London shows were very well received by the critics and fans alike. At the end of the set on 5 December 1974, Eric announced Pete Townshend on stage to jam on the last two numbers. In fact it was Ronnie Wood who walked on, much to the crowd's bemusement. On the original reel boxes stored in Polygram's New Jersey tape facility it was Pete's name that appeared, until I mentioned Eric's little joke to them!

Also available on
8 Track Cartridge and
Musicassette

MARKETED BY POLYDOR LIMITED

SLOWHAND WAS HERE

1975–1977

Eric's first session of the year was quite a controversial one. Arthur Louis, a thirtyish Jamaican who'd lived most of his life in New York before settling in the UK, recorded some two and a half hours of material with Eric. Included was a reggae version of Dylan's 'Knockin' On Heaven's Door', which was released as a single by Plum, Arthur's record company, on 29 July 1975. It started to receive a fair amount of radio interest, mainly on Radio One. However, ten days later RSO released Eric's version, which had a similar arrangement and guitar licks. Needless to say, neither Plum nor Arthur were too pleased to see their single disappear overnight in the face of such eminent opposition.

ERIC CLAPTON: *I played guitar on his version and that's how it all started. His version was a demo at the time. I though it was such a good idea to do a reggae version of the song. As he hadn't signed up with anybody, I released it myself. I figured it could only help him out. I even put one of his songs on the B side. Then he suddenly said, 'No, you can't put that out.' Eventually we worked out a deal.*

Studio Session
January 1975
Essex Sound Studios, London

Knockin' On Heaven's Door	A side/FIRST ALBUM
Plum	B side/FIRST ALBUM
The Dealer	B side/FIRST ALBUM
Still It Feels Good	A side/FIRST ALBUM
Come On And Love Me	B side/FIRST ALBUM
Layla Part 2	*Unissued*
Train 444	FIRST ALBUM
Go Out And Make It Happen	FIRST ALBUM

Guitar: Eric Clapton
Guitar/vocals: Arthur Louis
Vocals: Gene Chandler (The Dealer)
Guitar: Winston Deleando
Bass: Peter Dafrey
Vocals: Ernestine Pierce
Drums: Richard Bailey
Keyboards: Robert Bailey

Guitar used: Gibson Explorer

Producer: Arthur Louis
Engineer: ——

Plum did not survive very long, and its artists were taken over by Island Records who re-released 'Knockin' On Heaven's Door' backed with a different B side, 'The Dealer', to see if they could stir enough interest to release an album. Nothing happened, and Arthur was dropped – only to be taken over later by yet another label, Mainstreet. They also released a single from the same sessions, 'Still It Feels Good', backed with 'Come On And Love Me', but it did nothing saleswide and was doomed to litter deletion bins around the country. Eric played on all the A and B sides and they are therefore very collectable, particularly the Plum release.

The album, titled FIRST ALBUM (WITH GUEST APPEARANCE BY ERIC CLAPTON), was released by Polydor in 1976 in Japan, where it reached number 5 in the charts before quickly disappearing. It remains a rarity in its original mix, because in early 1988 PRT Records bought the rights to issue all the material by Arthur Louis and promptly remixed everything to give it an updated sound, as well as giving more prominence to Eric's guitar.

Studio Session
16 June 1975
Criteria Studios, Miami

Knockin' On Heaven's Door   A side

Guitar/vocals: Eric Clapton
Guitar: George Terry
Bass: Carl Radle
Keyboards: Dick Sims
Drums: Jamie Oldaker
Backing vocals: Yvonne Elliman
           Marcy Levy

Guitar used: 'Blackie' Fender Stratocaster

Producer: ——
Engineer: ——

Eric's 1975 US tour coincided with the infamous BLACK AND BLUES Rolling Stones tour. So it was no surprise that, when their itineraries crossed, a jam would occur. When the Stones played Madison Square Garden on 22 July 1975, Eric joined them for their encore, 'Sympathy For The Devil'. They returned the compliment by playing on a session for his new album. The song, titled 'Carnival To Rio', was later re-recorded as the contractual work to get all the names to appear would have taken too long. The song's title was also shortened to 'Carnival'.

'Carnival To Rio' is not that different from the later version recorded for Eric's NO REASON TO CRY album. It has a kind of samba feel to it, with all the guitarists riffing away to the beat with Eric and Mick Jagger on vocals, and Ronnie, Eric and George taking turns to solo while Keith holds down the rhythm. The best take lasts for around eight minutes and is surprisingly good, considering the amount of time they had to rehearse and the amount of brandy consumed.

Studio Session
25–30 June 1975
Electric Lady Studios, New York

Carnival To Rio (10 takes)   *Unissued*

Guitar/vocals: Eric Clapton
Vocals: Mick Jagger
Guitar: George Terry
       Keith Richards
       Ronnie Wood
Bass: Carl Radle
      Bill Wyman
Keyboards: Dick Sims
          Billy Preston
Drums: Jamie Oldaker
      Charlie Watts
Percussion: Ollie Brown
Backing vocals: Yvonne Elliman
           Marcy Levy

Guitar used: 'Blackie' Fender Stratocaster

Producer: ——
Engineer: ——

ERIC CLAPTON: *Ronnie Wood, Keith and I all played lead. The best takes were early on when nobody knew what they were doing. Later on, when everyone worked out what part to play, it got too sophisticated. It's very good actually. If it works out legally, I'll put it on the album.*

RONNIE WOOD: *That session with Eric was great – I didn't even know whose song it was till Eric said it was his. I told him that he better start leading before everyone demanded writing royalties. You'd never fit all the names on the label copy!*

Also recorded was a number by Arthur Louis.

Someone Like You   B side

Guitar/vocals: Eric Clapton
Guitar: George Terry
Bass: Carl Radle
Keyboards: Dick Sims
Drums: Jamie Oldaker
Backing vocals: Yvonne Elliman
           Marcy Levy

Guitar used: 'Blackie' Fender Stratocaster

Producer: ——
Engineer: ——

electric lady studios

52 west 8 street   new york city ny 10011   212 777-0150

CLIENT: RSO Records	REEL NO. 3/4	W.O.# M 6999		
ARTIST: Eric Clapton	TAPE NO. M6999-2			
PRODUCER:		MASTER: ✔	30 I.P.S. ✔	NAB
ENGINEER: RM - RGM	STUDIO A ✔ REMIX A ☐	COPY	15 I.P.S.	IEC
DATE: 6·25·75	STUDIO B ☐ REMIX B ☐	DOLBY: ✔	7½ I.P.S.	CCIR
24 TR ✔ 16 TR ☐	12 TR ☐ 8 TR ☐	4 TR ☐ 2 TR ☐		MONO ☐

TAKE	START	STOP	TITLE	COMMENTS	EDITS
#F000 3	065	073	Some ~~like~~ ~~or~~ You		
4	016	125	One Like	FS	
5	142	232		FS	
6	366	760		CT	
7	815	1316		PB CT Hot Good	
			↓		
			~~Continued on Reel #3~~		
			Carnival To Rio 6·30·75		
4.9	044	700			
4 4	065	075		FS	
5 3	080	126		FS	
6	125	210		FS	
7	215	553		IC	
8	680	1038		CT	
~~1050~~			6·30·75		
(9.)	1210	1937	MCR # M2623 A PB CT		
10	2070	3110		PB CT	

□□ Dolby A

Track Sheet 1 — REEL NO.: JG999-2

DATE: 6.25.75	TITLE: Someone Like You						
1 BD	2 SN	3 Drums-L	4 Drums-R	5 Guit Eric Vocal	6	7	8
9	10 Bass	11	12 EL Guitar	13 Organ-B	14 Organ-T	15	16
17	18	19	20	21	22	23	24

Track Sheet 2 — REEL NO.:

DATE: 6.30.75	TITLE: Carnival						
1 BD	2 SN	3 KiT	4 BD	5 SN	6 Kit	7 Vocal-1	8 Vocal-2
9 Vocal-3	10 Vocal-4	11 Kieth	12 George	13 Eric	14 Woody	15	16
17	18	19	20	21	22	23	24

Track Sheet 3 — REEL NO.:

DATE:	TITLE:						
1 BD	2 SN	3 Kit-Charlie	4 BD	5 SN	6 Kit-Jamie	7 Vocal-1	8 Vocal-2
9 Vocal-3	10 Vocal-4	11 Keith	12 George	13 Eric	14 Woody	15	16
17	18	19	20	21	22	23	24

Track Sheet 4 — REEL NO.:

DATE: 6.30.75	TITLE: Carnival To Rio						
1 BD	2 SN	3 Kit-Charlie	4 BD	5 SN	6 Kit-Jamie	7 Vocal-1	8 Vocal-2 Woody
9 Vocal-3	10 Vocal-4	11 Bass	12 Bass	13 Keith	14 George Eric	15	16 echo
17 Organ-B	18 Organ-T	19 Fender	20	21 Timbale	22 Conga	23	24

Track Sheet 5 — REEL NO.:

DATE:	TITLE: Same above Take 10 on						
1 BD	2 SN	3 Kit-Charlie	4 BD	5 SN	6 Kit-Ollie	7 Vocal-1	8 Vocal-2 Woody
9 Vocal-3?	10 Tamb	11 Bass	12 Bass	13 Keith	14 George	15 Eric	16
17 Organ-B	18 Organ						

Track Sheet 6 — REEL NO.:

DATE:	TITLE:						
1	2					7	8
9	10					15	16
17	18						

Track Sheet A — REEL NO.: M6999-4

DATE: 6.25.75	TITLE: Some One Like You						
1 BD	2 SN	3 Drums-L	4 Drums-R	5 Guitar ↔ Vocal Acc	6 Eric	7	8
9	10 Bass	11	12 El.Guitar	13	14 Organ-B	15 Organ-T	16
17	18	19	20	21	22	23	24

Track Sheet B — REEL NO.:

DATE: 6.28.75	TITLE: Carnival In Rio						
1 BD	2 SN	3 Sm Tom	4 FL Tom	5 OH Dick	6 OH	7 Bass carl	8 Bass
9 Guitar Ron?	10 Guitar Keith?	11 Guitar Eric?	12 Organ-B	13 Organ-1	14	15	16 Mick
17 Tamb	18 Eric	19 Keith + Ron	20 El. Piano	21 El Piano	22	23	24

Track Sheet C — REEL NO.:

DATE:	TITLE:						
1 BD	2 SN	3 KiT	4 BD	5 SN	6 KiT	7 Vocal-1	8 Vocal-2
9 Vocal-3	10 Vocal-4	11 Bass	12 Bass	13 Keith	14 George	15 Eric	16 Woody
17 Organ-B	18 Organ-T	19 Fender	20 Fender	21 Timbal	22 Conga	23 Clau	24 echo

---

Track Sheet (bottom) — REEL NO.: M6999

DATE: 6.25.75	TITLE: Some one Like You						
1 BD	2 SN	3 Drums-L	4 Drums-R	5 Acc Guitar ↔ Vocal	6 Eric	7 Acc Guitar	8 Guitar-1
9 Guitar NG2	10 Bass	11 Bass O/D	12 El Guitar	13 Piano-B	14 Organ-B Organ-T	15	16 BKG-1
17 BKG-2	18 Vocal	19 BKG-2	20 BKG-2	21 Harm Vocal	22 BKG Harm	23 Guitar 8+9	24 Piano-T

to BRIDGE ONLY

DATE:	TITLE:						
1	2	3	4	5	6	7	8
9	10	11	12	13	14	15	16
17	18	19	20	21	22	23	24

REEL NO.:

DATE:	TITLE:						
1	2	3	4	5	6	7	8
9	10	11	12	13	14	15	16
17	18	19	20	21	22	23	24

Live Session
25 June 1975
Civic Center, Providence, Rhode Island

Layla	*Unissued*
Further On Up The Road	*Unissued*
I Shot The Sheriff	*Unissued*
Make It Through Today	*Unissued*
Keep On Growing	*Unissued*
Can't Find My Way Home	*Unissued*
Driftin' Blues	*Unissued*
Sunshine Of Your Love	*Unissued*
Motherless Children	*Unissued*
Mean Old World	*Unissued*
Teach Me To Be Your Woman	*Unissued*
Bell Bottom Blues	*Unissued*
Badge	*Unissued*
Knockin' On Heaven's Door	*Unissued*
Tell The Truth	*Unissued*
Eyesight To The Blind	*Unissued*
Why Does Love Got To Be So Sad	*Unissued*

Guitar/vocals: Eric Clapton
Guitar: George Terry
      Carlos Santana (Eyesight To The Blind, Why Does Love
        Got To Be So Sad)
Bass: Carl Radle
Keyboards: Dick Sims
Drums: Jamie Oldaker
Backing vocals: Yvonne Elliman
         Marcy Levy

Guitars used: 'Blackie' Fender Stratocaster, Sunburst Fender
   Stratocaster

Producer: Tom Dowd
Engineer: ——
Recorded by: Record Plant Mobile

Live Session
28 June 1975
Nassau Coliseum, Uniondale, New York

Layla	*Unissued*
Key To The Highway	*Unissued*
Badge	*Unissued*
Bell Bottom Blues	*Unissued*
I Shot The Sheriff	*Unissued*
Can't Find My Way Home	*Unissued*
Further On Up The Road	EC WAS HERE
Better Make It Through Today	*Unissued*
Blues Power	*Unissued*
Teach Me To Be Your Woman	*Unissued*
Sunshine Of Your Love	*Unissued*
Crossroads	*Unissued*
Tell The Truth	*Unissued*
Stormy Monday	*Unissued*
Eyesight To The Blind	*Unissued*

Guitar/vocals: Eric Clapton
Guitar: George Terry
      Carlos Santana (Stormy Monday, Eyesight To The Blind)
      John McLaughlin (Stormy Monday, Eyesight To The
        Blind)
Bass: Carl Radle
Keyboards: Dick Sims
Drums: Jamie Oldaker
      Alphonze Mouzon (Stormy Monday, Eyesight To The
        Blind)
Backing vocals: Yvonne Elliman
         Marcy Levy

Guitars used: 'Blackie' Fender Stratocaster, Sunburst Fender
   Stratocaster

Producer: ——
Engineer: ——
Recorded by: Record Plant Mobile

Eric's 1975 tour was even better than the 1974 one. The band were tighter and the set would differ nightly, with Eric throwing in some of his favourite blues numbers such as 'Stormy Monday', 'Mean Old World', 'Crossroads', 'Key To The Highway' and 'Further On Up The Road'. The latter song was released on EC WAS HERE, and it gives the listener a good idea of how Eric and his band were sounding at the time. Carlos Santana would jam with them on most nights during the encore, giving fans a good opportunity to see these two great talents playing, not against each other, but in unison. On certain night they would almost take off with the sheer intensity of their solos. It is unfortunate that none of these tracks have, to date, been released officially. However, I hope that at some stage in the not too distant future Polygram will bring out a live blues-based box set covering all the groups that Eric has been involved in. There is certainly more than enough good material in the vaults, both at Polygram and his current label, Warner Reprise, to make a stunning retrospective that would equal, if not surpass, the excellent CROSSROADS boxed set, which teased more than it satisfied the serious collector.

92

Studio Session for Bob Dylan
28 July 1975
Columbia Studios, New York

Romance In Durango (five takes)	DESIRE
Oh Sister	*Unissued*
Mozambique	*Unissued*
Hurricane	*Unissued*
Catfish	*Unissued*
Money Blues	*Unissued*
Wiretappin'	*Unissued*

Guitar: Eric Clapton
Guitar/vocals: Bob Dylan
Guitar: Neil Hubbard
      Jim Mullen
      Hugh McCracken
      Eric Frandsen
Saxes: Mel Collins
Drums: John Sussewell
Piano: Tony O'Malley
Bass: Alan Spenner
      Rob Stoner
Violin: Scarlett Rivera

Mandolin/accordion: Dom Cortese
Backing vocals: Emmylou Harris
               Frank Collins
               Paddy McHugh
               Dyan Birch
Harmonica: Sugar Blue

Guitars used: various hired dobros and electric guitars

Producer: ———
Engineer: ———

ERIC CLAPTON: *It ended up with something like twenty-four musicians in the studio, all playing these incredibly incongruous instruments. Accordion, violin … and it really didn't work. He was after a large sound, but the songs were so personal that he wasn't comfortable with all the people around. But anyway, we did takes on about twelve songs. He even wrote one on the spot. All in one night.*

It was very hard to keep up with him. He wasn't sure what he wanted. He was really looking, racing from song to song. The songs were amazing.

Studio Session for Tom And Don
November–December 1975
Criteria Studios, Miami

Greyhound Bus (two takes)	*Unissued*
The Time Is Now	*Unissued*
I've Just Seen A Face	*Unissued*
Never Had It So Good	*Unissued*
Daybreak	*Unissued*
My Time	*Unissued*
Fool On The Hill	*Unissued*
Vincent	*Unissued*
Apple Scruff	*Unissued*
After The Thrill Is Gone (two takes)	*Unissued*
Beau Jangles	*Unissued*

Guitar: Eric Clapton
Guitars/vocals: Tom And Don
Bass: ——
Drums: ——
Keyboards: ——

Producers: Eric Clapton, Albhy Galuten
Engineer: ——

Not much is known about this session, other than that it happened and that Tom And Don were a Beatles-influenced folk duo. Nothing from the session was ever released. The master reels are located in Polygram's New Jersey tape complex.

94

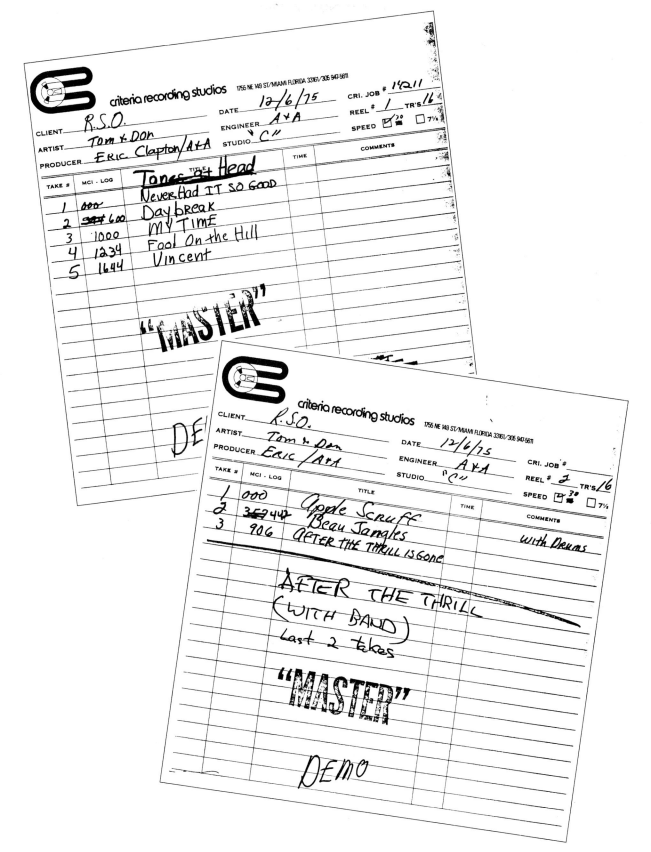

Studio Session
February–April 1976
Shangri-La Studios, Malibu, California

Daylight	*Unissued*	Buried Alive	*Unissued*
Beauty Spot	*Unissued*	Sooner Or Later	*Unissued*
Carnival	NO REASON TO CRY	I Got You On My Mind	*Unissued*
Let It Down	*Unissued*	Golden Slipper	*Unissued*
Disco	*Unissued*	Fever	*Unissued*
I Can See Myself In Your Eyes	*Unissued*	Seven Days	*Unissued*
Blues jam	*Unissued*	All Our Pastimes	NO REASON TO CRY
Hungry	NO REASON TO CRY	Hello Old Friend	NO REASON TO CRY
Do Bye Ah	*Unissued*	Innocent Times	NO REASON TO CRY
Billy Joe	*Unissued*	Beautiful Thing	NO REASON TO CRY
Double Trouble	NO REASON TO CRY	Sign Language	NO REASON TO CRY
Jam	*Unissued*	County Jail Blues	NO REASON TO CRY
Could This Be Called A Song	*Unissued*	Black Summer Rain	NO REASON TO CRY
Tuesday's Tune	*Unissued*	Last Night	NO REASON TO CRY CD only
Tenho Sede	*Unissued*	Stormy Monday	*Unissued*
		Hard Times	*Unissued*
		Who Do You Love	*Unissued*
		It's Eric Clapton's Birthday	*Unissued*
		The Path	*Unissued*

Guitar/vocals: Eric Clapton
Guitar: George Terry
Bass: Carl Radle
Keyboards: Dick Sims
Drums: Jamie Oldaker
Backing vocals: Yvonne Elliman
                   Marcy Levy
Guitar: Robbie Robertson
     Ronnie Wood
Guitar/vocals: Bob Dylan (Sign Language)
Keyboards/vocals: Billy Preston
Keyboards: George Fame (County Jail Blues)
Percussion: Sergio Pastora
Vocals: Van Morrison (Stormy Monday)
Vocals/bass: Rick Danko
Guitar: Pete Townshend (The Path)
Organ: Garth Hudson
Vocals/piano: Richard Manuel
Vocals/drums: Levon Helm

Guitar used: 'Blackie' Fender Stratocaster

Producer: Rob Fraboni in association with Eric Clapton and Carl Dean Radle
Engineer: Rob Fraboni

ERIC CLAPTON: *I think my best stuff has been done in American studios. Shangri-La, where we did* NO REASON TO CRY, *was the finest studio of all to work in. It's on the Pacific Coast Highway, north of Malibu on the way to San Francisco, and it was great because it was all wood and the room you record in was originally a master bedroom or a playroom, because it was a bordello. It probably had about twenty waterbeds in and a couple of sliding glass doors that you could just leave open to the outside, with the sea not more than a hundred feet away, lapping on the beach. And you would record like that, and that would go on the machine. It was something you couldn't do anywhere else – that was it!*

We sort of produced it ourselves, because we weren't allowed to work with Tom Dowd any more. There was a split between RSO and Warner Brothers, and Tom was under contract to Atlantic who were under contract to Warners, so he was told he couldn't work for anyone from RSO, and that went on for a long time. Rob Fraboni came in to mix it, that's all. It was a shame he came in so late. He engineered it when he mixed it and when we did overdubs, but he came in halfway through, and up until that point we were just using Ed Anderson, who's the sound man for the Band.

It was really rough, but I enjoyed that kind of feeling about it. I've got the original mixes of side one somewhere, and they're unbelievably different. They're great. And it's a shame, because Rob came in a different studio, and if he'd been able to mix it in Shangri-La, it would've kept that original feel. But we had to take it to Village Recorders and mix it there in a totally different atmosphere. It lost a little, it gained a little, but it wasn't the same as the original concept. We cut something like twenty-five tracks in three weeks out of nowhere, out of the blue – it was just like falling rain. And the out-takes – whoever's got them is sitting on a mint, because they're beautiful. Some of the best stuff didn't get on the album, like instrumentals.

It's one of my favourite albums – good groove, voice improving.

The NO REASON TO CRY sessions were very special, and while to outsiders it may seem like some sort of supersession, the fact remains that these sessions produced one of Eric's finest albums of the seventies. My personal favourite has to be 'Black Summer Rain', where Eric brings Layla to Shangri-La and a solo that would melt the heart of even the sternest critic.

◆

Eric also contributed to several sessions for friends such as Rick Danko, Joe Cocker, Kinki Friedman, Ringo Starr, Stephen Bishop and Corky Laing.

Studio Session for Rick Danko
April 1976
Village Recorders, Los Angeles

New Mexico   RICK DANKO

Guitar: Eric Clapton
Bass/vocals: Rick Danko
Drums: Denny Sewell
Accordion: Garth Hudson
Tambourine: Rob Fraboni

Guitar used: 'Blackie' Fender Stratocaster

Producers: Rick Danko and Rob Fraboni
Engineer: ———

Studio Session for Kinky Friedman
April 1976
Shangri-La Studios, Malibu, California

Kinky   LASSO FROM EL PASO
Ol' Ben Lucas   LASSO FROM EL PASO

Dobro: Eric Clapton
Vocals: Kinky Friedman
Bass: Rick Danko
Toy piano: Dr John (Ol' Ben Lucas)
Drums: Levon Helm

Guitar used: dobro

Producer: Kinky Friedman
Engineer: ——

Studio Session for Joe Cocker
April 1976
Shangri-La Studios, Malibu, California

Worrier   STINGRAY

Guitar: Eric Clapton
Vocals: Joe Cocker
Guitar: Cornell Dupree
      Eric Gale
Bass: Gordon Edwards
Drums: Steve Gadd
Keyboards: Richard Tee
Backing vocals: Bonnie Bramlett

Guitar used: 'Blackie' Fender Stratocaster

Producer: Rob Fraboni
Engineer: Rob Fraboni

Studio Session for Stephen Bishop
June 1976
ABC Studios/A&M Studios, Los Angeles

Save It For A Rainy Day   CARELESS
Sinking In An Ocean Of Tears   CARELESS

Guitar: Eric Clapton
Acoustic guitar/vocals: Stephen Bishop
Guitar: Jay Graydon (Sinking In An Ocean Of Tears)
      Jeffrey Staton (Save It For A Rainy Day)
Bass: Mac Cridlin (Sinking In An Ocean Of Tears)
Piano: Barlow Jarvis
Drums: Larry Brown (Sinking In An Ocean Of Tears)
Sax: Ray Pizzi (Sinking In An Ocean Of Tears)

Synthesizers: Alan Lindgren (Sinking In An Ocean Of Tears)
Drums: Russ Kunkel (Save It For A Rainy Day)
Backing vocals: Chaka Khan (Save It For A Rainy day)
Horns: arranged by Ian Freebairn Smith

Guitar used: 'Blackie' Fender Stratocaster

Producers: Henry Lewy, Stephen Bishop
Engineer: Henry Lewy

Studio Session for Ringo Starr
June 1976
Cherokee Studios, Los Angeles

This Be Called A Song   ROTOGRAVURE

Guitar: Eric Clapton
      Lon Van Eaton
Bass: Klaus Voorman
Vocals/drums: Ringo Starr
Drums: Jim Keltner
Piano: Jane Getz
Steel drums: Robert Greenidge
Backing vocals: Melissa Manchester
               Vini Poncia
               Joe Bean

Guitar used: 'Blackie' Fender Stratocaster

Producer: Arif Martin
Engineer: Lew Hahn

Studio Session for Corky Laing
June 1976
Westlake Audio, Los Angeles

On My Way   MAKIN' IT ON THE STREET

Guitar: Eric Clapton
      Corky Laing
      George Terry
      Dicky Betts
Drums: Corky Laing
Bass: Calvin Arline
Keyboards: Neal Larson

Guitar used: 'Blackie' Fender Stratocaster

Producer: John Sandlin
Engineer: Steve Hodge

On his return to the UK, Eric toured the seaside resorts to promote his album NO REASON TO CRY, which was released in August. It reached number 15 in the US and made the UK top ten.

◆

A US tour followed in November.

Live Session
15 November 1976
Convention Center, Dallas, Texas

Hello Old Friend	Radio broadcast
Sign Language	Radio broadcast
Badge	Radio broadcast
Knockin' On Heaven's Door	Radio broadcast
Key To The Highway	Not broadcast
Can't Find My Way Home	Radio broadcast
Tell The Truth	Radio broadcast
All Our Pastimes	Not broadcast
Blues Power	Radio broadcast
One Night	Radio broadcast
Layla	Radio broadcast
Further On Up The Road	FREDDIE KING 1934–1976

Guitar/vocals: Eric Clapton
Guitar: George Terry
Bass: Carl Radle
Drums: Jamie Oldaker
Keyboards: Dick Sims
Percussion: Sergio Pastora
Backing vocals: Yvonne Elliman
Backing vocals/harp: Marcy Levy
Guitar: Freddie King (Further On Up The Road)

Guitars used: Martin acoustic, 'Blackie' Fender Stratocaster

Producer: King Biscuit Flower Hour Radio Show
Engineer: ——

Eric's North American tour was a relatively short one, and was promoting NO REASON TO CRY. To this end one of the shows was recorded for radio syndication throughout the USA and the world. In the UK, it was eventually played on John Peel's late night BBC Radio 1 show.

◆

At the end of his tour, Eric, headed to San Francisco to rehearse with his friends, The Band, who were quitting the road for good with a huge farewell concert. This event was filmed by Martin Scorsese and released as THE LAST WALTZ. The concert featured guest artists who had been involved with them at various stages in their career, including Van Morrison, Neil Young, Joni Mitchell, Ronnie Hawkins, Bob Dylan and Muddy Waters.

Live Session
26 November 1976
Winterland, San Francisco

All Our Pastimes	*Unissued*
Further On Up The Road	THE LAST WALTZ

Guitar/vocals: Eric Clapton
Guitar: Robbie Robertson
Bass: Rick Danko
Drums: Levon Helm
Keyboards: Richard Manuel
Organ: Garth Hudson

I Shall Be Released	THE LAST WALTZ

Guitar/vocals: Eric Clapton
           Robbie Robertson
Bass: Rick Danko
Drums: Levon Helm
Keyboards/vocals: Richard Manuel
Organ: Garth Hudson
Guitar: Ronnie Wood
Drums: Ringo Starr
Vocals: Bob Dylan
        Neil Young
        Joni Mitchell
        Neil Diamond
        Ronnie Hawkins
        Dr John
        Paul Butterfield
        Bobby Charles
        Van Morrison

Instrumental jam	*Unissued*

Guitar: Eric Clapton
      Robbie Robertson
      Neil Young
      Ronnie Wood
Bass: Carl Radle
Drums: Levon Helm
      Ringo Starr
Harmonica: Paul Butterfield
Keyboards: Dr John

Guitar used: 'Blackie' Fender Stratocaster

Producer: Robbie Robertson
Engineers: Terry Becker, Tim Kramer, Elliot Mazer, Wayne Neuendorf, Ed Anderson, Neil Brody

THE LAST WALTZ

IF THE LAST WALTZ MEANS CHOOSING YOUR PARTNERS...
...THEN WHO BETTER THAN THESE?

The Band – Rick Danko, Levon Helm, Garth Hudson, Richard Manuel, Robbie Robertson.
Special guests – Paul Butterfield, Eric Clapton, Neil Diamond, Bob Dylan, Emmylou Harris, Ronnie Hawkins, Dr. John, Joni Mitchell, Van Morrison,
The Staples, Ringo Starr, Muddy Waters, Ron Wood, Neil Young.

"The road was our school. It gave us a sense of survival; it taught us everything we know and out of respect, we don't want to drive it into the ground . . . or maybe it's just
superstition but the road has taken a lot of the great ones. It's a goddam impossible way of life.
The Band has been together sixteen years, together on the road; eight years in dance halls, in dives and bars, eight years of concerts, arenas and stadiums. Our first concert as
The Band had been at Winterland, so we wrapped it up there on Thanksgiving Day. There was a dinner for 5,000, a waltz orchestra, a hell of a party and some friends showed
up to help us take it home. But they are much more than friends. They are some of the greatest influences on music and on a whole generation.
We wanted it to be more than a 'final concert.' We wanted it to be a celebration."

The Band
'The Last Waltz'
K66076
On Warner Brothers
Records and Tapes.

Marketed and distributed by WEA Records Ltd, P.O. Box 59, Alperton Lane, Wembley, Middx. HA0 1FJ. Phone 01-998-5929 or order through your WEA salesman.

The concert lasted some three hours. At the end the obligatory jam took place, with Eric having to be forcibly carried back on stage by the concert's promoter, Bill Graham.

Studio Session for Roger Daltrey
January 1977
Ramport Studios, Battersea, London

Although Eric participated in these sessions, it is not known what guitar parts survived, if any, onto the album. One of the reasons could have been Roger's idea of buying a huge barrel of beer for all to consume before recording! I have listened very closely to the album and various B sides and cannot find any trace of Eric, but he is credited on the sleeve. The album is titled ONE OF THE BOYS.

Studio Session for Ronnie Lane and Pete Townshend
February 1977
Olympic Sound Studios, Barnes, London

Rough Mix   ROUGH MIX

Guitar: Eric Clapton
         Pete Townshend
Bass: Ronnie Lane
Organ: Rabbit
Drums: Henry Spinetti

Annie   ROUGH MIX

Açoustic guitar: Eric Clapton
                  Pete Townshend
                  Ronnie Lane
                  Graham Lyle
Accordion: Benny Gallagher
Violin: Charlie Hart
String bass: Dave Markee

April Fool   ROUGH MIX

Dobro: Eric Clapton
Guitar: Pete Townshend
Guitar: Ronnie Lane
Double bass: Dave Markee

Till The Rivers Run Dry   ROUGH MIX

Dobro: Eric Clapton
Guitar: Pete Townshend
         Ronnie Lane
Drums: Henry Spinetti
Bass: Boz Burrell
Backing vocals: John Entwistle
                 Billy Nicholls

Guitars used: 'Blackie' Fender Stratocaster, dobro, Martin
               acoustic

Producer: Glyn Johns
Engineer: Glyn Johns

Eric and his band were invited to perform an exclusive concert for the influential *Old Grey Whistle Test* television show. The show took place during his UK tour of 1977, just before playing three London shows. Two of these were recorded for a proposed double live album with a view to a Christmas release. Sadly, like a lot of his live recordings, these were never released except for a version of 'Further On Up The Road' on the CROSSROADS retrospective. These two Hammersmith Odeon shows are quite exceptional, and hopefully will one day see an official release.

Live Session
26 April 1977
BBC Studios, Shepherds Bush, London

Hello Old Friend	Broadcast on *Whistle Test*
Sign Language	Broadcast on *Whistle Test*
Alberta	Broadcast on *Whistle Test*
Tell The Truth	Broadcast on *Whistle Test*
Can't Find My Way Home	Broadcast on *Whistle Test*
Double Trouble	Broadcast on *Whistle Test*
I Shot The Sheriff	Broadcast on *Whistle Test*
Knockin' On Heaven's Door	Broadcast on *Whistle Test*
Further On Up The Road	Broadcast on *Whistle Test*
Badge	Broadcast on *Whistle Test*
Key To The Highway	*Unissued*

Guitars used: Martin acoustic, 'Blackie' Fender Stratocaster

Producer: Michael Appleton

Live Session
27 April 1977
Hammersmith Odeon, London

Hello Old Friend	*Unissued*
Sign Language	*Unissued*
Alberta	*Unissued*
Tell The Truth	*Unissued*
Knockin' On Heaven's Door	*Unissued*
Steady Rollin' Man	*Unissued*
Can't Find My Way Home	*Unissued*
Further On Up The Road	CROSSROADS
Stormy Monday	*Unissued*
Badge	*Unissued*
Nobody Knows You When You're Down And Out	*Unissued*
I Shot The Sheriff	*Unissued*
Layla	*Unissued*
Key To The Highway	*Unissued*

Guitars used: Martin acoustic, Gold Top Gibson Les Paul, 'Blackie' Fender Stratocaster

Live Session
28 April 1977
Hammersmith Odeon, London

Hello Old Friend	*Unissued*
Sign Language	*Unissued*
Alberta	*Unissued*
All Our Pastimes	*Unissued*
Tell The Truth	*Unissued*
Knockin' On Heaven's Door	*Unissued*
Can't Find My Way Home	*Unissued*
Crossroads	*Unissued*
I Shot The Sheriff	*Unissued*
Nobody Knows You When You're Down And Out	*Unissued*
Further On Up The Road	*Unissued*
Stormy Monday	*Unissued*
Willie And The Hand Jive	*Unissued*
Layla	*Unissued*
All I Have To Do Is Dream	*Unissued*

Guitar/vocals: Eric Clapton
Guitar: George Terry
Bass: Carl Radle
Drums: Jamie Oldaker
Keyboards: Dick Sims
Backing vocals: Yvonne Elliman
Marcy Levy

Percussion: Sergio Pastora
Vocals/guitar: Ronnie Lane (Willie And The Hand Jive)

Guitars used: Martin acoustic, 'Blackie' Fender Stratocaster

Producer: ——
Engineer: ——
Recorded by: Ronnie Lane Mobile

Eric and his band went to Olympic Sound Studios in Barnes to record their next album only a few days after the end of their UK tour. Being in Olympic must have brought back memories to both Eric and Carl, as the last time they had been here together was during the infamous Derek And The Dominos second album sessions, when the band disintegrated among arguments and recriminations. Some good came out of it, though, as they decided to record a new version of 'Mean Old Frisco', which dated back to those April 1971 sessions. Maybe they hoped to lay the ghost of the past. If that was the case, it certainly worked. On its release in America in November, SLOWHAND went straight in at number 2 and the single 'Lay Down Sally' reached number 3.

Studio Session
May 1977
Olympic Sound Studios, Barnes, London

Reel 1 (2 May 1977)
Wonderful Tonight (eight takes)	SLOWHAND
Next Time You See Her (two takes)	SLOWHAND

Reel 2 (3–4 May 1977)
Next Time You See Her (one take)	SLOWHAND
Alberta (one take)	*Unissued*

Reel 3 (5 May 1977)
May You Never (eight takes)	SLOWHAND
Dumb Waiter (eight takes)	*Unissued*
Drowning On Dry Land (five takes)	*Unissued*

Reel 4 (5 May 1977)
Drowning On Dry Land (four takes)	*Unissued*

Reel 5 (6 May 1977)
Cocaine (two takes)	SLOWHAND
Alberta (six takes)	*Unissued*
Looking At The Rain	*Unissued*

Reel 6 (9 May 1977)
Mean Old Frisco (seven takes)	SLOWHAND

Reel 7 (9 May 1977)
Mean Old Frisco (two takes) — SLOWHAND
Be Bop And Holla (one take) — *Unissued*

Reel 8 (12 May 1977)
Peaches And Diesel (eight takes) — SLOWHAND

Reel 9 (12 May 1977)
Peaches And Diesel (eight takes) — SLOWHAND

Reel 9 (19 May 1977)
Lay Down Sally (five takes) — SLOWHAND

Reel 10 (19 May 1977)
Lay Down Sally (three takes) — SLOWHAND
Greyhound (one take) — *Unissued*
The Riff (The Core) — SLOWHAND
Jam — *Unissued*

Reel 11 (20 May 1977)
Greyhound (nine takes) — *Unissued*

Reel 12 (25 May 1977)
We're All The Way (five takes) — SLOWHAND
Stars Strays And Ashtrays (two takes) — *Unissued*

Reel 13 (25 May 1977)
Stars Strays And Ashtrays (five takes) — *Unissued*

Guitar/vocals: Eric Clapton
Guitar: George Terry
Bass: Carl Radle
Drums: Jamie Oldaker
Keyboards: Dick Sims
Backing vocals: Yvonne Elliman
　　　　　　　 Marcy Levy
Sax: Mel Collins (The Riff)

Guitar used: 'Blackie' Fender Stratocaster

Producer: Glyn Johns
Engineer: ——

ERIC CLAPTON: SLOWHAND *for me is a very nervous sung album, especially after* NO REASON TO CRY. *Maybe it was because of the lack of material we had when we went into the studio or the difference in surroundings.*

And laid back is not the word for it! LAYLA *wasn't a success – it died a death. But as far as I was concerned, I'd have put that album up against anybody's that was out at the time. With* SLOWHAND *it was a completely different story. It was lightweight, really lightweight, and the reason for that, I think, is partly due to the fact that some of the stuff that we wanted to put on the record I wrote, say, six months before. We were on the road and we wrote some songs and we couldn't get to the studio soon enough, or we wanted a couple of weeks off or something like that. And by the time we got in there, everyone knew the song so well, we were so sort of limp about it that it was lazy.*

Anyway, for me, I think the best track has got to be 'Wonderful Tonight', because the song is nice. It was written about my sweetheart, and whether or not it was recorded well or I played it well doesn't make any difference, because the song is still nice.

Studio Session for Ijahman Levi
December 1977
Joe Gibbs Studio, London

Eric definitely laid down some guitar parts alongside Stevie Winwood's keyboards, but it would appear that his guitar was either mixed very low or not used at all. The complete sessions came out on two separate albums, HAILE I HYMN and ARE WE A WARRIOR.

WHITE MANSIONS

A tale from the American Civil War 1861–1865

 DOLBY SYSTEM

BACKLESS ON THE ROAD AGAIN

1978–1979

Studio Session for WHITE MANSIONS project
January 1978
Olympic Sound Studios, Barnes, London

White Trash	WHITE MANSIONS
Kentucky Racehorse	WHITE MANSIONS

Guitar (slide): Eric Clapton (White Trash)
Guitar (dobro): Eric Clapton (Kentucky Racehorse)
Drums: Henry Spinetti
Bass: Dave Markee
Harmonica: Steve Cash
Piano: Tim Hinkley (White Trash)
Acoustic guitar/piano/backing vocals: John Dillon
Backing vocals: Bernie Leadon
                Paul Kennerley

Guitars used: 'Blackie' Fender Stratocaster, dobro

Producer: Glyn Johns
Engineer: Glyn Johns

Eric's US tour of 1978 was a lengthy one, promoting his successful SLOWHAND album. A radio broadcast took place, as did the recording of three concerts in Florida.

Live Session
26 March 1978
and 11 February 1978
Civic Auditorium, Santa Monica, California

Peaches And Diesel	Radio broadcast
Wonderful Tonight	Radio broadcast
Lay Down Sally	Radio broadcast
Next Time You See Her	Radio broadcast
The Core	Not broadcast
We're All The Way	Not broadcast
Rodeo Man	Not broadcast
Fools Paradise	Not broadcast

Cocaine	Radio broadcast
Badge	Radio broadcast
Double Trouble	Not broadcast
Nobody Knows You When You're Down And Out	Not broadcast
Knockin' On Heaven's Door	Radio broadcast
Key To The Highway	Not broadcast
Going Down Slow	Not broadcast
Layla	Not broadcast
Bottle Of Red Wine	Not broadcast
You'll Never Walk Alone	Not broadcast

Guitar/vocals: Eric Clapton
Guitar: George Terry
Bass: Carl Radle
Keyboards: Dick Sims
Drums: Jamie Oldaker
Vocals: Marcy Levy

Guitar used: 'Blackie' Fender Stratocaster

Producer: King Biscuit Flower Hour
Engineer: ——
Recorded by: DIR Broadcasting 24-track mobile unit

Live Session
19 March 1978
Jai-Alai Frontun, Miami

Peaches And Diesel	*Unissued*
Wonderful Tonight	*Unissued*
Lay Down Sally	*Unissued*
Next Time You See Her	*Unissued*
The Core	*Unissued*
We're All The Way	*Unissued*
Rodeo Man	*Unissued*
Fools Paradise	*Unissued*
Cocaine	*Unissued*
Double Trouble	*Unissued*
Badge	*Unissued*

Nobody Knows You When You're	
Down And Out	*Unissued*
Knockin' On Heaven's Door	*Unissued*
Key To The Highway	*Unissued*
Let It Rain	*Unissued*
Layla	*Unissued*
Bottle Of Red Wine	*Unissued*

Live Session
20 March 1978
Civic Center Coliseum, Lakeland, Florida

Tracks as above for Miami	*Unissued*

Live Session
21 March 1978
Civic Center, Savannah, Georgia

The Core	*Unissued*
Peaches And Diesel	*Unissued*
Wonderful Tonight	*Unissued*
Lay Down Sally	*Unissued*
Next Time You See Her	*Unissued*
Mean Old Frisco	*Unissued*
Rodeo Man	*Unissued*
Fools Paradise	*Unissued*
Cocaine	*Unissued*
Double Trouble	*Unissued*
Badge	*Unissued*
Nobody Knows You When You're	
Down And Out	*Unissued*
Knockin' On Heaven's Door	*Unissued*
Key To The Highway	*Unissued*
Let It Rain	*Unissued*
Layla	*Unissued*
Bottle Of Red Wine	*Unissued*

Guitar/vocals: Eric Clapton
Guitar: George Terry
Bass: Carl Radle
Keyboards: Dick Sims
Drums: Jamie Oldaker
Backing vocals: Marcy Levy

Guitar used: 'Blackie' Fender Stratocaster

Producer: ——
Engineer: ——

Live Session for Alexis Korner's fiftieth birthday party
19 April 1978
The Gatsby Room, Pinewood Studios

Hey Pretty Mama	THE PARTY ALBUM
Can't Get You Out Of My Mind	*Unissued*
Hi-Heel Sneakers	THE PARTY ALBUM
Stormy Monday Blues	THE PARTY ALBUM

Guitar: Eric Clapton
Guitar/vocals: Alexis Korner
Bass: Colin Hodgkinson
Electric piano/vocals: Zoot Money
Drums: Stu Spears
Tenor sax: Dick Morrissey
Tenor sax/soprano sax: Dick Heckstall-Smith
Tenor sax/soprano sax: Art Themen
Tenor sax/soprano sax/baritone sax: Mel Collins
Baritone sax/soprano sax: John Surman
Trombone/bass trumpet: Mike Zwerin
Vocals: Chris Farlowe
Harmonica: Duffy Power
               Paul Jones
Guitar: Neil Ford

Guitar used: 'Blackie' Fender Stratocaster

Producer: Alexis Korner
Engineer: Mike Robinson
Recorded by: BBC Mobile

Eric's main influences during this part of the seventies were Don Williams, J.J. Cale and Bob Dylan, although his mainstay was still the blues. All these different styles, which had originated during the recording of SLOWHAND, were to continue for its follow-up, BACKLESS.

Studio Session for Backless
May–September 1978
Olympic Sound Studios, Barnes, London

Tulsa Time (six takes)	BACKLESS
Sweet Lorraine	*Unissued*
It's A Shame (two takes)	*Unissued*
If I Don't Be There By Morning (five takes)	BACKLESS
Eric's Thing	*Unissued*
Early In The Morning	BACKLESS
Country jam	*Unissued*
Tell Me That You Love Me	BACKLESS

Watch Out For Lucy	BACKLESS
One Chord Tune (two takes)	*Unissued*
Walk Out In The Rain	BACKLESS
I'll Make Love To You Anytime	BACKLESS
Roll It	BACKLESS
Golden Ring	BACKLESS
Promises (originally titled You)	BACKLESS
Depend On Me	*Unissued*
The Road Is Long	*Unissued*
Dickie's Song	*Unissued*
Before You Accuse Me	*Unissued*
Give It Away	*Unissued*

Guitar/vocals: Eric Clapton
Guitar: George Terry
Bass: Carl Radle
Drums: Jamie Oldaker
Keyboards: Dick Sims
Backing vocals: Marcy Levy
                  Benny Gallagher (Golden Ring)
                  Graham Lyle (Golden Ring)

Guitar used: 'Blackie' Fender Stratocaster

Producer: Glyn Johns
Engineer: ——

ERIC CLAPTON: *Well, he [Bob Dylan] just laid this cassette on me with* 'If I Don't Be There By Morning' *and* 'Walk Out In The Rain'. *He was hooked up with this girl called Helena Springs. They were co-writing, and I think he was very proud of it and laid it on me when we were in Nuremberg. I've still got that on cassette of them two. That's another bootleg. I've got a private copy of that. When I get down sometimes, I listen to them and it will bring me right out, because I know that no one else has got it. This was a gift to me. The funny thing was, when we next met was at Blackbushe in fact. We did Nuremberg first. At Blackbushe I sat in a coach and played him – I'd gone into the studio by then and done the two numbers – and I played them back and he said, 'Well, when are they going to be finished?' [laughs] and I realized I was dealing with a master. Still is. Always will be. The man's a master.*

The title of the album, BACKLESS, *came from the Dylan Blackbushe gig, where it became very apparent that he knew exactly what was going on everywhere around him all the time. So it's a tribute to Bob, really. I mean, if you were backstage, he expected you to be putting as much into it as he was. You couldn't just stand there and be one of the roadies, you had to actually focus all your attention on him, and if you didn't he knew it, and he'd turn around and he'd look at you and you'd get daggers.*

The best things that happened on BACKLESS *were the things that happened at the time. I got away with one song on there,* 'Golden Ring', *which I think is the strongest song on the album, because I wrote it because I was fed up with the general apathy of everyone involved, and I just thought, 'Well, I'll take a song in there and whether they like it or not, we'll do it, they'll learn it and record it and we'll put it on the record, and that's that!' And that kind of conviction carried the thing through.*

Being critical of your own work is very difficult, especially when you can just say 'Bow wow' instead. In the case of BACKLESS *I think we were very lazy. In fact, I think all musicians are lazy. I think that's one of the best parts about us. The trouble with being lazy is you either don't try hard enough or you try too hard, and you don't like being told what to do.*

The UK tour of 1978 started in Glasgow. The band were now down to a four-piece, which meant Eric had to do all the guitar solos with no foil on rhythm. Fans were rewarded with some of his best playing of the seventies. In Glasgow, the lucky Scots were treated to a version of Robert Johnson's 'Kindhearted Woman Blues'. Several shows were filmed and recorded for a proposed documentary of Eric on the road in the UK and Europe. The film *Eric Clapton And His Rolling Hotel* was shown only at a few film festivals before being withdrawn, because although it was a true reflection of that tour, it didn't present Eric at his best. However, it does contain some fascinating footage on the Orient Express, which had been hired out as transportation for the European tour, of Eric playing some of his favourite acoustic blues numbers. The climax of the film is the hometown gig at Guildford's Civic Hall, which featured George Harrison and Elton John on the encore, 'Further On Up The Road'.

Live Session
24 November 1978
Apollo, Glasgow

Layla	*Unissued*
Worried Life Blues	*Unissued*
Tulsa Time	*Unissued*
Early In The Morning	*Unissued*
Badge	*Unissued*
Wonderful Tonight	*Unissued*
Kindhearted Woman Blues	*Unissued*
Key To The Highway	*Unissued*
Further On Up The Road	*Unissued*
Cocaine	*Unissued*
Double Trouble	*Unissued*
Crossroads	*Unissued*

Guitar/vocals: Eric Clapton
Bass: Carl Radle
Drums: Jamie Oldaker
Keyboards: Dick Sims
Piano: Ian Stewart (Key To The Highway, Further On Up The Road)
Harmonica: Jerry Portnoy (Key To The Highway, Further On Up The Road)
Guitar: Bob Margolin (Key To The Highway, Further On Up The Road)

Producer: ——
Engineer: ——
Recorded by: Rolling Stones Mobile

Live Session
25 November 1978
City Hall, Newcastle

Layla	*Unissued*
Worried Life Blues	*Unissued*
Wonderful Tonight	*Unissued*
If I Don't Be There By Morning	*Unissued*
Double Trouble	*Unissued*
I'll Make Love To You Anytime	*Unissued*
Badge	*Unissued*
Key To The Highway	*Unissued*
Cocaine	*Unissued*
Blues jam 1	*Unissued*
Blues jam 2	*Unissued*
Crossroads	*Unissued*

Producer: ——
Engineer: ——
Recorded by: Rolling Stones Mobile

Live Session
7 December 1978
Civic Hall, Guildford

Loving You Is Sweeter Than Ever	*Unissued*
Worried Life Blues	*Unissued*
Badge	*Unissued*
Tulsa Time	*Unissued*
Early In The Morning	*Unissued*
Wonderful Tonight	*Unissued*
Crossroads	*Unissued*
Cocaine	*Unissued*
Double Trouble	*Unissued*
Layla	*Unissued*
Standin' Around Crying/Sad Sad Day	*Unissued*
Further On Up The Road	*Rolling Hotel* film

Guitar/vocals: Eric Clapton
Guitar: George Terry
Bass: Carl Radle
Drums: Jamie Oldaker
Piano: Pinetop Perkins (Standing Around Crying)
      Elton John (Further On Up The Road)
Guitar: Bob Margolin (Standing Around Crying)
      George Harrison (Further On Up The Road)
Harmonica: Jerry Portnoy (Standing Around Crying)

Guitar used: 'Blackie' Fender Stratocaster

Producer: ——
Engineer: ——

Studio Session for George Harrison
December 1978
FPSHOT (Friar Park Studios, Henley-on-Thames, Oxon)

Love Comes To Everyone	GEORGE HARRISON

Guitar: Eric Clapton
Guitar/vocals: George Harrison
Drums: Andy Newmark
Bass: Willie Weeks
Keyboards: Neil Larsen
Percussion: Ray Cooper
Moogs/backing vocals: Stevie Winwood

Guitar used: 'Blackie' Fender Stratocaster

Producers: George Harrison, Russ Titelman
Engineer: Phil MacDonald

At the end of 1978, Eric went back to Olympic Sound Studios to record three demos with a new British rhythm section that would soon become part of his backing band.

Studio Session
28–29 December 1978
Olympic Sound Studios, Barnes, London

To Make Somebody Happy	*Unissued*
Water On The Ground	*Unissued*
Cryin'	*Unissued*

Guitar/vocals: Eric Clapton
Bass: Dave Markee (probably)
Drums: Henry Spinetti (probably)

Producer: Glyn Johns
Engineer: Glyn Johns

Studio Session for Marc Benno
January 1979
Olympic Sound Studios, Barnes, London

Hotfoot Blues	LOST IN AUSTIN
Chasin' Rainbows	LOST IN AUSTIN
Me And A Friend Of Mine	LOST IN AUSTIN
New Romance	LOST IN AUSTIN
Last Train	LOST IN AUSTIN
Lost In Austin	LOST IN AUSTIN
Splish Splash	LOST IN AUSTIN
Monterrey Pen	LOST IN AUSTIN
The Drifter	LOST IN AUSTIN
Hey There Senorita	LOST IN AUSTIN

Guitar: Eric Clapton
Guitar/vocals/piano: Marc Benno
Guitar: Albert Lee
Bass: Carl Radle
Drums: Jim Keltner
Keyboards: Dick Sims
Sax: Dickie Morresey

Guitar used: 'Blackie' Fender Stratocaster

Producer: Glyn Johns
Engineer: Glyn Johns

This next guest session was an interesting one, reuniting Eric with his fellow Blues Breaker John McVie.

Studio Session for Danny Douma
March 1979
Village Recorder, Los Angeles

I Hate You	NIGHT EYES

Guitar: Eric Clapton
Guitar/vocals: Danny Douma
Drums: Mick Fleetwood
Bass: John McVie
Keyboards: Christine McVie

Guitar used: 'Blackie' Fender Stratocaster

Producers: Danny Douma, Nick Van Maarth
Engineer: Nick Van Maarth

Eric's new all British band recorded a live album as a debut. They couldn't have chosen a better venue, as the sound at the Budokan in Tokyo is superb.

Live Session for JUST ONE NIGHT
3 December 1979
Budokan, Tokyo

Reel 1

Tulsa Time	JUST ONE NIGHT
Early In The Morning	JUST ONE NIGHT
Lay Down Sally	JUST ONE NIGHT

Reel 2

Wonderful Tonight	JUST ONE NIGHT
If I Don't Be There By Morning	JUST ONE NIGHT
Worried Life Blues	JUST ONE NIGHT

Reel 3

Country Boy	*Unissued*

Reel 4

All Our Pastimes	JUST ONE NIGHT
Blues Power	JUST ONE NIGHT

Reel 5

Knockin' on Heaven's Door	TIME PIECES 2
Setting Me Up	JUST ONE NIGHT

Reel 6

Ramblin' On My Mind	JUST ONE NIGHT

Reel 7

After Midnight	JUST ONE NIGHT
Cocaine	JUST ONE NIGHT

Reel 8

Layla	*Unissued*
Further On Up The Road	JUST ONE NIGHT

Live Session
4 December 1979
Budokan, Tokyo

Reel 1

Tulsa Time	*Unissued*
Early In The Morning	*Unissued*

Reel 2

Lay Down Sally	*Unissued*
Wonderful Tonight	*Unissued*
If I Don't Be There By Morning	*Unissued*

Reel 3

Worried Life Blues	*Unissued*
Country Boy	*Unissued*

Reel 4

All Our Pastimes	*Unissued*
Blues Power	*Unissued*

Reel 5

Double Trouble	*Unissued*
Knockin' On Heaven's Door	*Unissued*

Reel 6

Setting Me Up	*Unissued*
Ramblin' On My Mind	*Unissued*

Reel 7

Cocaine	*Unissued*
Layla	*Unissued*

Reel 8

Further On Up The Road	*Unissued*

Guitar/vocals: Eric Clapton
Guitar/keyboards/vocals: Albert Lee
Bass: Dave Markee
Drums: Henry Spinetti
Keyboards: Chris Stainton

ERIC CLAPTON: *I really didn't want to record it. There's a natural shyness about me when I'm playing onstage. For me it's something that should only happen once, you know, and then it's gone.*

The album was one show. We did two nights, and recorded both. I think they chose the one I didn't like [3 December].

JUST ONE NIGHT was a very successful double live album, making the top five in both the UK and the USA.

Odeon Hammersmith, London, 1980

MONEY, TICKETS, CIGARETTES

1980–1982

In between his own recording and touring commitments, Eric continued to play on friends' sessions at regular intervals.

Studio Session for Ronnie Lane
January 1980
Studio not known

When Lad Has Money   SEE ME

Guitar: Eric Clapton
        Alun Daves
Vocals: Ronnie Lane
Bass: Brian Belshaw
Drums: Bruce Rowland
Piano: Bill Livsey
Backing vocals: Carol Grimes

Barcelona   SEE ME

Guitar: Eric Clapton
Vocals: Ronnie Lane
Bass: Brian Belshaw
Drums: Bruce Rowland
Piano: Bill Livsey
        Henry McCullough
Backing vocals: Carol Grimes
Strings: Charlie Hart
Steve Simpson

Way Up Yonder   SEE ME

Guitar: Eric Clapton
        Alun Daves
Vocals: Ronnie Lane
Bass: Brian Belshaw
Drums: Bruce Rowland
Piano: Bill Livsey
        Ian Stewart
Backing vocals: White Grit Gang

Guitar used: 'Blackie' Fender Stratocaster

Producer: Fishpool Productions
Engineer: Bob Potter

Studio Session for Gary Brooker
March 1980
Surrey Sound Studios, Leatherhead, Surrey

Leave The Candle   A side
Chasing The Chop   B side

Guitar: Eric Clapton
Vocals/keyboards: Gary Brooker
Bass: Dave Markee
Drums: Henry Spinetti
Backing vocals: Gallagher and Lyle

Guitar used: 'Blackie' Fender Stratocaster

Producer: ——
Engineer: ——

Studio Session for Stephen Bishop
March 1980
Air Studios, London

Little Moon   RED CAB TO MANHATTAN
Sex Kittens Go To College   RED CAB TO MANHATTAN

Guitar: Eric Clapton
Acoustic guitar: Stephen Bishop
Keyboards: Gary Brooker
           Chris Stainton
Bass: John Giblun
Drums: Phil Collins
Cello: Clive Anstree (Little Moon only)

Eric had recruited Gary Brooker as unofficial musical director for the group, and immediately set about recording his new album. The sessions produced some fairly uninspired results. It is difficult to pinpoint blame; maybe it was Eric simply being lazy, maybe it was the band being too laid back, or perhaps Glyn Johns in his role as producer was not assertive enough. Whatever the reason, the album was finished and mastered and cassette copies were sent round to various RSO executives. It was to be called TURN UP DOWN, but all concerned decided that it was not good enough to release.

Studio Session for TURN UP DOWN
March–April 1980
Surrey Sound Studios, Leatherhead, Surrey

Blues Instrumental	*Unissued*
There Ain't No Money	*Unissued*
Games Up	*Unissued*
Rita Mae	*Unissued*
Freedom	*Unissued*
Evangelina	*Unissued*
Home Lovin'	*Unissued*
Hold Me Lord	*Unissued*
Something Special	*Unissued*
I'd Love To Say I Love You	*Unissued*
Catch Me If You Can	*Unissued*
Thunder And Lightning	*Unissued*
Oh How I Miss My Baby's Love	*Unissued*

Guitar/vocals: Eric Clapton
          Albert Lee
Keyboards: Chris Stainton
Keyboards/vocals: Gary Brooker
Drums: Henry Spinetti
Bass: Dave Markee

Guitars used: 'Blackie' Fender Stratocaster, Sunburst Fender
   Stratocaster

Producer: Glyn Johns
Engineer: Glyn Johns

Studio Session for ANOTHER TICKET
July–August 1980
Compass Point Studios, Nassau, Bahamas

Say Hello To Billy Jean	*Unissued*
Something Special	ANOTHER TICKET
Black Rose	B side/ANOTHER TICKET
Blow Wind Blow	ANOTHER TICKET
Another Ticket	A side/ANOTHER TICKET
I Can't Stand It	A side/ANOTHER TICKET
Hold Me Lord	ANOTHER TICKET
Floating Bridge	ANOTHER TICKET
Catch Me If You Can	ANOTHER TICKET
Rita Mae	B side/ANOTHER TICKET
Lead Me To The Water	LEAD ME TO THE WATER
Home Lovin'	LEAD ME TO THE WATER

Guitar/vocals: Eric Clapton
          Albert Lee
Keyboards: Chris Stainton
Keyboards/vocals: Gary Brooker
Drums: Henry Spinetti
Bass: Dave Markee

Guitars used: 'Blackie' Fender Stratocaster, Gibson 335,
   Sunburst Fender Stratocaster

Producer: Tom Dowd
Engineer: Tom Dowd

ERIC CLAPTON: *Most of it is very bluesy. A couple of them are exceptionally bluesy. It took a long time to make that album because I was totally fed up with writing ditties and pleasant melodies, and I thought it was time for me to reconnect myself to what I know best.*

LEE DICKSON *(Eric's guitar tech): When Eric was recording* ANOTHER TICKET, *he went through a number of guitars trying to get a particular sound on 'Rita Mae'. He finally settled on his Gibson 335. He'll dabble with a Gibson Explorer or a Les Paul, but he'll always be drawn back to his true love – the Fender Stratocaster. There's something about the Strat sound that's perfect for him. Plus, he can get everything out of a Strat that he can out from a Les Paul or a Telecaster, so why depend on another guitar? His favourite is his 'Blackie' 56 Strat. Then there's a brown '57 model that we use as back-up, and a '54 with raised action in an open tuning for slide tunes.*

ANOTHER TICKET is a superb album. The first single, 'I Can't Stand It', received a lot of air play, and both album and single were set to do well. Unfortunately, Eric became seriously ill only eight dates into a huge US tour, resulting in the cancellation of the remainder of the itinerary. With no promotion, the album disappeared fairly quickly from the charts. A great shame, as it is one of the bluesiest albums Eric produced. The last two numbers were released on Gary Brooker's second solo album LEAD ME TO THE WATER.

Studio Session for Phil Collins
October 1980
Townhouse Studios, London

If Leaving Me Is Easy   FACE VALUE

Guitar: Eric Clapton
Drums/vocals: Phil Collins
Guitar: Daryl Stuermer
Bass: Alphonso Johnson
Sax: Don Myrick
Flugelhorn: Rahmlee Michael Davis
              Michael Harris

Guitar used: ——

Producer: Phil Collins
Engineer: Hugh Padgham

Studio Session for John Martyn
February 1981
Townhouse Studios, London

Couldn't Love You More   GLORIOUS FOOL

Guitar: Eric Clapton
Guitar/vocals: John Martyn
Drums/additional vocals: Phil Collins
Bass: Alan Thomson
Keyboards: Max Middleton
Percussion: Danny Cummings

Guitar used: 'Blackie' Fender Stratocaster

Producer: Phil Collins
Engineer: Nick Launay

Live Session
9 September 1981
Theatre Royal, Drury Lane, London

'Cause We Ended As Lovers   *Unissued*
Crossroads   THE MUSIC

Guitar/vocals: Eric Clapton
Guitar: Jeff Beck
Bass: Neil Murray
Drums: Simon Philips

I Shall Be Released   *Unissued*

Guitar: Eric Clapton
Guitar/vocals: Sting

Guitar: Jeff Beck
        John Etheridge
        Neil Innes
        Ray Russell
Bass: Neil Murray
      Mo Foster
Drums: Simon Phillips
Keyboards: John Altman
           Chas Jankel
Horns: Mel Collins
       Paul Cosh
       Jeff Daly
       Martin Drover
       Digby Fairweather
       Malcolm Griffiths
       Mike Henry
       Mark Isham
Backing vocals: Victoria Wood
                Pamela Stephenson
                Sharon Campbell

Live Session
10 September 1981
Theatre Royal, Drury Lane, London

'Cause We Ended As Lovers   THE MUSIC
Further On Up The Road   THE MUSIC

Guitar/vocals: Eric Clapton
Guitar: Jeff Beck
Bass: Neil Murray
Drums: Simon Phillips

I Shall Be Released   *Unissued*

Guitar: Eric Clapton
Guitar/vocals: Sting
Guitar: Jeff Beck
        John Etheridge
        Neil Innes
        Ray Russell
Bass: Neil Murray
      Mo Foster
Drums: Simon Phillips
Keyboards: John Altman
           Chas Jankel
Horns: Mel Collins
       Paul Cosh
       Jeff Daly
       Martin Drover
       Digby Fairweather
       Malcolm Griffiths
       Mike Henry
       Mark Isham

Backing vocals: Phil Collins
Donovan
Doreen Chanter
Sharon Campbell
Bob Geldof

Live Session
12 September 1981
Theatre Royal, Drury Lane, London

I Shall Be Released   THE MUSIC

As above plus:
Backing vocals: Tom Robinson
Sheena Easton
Midge Ure
Linda Taylor
Micky Moody
Chris Cross

Guitar used: 'Blackie' Fender Stratocaster

Producer: Martin Lewis
Engineer: Tim Summerhayes
Recorded by: The Rak Mobile

ERIC CLAPTON: *During rehearsals, Jeff and I were sending Sting up. He was going through all the motions of leaping about, when there was no one there. No audience. 'Bit green, isn't he?' we were saying. 'Only been in the business three weeks – look at him.' But then we saw him in front of an audience – so composed, so confident. Obviously with a performance such as he gives you've got to practise it. He's very good.*

Studio Session
September–November 1982
Compass Point Studios, Nassau, Bahamas

I've Got A Rock 'n' Roll Heart	A side/MONEY AND CIGARETTES
Man In Love	B side/MONEY AND CIGARETTES
The Shape You're In	A side/MONEY AND CIGARETTES
Crosscut Saw	B side/MONEY AND CIGARETTES
Slow Down Linda	A side/MONEY AND CIGARETTES
Crazy Country Hop	B side/MONEY AND CIGARETTES
Everybody Oughta Make A Change	MONEY AND CIGARETTES

Ain't Going Down   MONEY AND CIGARETTES
Man Overboard   MONEY AND CIGARETTES
Pretty Girl   MONEY AND CIGARETTES

Guitar/vocals: Eric Clapton
Guitar: Ry Cooder
        Albert Lee
Bass: Duck Dunn
Keyboards: Chris Stainton
Drums: Roger Hawkins

Guitars used: 'Blackie' Fender Stratocaster, Sunburst Fender
  Stratocaster

Producer: Tom Dowd
Engineer: ——

ROGER HAWKINS: *Eric and Albert are on guitar, Chris Stainton on keyboards, Duck Dunn on bass and me on drums. We recorded ten numbers in the same number of days. Eric works slowly, but it was great fun doing that session.*

ERIC CLAPTON: *In terms of who joins my line-up, my hands are tied to a certain extent. If I could have the pick of anyone in the world – well, I wouldn't know where to start. So I have to choose from who's available, whose playing I like and whom I respect. I've loved Duck Dunn's playing as long as I can remember. He's the only bass player who's had a really marked effect on me.*

Studio Session for Ringo Starr
December 1982
Startling Studios (Ringo's home studio)

Everybody's In A Hurry But Me   OLD WAVE

Guitar: Eric Clapton
Vocals: Ringo Starr
Guitar: Waddy Wachtel
Drums: Russell Kunkel
Bass: John Entwistle
Percussion: Ray Cooper
Keyboards: Chris Stainton
Guitar: Joe Walsh

Guitar used: 'Blackie' Fender Stratocaster

Producer: Joe Walsh
Engineer: Jim Niper

Eric finished the year off by playing with Chas And Dave on their Christmas telvision special. The set was a makeshift East End pub with various entertainers, including Eric playing a new number from his recent studio sessions for his upcoming album.

Live Session for Chas And Dave
December 1982
Studio not known

Slow Down Linda   *Chas And Dave Xmas Show* (TV)
Goodnight Irene   *Chas And Dave Xmas Show* (TV)

Guitar/vocals: Eric Clapton
Piano/vocals: Chas Hodges
Bass/vocals: Dave Peacock
Drums: Mick Burt
Guitar/vocals: Albert Lee (Goodnight Irene)

Guitar used: Fender Stratocaster

Producer: ——
Engineer: ——

Odeon Hammersmith, London, 1983

BEHIND THE SUN

1983–1985

Studio Session for Christine McVie
June 1983
Olympic Sound Studios, Barnes, London

The Challenge   CHRISTINE McVIE

Guitar: Eric Clapton
Keyboards/vocals: Christine McVie
Guitar/vocals: Todd Sharp
Bass: George Hawkins
Drums: Steve Ferrone

Guitar used: 'Blackie' Fender Stratocaster

Producer: Russ Titelman
Engineer: David Richards

In August 1983, Eric joined Roger Waters for sessions for his first solo venture. Eric's playing throughout is superb, particularly on 'Sexual Revolution'.

Studio Session for Roger Waters
August 1983
The Billiard Room, Eel Pie, Olympic Studios, London

4.30am (Apparently They Were Travelling Abroad)
THE PROS AND CONS OF HITCH-HIKING
4.33am (Running Shoes)
THE PROS AND CONS OF HITCH-HIKING
4.37am (Arabs With Knives And West German Skies)
THE PROS AND CONS OF HITCH-HIKING
4.39am (For The First Time Today – part 2)
THE PROS AND CONS OF HITCH-HIKING
4.41am (Sexual Revolution)
THE PROS AND CONS OF HITCH-HIKING
4.47am (The Remains Of Our Love)
THE PROS AND CONS OF HITCH-HIKING
4.50am (Go Fishing)   THE PROS AND CONS OF HITCH-HIKING

4.56am (For The First Time Today – part 1)
THE PROS AND CONS OF HITCH-HIKING
4.58am (Dunroamin Duncarin Dunlivin)
THE PROS AND CONS OF HITCH-HIKING
5.01am (The Pros And Cons of Hitch-Hiking)
THE PROS AND CONS OF HITCH-HIKING
5.06am (Every Stranger's Eyes)
THE PROS AND CONS OF HITCH-HIKING
5.11am (The Moment of Clarity)
THE PROS AND CONS OF HITCH-HIKING

Guitar: Eric Clapton
Guitar/bass/vocals: Roger Waters
Hammond organ/12-string guitar: Andy Bown
Percussion: Ray Cooper
Piano: Michael Kamen
Drums: Andy Newmark
Saxophone: David Sanborn
Horns: Raphael Ravenscroft
        Kevin Flanagan
        Vic Sullivan
Backing vocals: Katie Kissoon
              Doreen Chanter
              Madeline Bell

Guitar used: 'Blackie' Fender Stratocaster

Producers: Roger Waters and Michael Kamen
Engineer: Andy Jackson

1983 was the year in which Eric celebrated twenty years on the road. He decided to play two special shows at London's Royal Albert Hall along with some friends. The concerts were done for charity, the first night being for ARMS (Action Research into Multiple Sclerosis) and the second for the Prince's Trust.

Live Session
20 September 1983
Royal Albert Hall, London

Main artist: Eric Clapton

Everybody Oughta Make A Change	*ARMS* video
Lay Down Sally	*ARMS* video
Wonderful Tonight	*ARMS* video
Ramblin' On My Mind	*ARMS* video
Have You Ever Loved A Woman	*ARMS* video
Rita Mae	*ARMS* video
Cocaine	*ARMS* video

Main artist: Andy Fairweather-Low

Man Smart Woman Smarter	*ARMS* video

Main artist: Stevie Winwood

Hound Dog	*Unissued*
Best That I Can	*Unissued*
Road Runner	*ARMS* video
Slowdown Sundown	*ARMS* video
Take Me To The River	*ARMS* video
Gimme Some Lovin'	*ARMS* video

All members

Tulsa Time	*ARMS* video
Wee Wee Baby	*Unissued*
Layla	*ARMS* video

Main artist: Ronnie Lane plus all

Bomber's Moon	*Unissued*
Goodnight Irene	*ARMS* video

Guitar/vocals: Eric Clapton
                Andy Fairweather-Low
Keyboards/vocals: Stevie Winwood
Drums: Charlie Watts
       Simon Phillips
       Kenney Jones
Bass: Bill Wyman
      Fernando Saunders
Percussion: Ray Cooper
Keyboards: Chris Stainton
           Jamer Hooker
Guitar: Jimmy Page
        Jeff Beck
Vocals: Ronnie Lane

The London shows of this dream outfit proved so successful and popular that a short US tour was organized. Three shows in San Francisco were filmed, but never released. The American shows were as good as, if not better than, the UK ones. The highlight was Eric and Jeff Beck soloing with Jimmy Page on the classic 'Stairway To Heaven'.

Live Session
1–3 December 1983
Cow Palace, San Francisco

Main artist: Eric Clapton

Everybody Oughta Make A Change	*Unissued*
Lay Down Sally	*Unissued*
Wonderful Tonight	*Unissued*
Rita Mae	*Unissued*
Have You Ever Loved A Woman	*Unissued*
Ramblin' On My Mind	*Unissued*
Cocaine	*Unissued*

Main artist: Joe Cocker

Don't Talk To Me	*Unissued*
Watching The River Flow	*Unissued*
Worried Life Blues	*Unissued*
You Are So Beautiful	*Unissued*
Seven Days	*Unissued*
Feelin' Alright	*Unissued*

Main artist: Jimmy Page

Stairway To Heaven   *Unissued*

All

Layla   *Unissued*
With A Little Help From My Friends   *Unissued*

Main artist: Ronnie Lane plus all

April Fool   *Unissued*
Goodnight Irene   *Unissued*

Guitar/vocals: Eric Clapton
                Andy Fairweather-Low
Guitar: Jimmy Page (Stairway To Heaven onwards)
Guitar: Jeff Beck (Stairway To Heaven onwards)
Vocals: Joe Cocker
Keyboards: Chris Stainton
            James Hooker
Bass: Fernando Saunders
       Bill Wyman
Drums: Charlie Watts
        Simon Phillips
        Kenney Jones
Percussion: Ray Cooper
Vocals: Paul Rodgers
Keyboards: Jan Hammer

Guitar used: 'Blackie' Fender Stratocaster

Producer: Glyn Johns
Engineer: Glyn Johns

◆

Eric's first session of the year was also his first of
many film soundtracks, although in this case it was
just the title music. An impressive, moody piece,
none the less.

Studio Session for *The Hit*
January 1984
Rock City Studios, Shepperton, Middlesex

The Hit   *Unissued*

Guitar: Eric Clapton

Guitar used: 'Blackie' Fender Stratocaster

Producer: ——
Engineer: ——

Studio Session for Corey Hart
February 1984
Eel Pie Studios, London

Jenney Fey   FIRST OFFENCE

Dobro: Eric Clapton
Vocals: Corey Hart
Bass: Gary Tibbs
Drums: Paul Burgess
Rhythm guitar: Mike Hehir
                Jon Astley
                Andy Mac
Lead guitar: Andy Barnett
Keyboards: Richie Close

Guitar used: dobro

Producer: Jon Astley
Engineer: Andy MacPherson

Studio Session for BEHIND THE SUN
March–April 1984
Air Studios, Montserrat

You Don't Know Like I Know	A side (Australia only)
Knock On Wood	B side/BEHIND THE SUN
Heaven Is One Step Away	B side (12in only)/ CROSSROADS
Too Bad	B side
One Jump Ahead Of The Storm	*Unissued*
Same Old Blues	BEHIND THE SUN
She's Waiting	BEHIND THE SUN
It All Depends	BEHIND THE SUN
Tangled In Love	BEHIND THE SUN
Never Make You Cry	BEHIND THE SUN
Just Like A Prisoner	BEHIND THE SUN
Jailbait	B side
Behind The Sun	BEHIND THE SUN

Guitar/vocals: Eric Clapton
Bass: Duck Dunn
Drums: Jamie Oldaker
Synthesizer: Peter Robinson
Percussion: Ray Cooper
Keyboards/synthesizer: Chris Stainton
Drums/percussion/backing vocals: Phil Collins
Backing vocals: Marcy Levy
                 Shaun Murphy

Guitar used: 'Blackie' Fender Stratocaster

Producer: Phil Collins
Engineer: Nick Launay

Warner's rejected the finished session, giving the reason as not enough singles material. Someone obviously had cotton wool in their ears, as 'She's Waiting', 'Heaven Is One Step Away' and 'One Jump Ahead Of The Storm' had hit single written all over them. However, Eric was asked to record some more commercial numbers with a session band to substitute for three other tracks. As Warner's were shedding some major artists at this time, including Van Morrison, it worried Eric that he might be a future victim.

PHIL COLLINS: *Eric's last couple of albums were a little bland, productionwise, so when Eric asked me to produce him, I thought it would be a great chance to shake up his music and make it stand again. He had written some great songs, was off the booze, playing and singing better than ever. When we finished the album I thought, 'Right, that's the album!' Then I get a call from Eric's manager saying that Lenny Waronker, the president of Warner Bros, didn't think there were any singles on the album and that Eric had to go back and record some more stuff. My heart sank. I spoke to Eric, and he was fuming. We had all felt so solid about the album, and suddenly these people, who had no input at all when the record was being made, came in and said there were no singles. We weren't even convinced that they'd listened to the album more than three or four times. I appreciated the fact that they put out the money for the thing and wanted something back for it, but they just didn't understand what Eric's music was about.*

Studio Session for Stephen Bishop
April 1984
Air Studios, Monserrat

Hall Light   BOWLING IN PARIS

Guitar: Eric Clapton
Vocals/acoustic guitar: Stephen Bishop
Drums: Phil Collins
Bass/harmony vocal: Sting
Piano/organ: Michael Omartian

Guitar used: 'Blackie' Fender Stratocaster

Producer: Phil Collins
Engineer: Nick Launay

Eric joined Roger Waters for a UK, European and US tour to promote his album. His solos were full of fire, quite unlike anything heard from him since his Blues Breaker days.

Live Session
21–22 June 1984
Earls Court Arena, London

Set The Controls For The Heart Of The Sun	*Unissued*
Money	*Unissued*
If	*Unissued*
Welcome To The Machine	*Unissued*
Have A Cigar	*Unissued*
Wish You Were Here	*Unissued*
Pigs On The Wing	*Unissued*
In The Flesh	*Unissued*
Nobody Home	*Unissued*
Hey You	*Unissued*
The Gunner's Dream	*Unissued*
4.30am (Apparently They Were Travelling Abroad)	*Unissued*
4.33am (Running Shoes)	*Unissued*
4.37am (Arabs With Knives And West German Skies)	*Unissued*
4.39am (For The First Time Today – part 2)	*Unissued*
4.41am (Sexual Revolution)	*Unissued*
4.47am (The Remains Of Our Love)	*Unissued*
4.50am (Go Fishing)	*Unissued*
4.56am (For The First Time Today – part 1)	*Unissued*
4.58am (Dunroamin Duncarin Dunlivin)	*Unissued*
5.01am (The Pros And Cons Of Hitch-Hiking)	*Unissued*
5.06am (Every Stranger's Eyes)	*Unissued*
5.11am (The Moment of Clarity)	*Unissued*
Brain Damage	*Unissued*

Guitar: Eric Clapton
Vocals/bass/guitar: Roger Waters
Guitar: Tim Renwick
Bass/keyboards: Chris Stainton
Drums: Andy Newmark
Keyboards: Michael Kamen
Saxophones: Mel Collins
Backing vocals: Doreen Chanter
                    Katie Kissoon

Guitars used: Gibson Les Paul, Fender Stratocaster, Ovation acoustic

Producer: ——
Engineer: ——

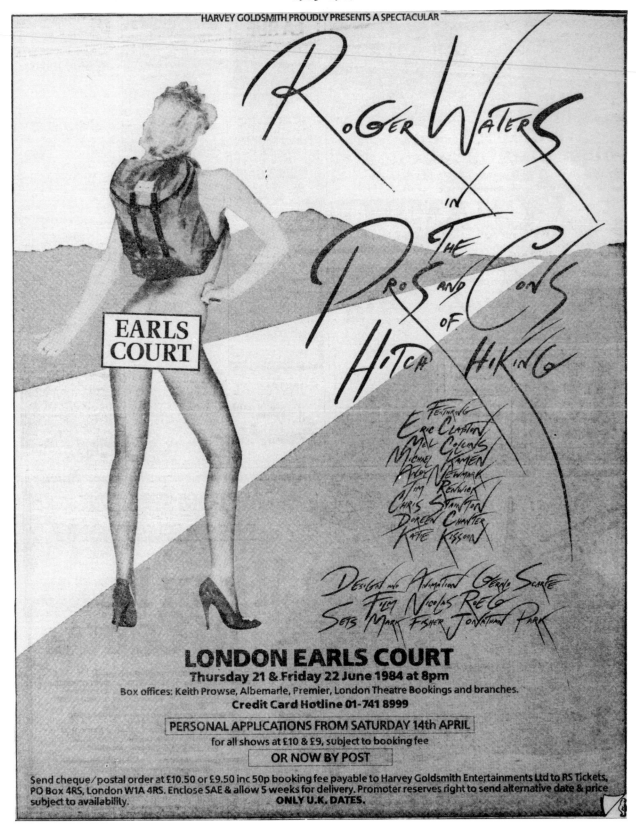

Live Session
7 July 1984
Wembley Stadium, London

Leopard Skin Pillbox Hat	*Unissued*
It's All Over Now Baby Blue	*Unissued*
Tombstone Blues	*Unissued*
Senor	*Unissued*
Times They Are A Changin'	*Unissued*
Blowin' In The Wind	*Unissued*
Knockin' On Heaven's Door	*Unissued*

Guitar: Eric Clapton
Guitar/vocals: Bob Dylan
Guitar: Mick Taylor
        Carlos Santana
Guitar/vocals: Van Morrison (It's All Over Now Baby Blue)
Vocals: Chrissie Hynde
Drums: Colin Allen
Bass: Greg Sutton
Keyboards: Ian MacLagen

Guitar used: Fender Stratocaster

Producer: ——
Engineer: ——

Eric finally got round to recording the more commercial tracks that Warner's required before they would release his new album.

Studio Session for BEHIND THE SUN
December 1984
Lion Share Studios, Los Angeles

Forever Man	BEHIND THE SUN
See What Love Can Do	BEHIND THE SUN
Something's Happening	BEHIND THE SUN
Loving Your Lovin'	WAYNE'S WORLD

Guitar: Eric Clapton
Drums: Jeff Porcaro
        John Robinson (Something's Happening)
Bass: Nathan East
Rhythm guitar: Steve Lukather
        Lindsay Buckingham (Something's Happening)
Synthesizers: Michael Omartian
        Greg Phillinganes (Something's Happening)
        Newton Howard (Something's Happening)
Congas: Lenny Castro
Backing vocals: Jerry Williams
        Marcy Levy

Timbales/tambourine/shaker: Ted Templeman

Guitar used: 'Blackie' Fender Stratocaster

Producers: Ted Templeman, Lenny Waronker
Engineer: Lee Herschberg

Studio Session for Gary Brooker
January 1985
Jacobs Studios, Farnham, Surrey

Echoes In The Night	ECHOES IN THE NIGHT

Guitar: Eric Clapton
Keyboards/vocals: Gary Brooker
Keyboards: Matthew Fisher
Drums:: Matt Lettley
Bass: John Giblin
Guitar: Tim Renwick
Backing vocals: Linda Page
        Jannette Sewell
        Shola Phillips

Guitar used: 'Blackie' Fender Stratocaster

Producers: Matthew Fisher, Gary Brooker

Engineer: Terry Barnham

Eric's 1985 tour was like a rebirth. The fiery guitar which he'd played with Roger Waters had not been extinguished; if anything, he was playing like a man possessed. Luckily, fans unable to attend the shows were treated to a radio broadcast from Richmond (Virginia, rather than Eric's home ground of Richmond in Surrey!), as well as a live video of a show in Hartford, Connecticut.

Live Session
22 April 1985
Coliseum, Richmond, Virginia

Tulsa Time	Radio broadcast
Motherless Children	Radio broadcast
I Shot The Sheriff	Radio broadcast
Same Old Blues	Not broadcast
Blues Power	Radio broadcast
Tangled In Love	Radio broadcast
Behind The Sun	Radio broadcast
Wonderful Tonight	Radio broadcast
Steppin' Out	Not broadcast
Never Make You Cry	Not broadcast

She's Waiting	Radio broadcast
Something Is Wrong With My Baby	Not broadcast
Lay Down Sally	Radio broadcast
Badge	Radio broadcast
Let It Rain	Radio broadcast
Double Trouble	Not broadcast
Cocaine	Not broadcast
Layla	Radio broadcast
Forever Man	Radio broadcast
Further On Up The Road	Radio broadcast

Guitar/vocals: Eric Clapton
Guitar: Tim Renwick
Bass: Duck Dunn
Drums: Jamie Oldaker
Keyboards: Chris Stainton
Backing vocals: Marcy Levy
              Shaun Murphy

Guitars used: 'Blackie' Fender Stratocaster, Sunburst Fender
   Stratocaster, Roland Synth

Producer: ——
Engineer: ——

Live Session
1 May 1985
Civic Center, Hartford, Connecticut

Tulsa Time	*Live 85* video
Motherless Children	*Live 85* video
I Shot The Sheriff	*Live 85* video
Same Old Blues	*Live 85* video
Blues Power	*Live 85* video
Tangled In Love	*Live 85* video
Behind The Sun	*Unissued*
Wonderful Tonight	*Live 85* video
Steppin' Out	*Unissued*
Never Make You Cry	*Unissued*
She's Waiting	*Live 85* video
Something Is Wrong With My Baby	*Unissued*
Lay Down Sally	*Live 85* video
Badge	*Live 85* video
Let It Rain	*Live 85* video
Double Trouble	*Unissued*
Cocaine	*Live 85* video
Layla	*Live 85* video

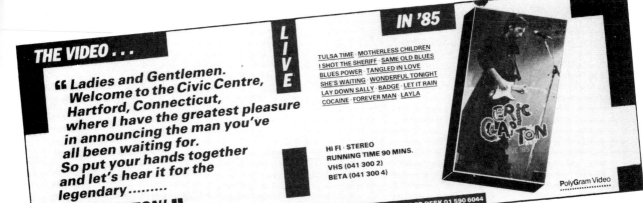

| Forever Man | *Live 85* video |
| Further On Up The Road | *Unissued* |

Band same as Richmond
Guitars used: 'Blackie' Fender Stratocaster, Sunburst Fender
   Stratocaster, Roland Synth

Producer: ——
Engineer: ——

Live Session
8 May 1985
David Letterman Television Show, New York

Late Night With David Letterman	
Theme Tune	TV broadcast
Layla	TV broadcast
Lay Down Sally	TV broadcast
White Room	TV broadcast
Forever Man	TV broadcast
Further On Up The Road	TV broadcast
Same Old Blues	TV broadcast
Knock On Wood	TV broadcast
End Theme	TV broadcast

Guitar: Eric Clapton
Keyboards: Paul Shaffer
Bass: Will Lee
Drums: Steve Jordan

Guitar used: 'Blackie' Fender Stratocaster

Producer: ——
Engineer: ——

Studio Session for EDGE OF DARKNESS
May–June 1985
Eel Pie Studios, London

Edge of Darkness	EDGE OF DARKNESS
Shoot Out	EDGE OF DARKNESS
Obituary	EDGE OF DARKNESS
Escape From Northmoor	EDGE OF DARKNESS
Oxford Circus	EDGE OF DARKNESS
Northmoor	EDGE OF DARKNESS

Guitar: Eric Clapton

Guitar used: 'Blackie' Fender Stratocaster

Producer: Michael Wearing
Engineer: Andy Jackson

Live Session for *Live Aid*
13 July 1985
JFK Stadium, Philadelphia

White Room	TV/radio broadcast
She's Waiting	TV/radio broadcast
Layla	TV/radio broadcast

Guitar/vocals: Eric Clapton
Guitar: Tim Renwick
Bass: Duck Dunn
Drums: Phil Collins
      Jamie Oldaker
Keyboards: Chris Stainton
Backing vocals: Marcy Levy
      Shaun Murphy

HARVEY GOLDSMITH, BOB GELDOF AND MAURICE JONES FOR THE BAND AID TRUST PRESENT

AT
WEMBLEY STADIUM LONDON

ADAM ANT
BOOMTOWN RATS
DAVID BOWIE
PHIL COLLINS
ELVIS COSTELLO
DIRE STRAITS
BRYAN FERRY
ELTON JOHN
HOWARD JONES
NIK KERSHAW
ALISON MOYET
QUEEN
SADE
SPANDAU BALLET
STATUS QUO
STYLE COUNCIL
STING
U2
ULTRAVOX
PAUL YOUNG
WHAM!
THE WHO

LIVE AID

AT
J.F.K. STADIUM PHILADELPHIA

BRYAN ADAMS
THE CARS
ERIC CLAPTON
DURAN DURAN
BOY GEORGE
HALL AND OATES
MICK JAGGER
BILLY JOEL
WAYLON JENNINGS
JUDAS PRIEST
KRIS KRISTOFFERSON
HUEY LEWIS & THE NEWS
ROBERT PLANT
POWER STATION
PRETENDERS
SANTANA
PAUL SIMON
SIMPLE MINDS
TEARS FOR FEARS
TEMPTATIONS
THOMPSON TWINS
NEIL YOUNG
STEVIE WONDER

JULY 13th

DOORS OPEN 10 AM, CONCERT STARTS 12 NOON FINISHES 10 PM
Tickets at £25 are on sale NOW from Wembley Stadium Box Office.

And subject to 50p booking fee per ticket for counter sales from
Keith Prowse, Premier, London Theatre Bookings, Stargreen Agencies.
And **BRIGHTON Centre, SOUTHAMPTON** Gaumont, **PORTSMOUTH** Guildhall, **OXFORD** Apollo.
And subject to £1 booking fee per ticket from
Keith Prowse Credit Card No 01-741 8999

SOLD OUT

Or see local press for inclusive coach and concert tickets. Tickets are limited to 6 per person.
DO NOT PAY MORE THAN THE LISTED PRICE FOR YOUR TICKETS.
OUR THANKS TO N.M.E. FOR DONATING THIS PAGE.
NO BOTTLES, NO CANS WILL BE ALLOWED IN THE STADIUM.
ANY DONATIONS WILL BE GRATEFULLY RECEIVED TO 'BAND AID TRUST'
c/o STOY HAYWARD 8 BAKER STREET, LONDON WIM IDJ.

We Are The World   TV/radio broadcast

Guitar: Eric Clapton
Vocals: Lionel Richie, plus most of the musicians from the
    concert joining in for the historic finale of *Live Aid*

Studio Session for Lionel Richie
July 1985
Bear Creek Recording Studios, Washington

Tonight Will Be Alright   DANCING ON THE CEILING

Guitar: Eric Clapton
Vocals/keyboards: Lionel Richie
Drums: Paul Leim
Bass: Joseph Chemay
Guitar: Tim May
    Carlos Rios
Percussion: Paulinho Da Costa
Keyboards: Greg Phillinganes
Synthesizers: Michael Boddicker
Backing vocals: Richard Marx
    Deborah Thomas
    Julia Waters Tillman
    Maxine Waters Willard

Guitar used: 'Blackie' Fender Stratocaster

Producer: Lionel Richie
Engineer: Calvin Harris

Studio Session for Paul Brady
November 1985
Utopia Sound Studios, London

Deep In Your Heart   BACK TO THE CENTRE

Guitar: Eric Clapton
Acoustic guitar/vocals/keyboards/tin whistles: Paul Brady
Drum: Ole Romo
Harmonica: Mitt Gamon
Guitar: Phil Palmer
Keyboards: Betsy Cook
Bass/percussion: Ian Maidman

Guitar used: 'Blackie' Fender Stratocaster

Producer: Ian Maidman
Engineer: John Lee

Towards the end of his huge 1985 world tour, Eric was invited to participate in celebrating thirty years of rockabilly music with Carl Perkins. The show was filmed in the Docklands area of London in a small television studio. Two of Carl's greatest fans were also playing – Ringo Starr and George Harrison! Eric's playing can be described as 'stinging'.

Live Session with Carl Perkins
21 December 1985
Limehouse Television Studios, London

Matchbox   *A Rockabilly Session* video

Guitar/vocals: Eric Clapton
    Carl Perkins
Drums: Ringo Starr
Bass: John David
Piano: Geraint Watkins
Guitar: Dave Edmunds
    Mickey Gee

Mean Woman Blues   *A Rockabilly Session* video

Guitar/vocals: Eric Clapton
    Carl Perkins
Drums: David Charles
Bass: John David
Piano: Geraint Watkins
Guitar: Dave Edmunds
    Mickey Gee

That's Alright Now Mama   *A Rockabilly Session* video
Blue Moon Of Kentucky   *A Rockabilly Session* video
Night Train   *A Rockabilly Session* video
Glad All Over   *A Rockabilly Session* video
Whole Lotta Shakin'
    Goin' On   *A Rockabilly Session* video
Gone Gone Gone   *A Rockabilly Session* video
Blue Suede Shoes   *A Rockabilly Session* video

Guitar/vocals: Eric Clapton
    Carl Perkins
    George Harrison
    Dave Edmunds
Guitar: Earl Slick
Percussion: Slim Jim Phantom
Bass: Lee Rocker
    John David
    Greg Perkins
Piano: Geraint Watkins
Vocals/tambourine: Rosanne Cash
    Ringo Starr
Drums: David Charles

Guitar used: 'Blackie' Fender Stratocaster

Producer: Dave Edmunds
Engineer: ———

Wembley, London, 1985

Eric during Soundcheck Europe, 1986

ONE MORE CAR, ONE MORE RIDER

1986–1987

Studio Session for Leona Boyd
February 1986
Audio International Studios, London

Labyrinth   PERSONA

Guitar: Eric Clapton
         Leona Boyd
Bass: Dean Garcia
Kurzweil drums/percussion/piano: Michael Kamen

Guitar used: Eric Clapton Signature Fender Stratocaster

Producer: Leona Boyd
Engineer: Andrew Jackson

Eric's next album was to be called ONE MORE CAR ONE MORE RIDER, but was changed to AUGUST as a celebration of the birth of his son Conor.

Studio Session for AUGUST
April–May 1986
Sunset Sound Studios, Los Angeles

Miss You	AUGUST
Tearing Us Apart	AUGUST
Behind The Mask	AUGUST
Run	AUGUST
Bad Influence	AUGUST
Walk Away	AUGUST
Hung Up On Your Love	AUGUST
Take A Chance	AUGUST
Hold On	AUGUST
Holy Mother	AUGUST
Grand Illusion	AUGUST CD only
Wanna Make Love To You	CROSSROADS
Lady Of Verona	*Unissued*
Walking The White Line	*Unissued*

Guitar/vocals: Eric Clapton
Bass: Nathan East
Keyboards/backing vocals: Greg Phillinganes
Drums/percussion/backing vocals: Phil Collins
Vocals: Tina Turner (Tearing Us Apart, Hold On)
Backing vocals: Tessa Niles
                 Katie Kissoon
Sax: Michael Brecker
Trumpet: Jon Faddis
          Randy Brecker
Trombone: Dave Bargerone

Producer: Phil Collins
Engineers: Magic Moreno, Peter Hefter, Paul Gommersall

ERIC CLAPTON: *People will say that* BEHIND THE SUN *and* AUGUST *are Phil Collins records. Fine – if that's all they can hear, they're not listening properly. I'm in there with as much as I've got, but not in a competitive way. If I did, it would be a mess. It works pretty good for me to allow people to be themselves rather than trying to lay down the law.*

Live Session for PRINCE'S TRUST 10TH BIRTHDAY PARTY
20 June 1986
Wembley Arena, London

Better Be Good To Me (Tina Turner)	CD/video
Tearing Us Apart (Tina Turner, Eric Clapton)	CD/video
Call Of The Wild (Midge Ure)	CD/video
Money For Nothing (Mark Knopfler, Sting)	CD/video
Everytime You Go Away (Paul Young)	CD/video
Reach Out (Joan Armatrading)	CD/video
No One Is To Blame (Howard Jones)	CD/video
Sailing (Rod Stewart)	CD/video
I'm Still Standing (Elton John)	CD/video
Everytime You Go Away (Paul Young, George Michael)	Video

I Saw Her Standing There (Paul McCartney)	Video
Long Tall Sally (Paul McCartney)	CD/video
Dancing In The Street (David Bowie, Mick Jagger)	*Unissued*
Get Back (Paul McCartney, plus everyone)	CD/video

Guitar/vocals: Eric Clapton
　　　　　　　 Midge Ure
　　　　　　　 Mark Knopfler
　　　　　　　 Bryan Adams
　　　　　　　 Paul McCartney
　　　　　　　 Joan Armatrading
Guitar: Rick Parfitt
　　　　 Francis Rossi
Percussion: Ray Cooper
Piano: Elton John
Vocals: David Bowie
　　　　 Mick Jagger
　　　　 Paul Young
　　　　 George Michael
　　　　 Sting
　　　　 Rod Stewart
Bass: Mark King
　　　 John Illsley
Keyboards/vocals: Howard Jones
Backing vocals: Vicki Brown
　　　　　　　　 Samantha Brown
　　　　　　　　 Jimmy Chambers
　　　　　　　　 George Chandler
　　　　　　　　 Jimmy Helms

Guitar used: Eric Clapton Signature Fender Stratocaster
　 prototype (Ferrari red)

Producer: Andre Sheehan
Engineer: Barry Sage
Recorded by: The Pumacrest Unit

Live Session for Otis Rush
9 July 1986
Casino de Montreux, Montreux, Switzerland

Crosscut Saw	Swiss radio broadcast
Double Trouble	Swiss radio broadcast
All Your Love	Swiss radio broadcast
Everyday I Have The Blues	Swiss radio broadcast

Guitar/vocals: Eric Clapton
　　　　　　　 Otis Rush
　　　　　　　 Luther Allison (Everyday I Have The Blues)
Bass: ——
Drums: ——
Keyboards: ——

Guitar used: Eric Clapton Signature Fender Stratocaster (Ferrari red)

Producer: ——
Engineer: ——

A double album/CD was part of Eric's contract with Warner's, so it seemed a good idea to record several shows with the new band. A total of eight shows were recorded in 1986 and 1987, and a track listing was worked out for the project's potential release in late 1987 (see 1987 for further details).

Live Session
10 July 1986
Casino de Montreux, Montreux, Switzerland

Crossroads	French radio broadcast
White Room	French radio broadcast
I Shot The Sheriff	French radio broadcast
Wanna Make Love To You	French radio broadcast
Run	French radio broadcast
Miss You	French radio broadcast
Same Old Blues	French radio broadcast
Tearing Us Apart	French radio broadcast
Holy Mother	French radio broadcast
Behind The Mask	French radio broadcast
Badge	French radio broadcast
Let It Rain	French radio broadcast
In The Air Tonight	French radio broadcast
Cocaine	French radio broadcast
Layla	French radio broadcast
Sunshine Of Your Love	French radio broadcast
Ramblin' On My Mind/Have You Ever Loved A Woman	French radio broadcast

Guitar/vocals: Eric Clapton
Drums/vocals: Phil Collins
Bass: Nathan East
Keyboards/vocals: Greg Phillinganes
Guitar/vocals: Robert Cray (Ramblin' On My Mind, Have You Ever Loved A Woman)

Guitars used: Eric Clapton Signature Fender Stratocasters (charcoal and Ferrari red)

Producer: ——
Engineer: ——

Live Session
14 July 1986
NEC Arena, Birmingham

Same set as 15 July, but nothing has been issued.
Also, the 15th is the only night to have been filmed.

Live Session
15 July 1986
NEC Arena, Birmingham

Crossroads	Free single/EC concert video
White Room	Free single/EC concert video
I Shot The Sheriff	B side
Wanna Make Love To You	*Unissued*
Run	12in single/EC concert video
Miss You	EC concert video
Same Old Blues	*Unissued*
Tearing Us Apart	EC concert video
Holy Mother	EC concert video
Behind The Mask	12in single
Badge	12in single/CD single
Let It Rain	12in single/CD single
In The Air Tonight	EC concert video
Cocaine	*Unissued*
Layla	EC concert video
Sunshine Of Your Love	EC concert video
Further On Up The Road	*Unissued*

Guitar/vocals: Eric Clapton
Robert Cray (Further On Up The Road)
Drums: Phil Collins
Bass: Nathan East
Keyboards: Greg Phillinganes

Guitars used: Eric Clapton Signature Fender Stratocasters
(charcoal and Ferrari red)

Producer: Mike Ponczek
Engineer: Mike Ponczek

Studio Session for Bob Geldof
August 1986
Studio not known

Love Like A Rocket   A side/DEEP IN THE HEART OF NOWHERE
August Was A
   Heavy Month   DEEP IN THE HEART OF NOWHERE
The Beat Of
   The Night   DEEP IN THE HEART OF NOWHERE
Good Boys In
   The Wrong   DEEP IN THE HEART OF NOWHERE

Guitar: Eric Clapton
Vocals: Bob Geldof

Guitar used: Eric Clapton Signature Fender Stratocaster

Producer: ——
Engineer: ——

ERIC CLAPTON: *I never thought I would be any good to Bob Geldof. But playing with him was great! He was so good to work with. He gave me complete carte blanche. Normally, I would find someone saying 'What do you think?' and I would say, 'Well, maybe I could do better', then they'd go, 'Okay, go ahead.' Bob said, 'No, you can't. Don't do it again. Keep what you've done, that's fine.' So I did a lot of work in a very short amount of time, because he was wise enought to catch me on my first and second takes, which is usually when I'm best. But I always think I can do better, and I blow it. He knew better than that, which is great. I think it was a good album.*

Studio Session for The Bunburys
14 August 1986
Surrey Sound Studios, Leatherhead, Surrey

Fight (The Good Fight)   A side/BUNBURY TAILS

Guitar/vocals: Eric Clapton
Bass: Lawrence Cottle
Keyboards: Duncan Mackay
Backing vocals: The Bee Gees
Additional vocals: David English
                    Ian Botham
Drums: Drum Machine

Producer: ——
Engineer: ——

ERIC CLAPTON: *David English invented the Bunburys as a cartoon, and he put out books first of all. And then he thought about making music to go with it. He's an old friend of Barry Gibb's and those two started writing. Barry wrote a song for me to do which hasn't been released yet, called 'Fight'! And that will be out on the next album the Bunburys put out. Elton's on it, as is George Harrison. It's all been held up for one reason or another, because I don't know what record label it's going to be on.*

The album BUNBURY TAILS was finally released in late 1992.

Studio Session for Bob Dylan
27–28 August 1986
Townhouse Studios, London

The Usual (three takes)   HEARTS OF FIRE
Song With No Name   *Unissued*
Had A Dream About You (seven takes) HEARTS OF FIRE
Five And Dimmer (three takes)   HEARTS OF FIRE
To Fall In Love   *Unissued*

Guitar: Eric Clapton
Guitar/vocals: Bob Dylan
Bass: Ronnie Wood
Drums: Henry Spinetti

Guitar used: Eric Clapton Signature Fender Stratocaster

Producer: Beau Hill
Engineer: Beau Hill

ERIC CLAPTON: *Bob came into London, looking to get a band together. He seemed to be flying pretty blind. He knew he had to get some music for his film and it was so early on in the stage of the game that he did not know what he wanted to sound like – what the part entailed in the film.*

He called me to help out and I got involved, but was actually pretty tightly scheduled to do other things as well, so I could only do two or three days and then I had to move on. Basically, I just played rhythm parts and a little bit of lead. I would have liked to get more involved, but at the time I was really busy, and couldn't commit myself to more than that.

Studio Session for COLOUR OF MONEY
August–September 1986
Studio not known

It's My Life Baby   *Unissued*

Guitar/vocals: Eric Clapton
Rest: Big Town Playboys

ERIC CLAPTON: *I would like to get into the studio with The Big Town Playboys again and make a blues album. That probably will come after my next solo album, which I think I am going to do as a commercial venture again. Pretty much like* AUGUST *– not perhaps as commercial as* AUGUST *was set out to be.*

Studio Session for COLOUR OF MONEY and AUGUST
September 1986
Studio not known

The Gift (It's In The Way That You Use It)   AUGUST

Guitar/vocals: Eric Clapton
Keyboards/vocals: Gary Brooker
Bass: Laurence Cottle
Drums: Henry Spinetti
Synthesizer: Richard Cottle

Guitar used: Eric Clapton Signature Fender Stratocaster

Producers: Tom Dowd, Eric Clapton
Engineers: John Jacobs, Steve Chase

ERIC CLAPTON: *I preferred the Bobby Bland song, which you didn't get to hear hardly at all, and it didn't get on to the soundtrack album. That was the better of the two cuts for me.*

Studio Session for Tina Turner
September 1986
Mayfair Studios, London

What You See Is What You Get   12in single

Guitar: Eric Clapton
Vocals: Tina Turner
Keyboards: Nick Glennie-Smith
Guitar/bass/drum programming: Terry Britten
Mandolin: Graham Lyle

Guitar used: Eric Clapton Signature Fender Stratocaster

Producer: Terry Britten
Engineer: John Hudson

TINA TURNER: *Terry Britten got so excited recording one of his heroes that he recorded it an octave lower than it was supposed to be.*

TERRY BRITTEN: *When you use big names, there's a temptation to give up your own responsibility when someone else comes in with an idea. And then you're going down a different road.*

Live Session for Chuck Berry's 60th birthday
16 October 1986
Fox Theatre, St Louis

Two shows

Wee Wee Hours   HAIL! HAIL! ROCK 'N' ROLL
                       (album and film)

Rock 'N' Roll Music   HAIL! HAIL! ROCK 'N' ROLL
                       (album and film)

Hail! Hail! Rock 'N' Roll   *Hail! Hail! Rock 'N' Roll*
                                      (film)

Guitar/vocals: Eric Clapton
               Chuck Berry
               Keith Richards
Guitar: Robert Cray
Bass: Joey Spampinato
Drums: Steve Jordan
Piano: Johnnie Johnson
Keyboards: Chuck Leavell
Sax: Bobby Keys
Vocals: Etta James (Rock 'N' Roll Music)
Backing vocals: Linda Ronstadt (Hail! Hail! Rock 'N' Roll)
                Julian Lennon (Hail! Hail! Rock 'N' Roll)
                Ingrid Berry

Guitar used: Gibson ES-350T

Producer: Keith Richards
Engineer: Bridget Daly
Recorded by: Remote Recording Services

ERIC CLAPTON: *I was very pleased with my perform- ance. In fact, having done very little rehearsing, there was little for me to do there except sit and kick my heels and wait for my chance. By the time I got to play, I was very frustrated and it came out. I attacked the guitar a bit.*

Live Session
29 October 1986
Nightlife TV Show, New York

Miss You	TV broadcast
It's In The Way That	
You Use It (The Gift)	TV broadcast
I Shot The Sheriff	TV broadcast

Guitar/vocals: Eric Clapton
Rest: *Nightlife* house band featuring Billy Preston

Guitar used: Eric Clapton Signature Fender Stratocaster

Producer: ——
Engineer: ——

Live Session
8 November 1986
Mean Fiddler, London

Smoking Gun	*Unissued*
Playing In The Dirt	*Unissued*

The Last Time	*Unissued*
Bad Influence	*Unissued*
Phone Booth	*Guitar Player* magazine (flexi-disc)

Guitar/vocals: Eric Clapton
           Robert Cray
Bass: Robert Cousins
Drums: David Olson
Keyboards: Peter Boe

ERIC CLAPTON: *It's a lovely band to play with. You can play along and not really have to learn anything or there's no awkward chords that are going to come up. It's pretty straightforward. And with a great feeling. It's great to play with Robert. Any time.*

The only number released from this show was 'Phone Booth', which was given away with the May 1987 issue of *Guitar Player* magazine.

Studio Session for *Lethal Weapon* soundtrack
8–16 December 1986
Townhouse Studios, London

Amanda	LETHAL WEAPON
Meet Martin Riggs	LETHAL WEAPON
Roger	LETHAL WEAPON
Coke Deal	LETHAL WEAPON
Mr Joshua	LETHAL WEAPON
They've Got My Daughter	LETHAL WEAPON
The Desert	LETHAL WEAPON
Nightclub	LETHAL WEAPON
The Weapon	LETHAL WEAPON

Guitar: Eric Clapton
Sax: David Sanborn
Keyboards: Michael Kamen
Drums: Henry Spinetti
Bass: Laurence Cottle
      Dean Garcia

Guitar used: Eric Clapton Signature Fender Stratocaster

Producer: Michael Kamen
Engineer: ——

Studio Session for Jon Astley
December 1986
Revolution Studios, Manchester

Jane's Getting Serious	EVERYONE LOVES THE PILOT

Guitar: Eric Clapton
Vocals/fairlight: Jon Astley
Keyboards: Richie Close

Guitar used: ——

Producer: Phil Chapman and Andy MacPherson
Engineer: ——

Live Session
10–12 January 1987
Royal Albert Hall, London

Crossroads	*Unissued*
White Room	*Unissued*
I Shot The Sheriff	*Unissued*
Hung Up On Your Love	*Unissued*
Wonderful Tonight	*Unissued*
Miss You	*Unissued*
Same Old Blues	*Unissued*

Tearing Us Apart	*Unissued*
Holy Mother	*Unissued*
Badge	*Unissued*
Let It Rain	*Unissued*
Cocaine	*Unissued*
Layla	*Unissued*
Money For Nothing	*Unissued*
Sunshine Of Your Love	*Unissued*

Guitar/vocals: Eric Clapton
Guitar: Mark Knopfler
Bass: Nathan East
Keyboards: Greg Phillinganes
Drums: Steve Ferrone
      Phil Collins (11 and 12 January)

Guitar used: Eric Clapton Signature Fender Stratocaster

Producer: ——
Engineer: ——

Studio Session for Jack Bruce
February 1987
Studio not known

Willpower	WILLPOWER

Guitar: Eric Clapton
Bass/keyboards/vocals: Jack Bruce
Guitar: Clem Clemson
Drums: Stuart Elliot

Ships In The Night	WILLPOWER

Guitar: Eric Clapton
Bass/keyboards/vocals/piano/cello: Jack Bruce
Vocals: Maggie Reilly
Acoustic guitars: Peter Weihe
Drums: Stuart Elliot

Guitar used: Eric Clapton Signature Fender Stratocaster

Producer: Jack Bruce
Engineer: ——

Studio Session for Sting
March 1987
Air Studios, Montserrat, West Indies

They Dance Alone	NOTHING LIKE THE SUN

Guitar: Eric Clapton
Vocals/bass: Sting
Guitar: Mark Knopfler
      Fareed Haque

Drums: Manu Katche
Keyboards: Kenny Kirkland
Vocoder/percussion: Mino Cinelu
Sax: Branford Marsalis
Spanish voice: Ruben Blades

Guitar used: Gibson Chet Atkins gut string acoustic

Producer: ——
Engineer: ——

ERIC CLAPTON: *I'm playing a Gibson Chet Atkins, which is that gut string solid guitar. But if you look at the credits on that track, you will see there are other guitar players on there. The way it is mixed, you can just hear me, very barely in some places. Because I know that I played, I can recognize it. Otherwise you wouldn't know.*

I don't know why. I think perhaps he's a perfectionist. I played on about three or four other tracks on the album. That was in Montserrat. Sting wasn't there because his mother had just died. I then went to New York where I knew he'd be, just to see what his reaction was, and he wanted me to change a few things. So I played some of it again and he seemed pleased. But then when he mixed it down, he obviously decided there was too much going on, so he mixed it out.

I think it is sad in a way that some of that stuff gets lost. However, it is not lost forever, because it has got to be there somewhere. He knows best. It's his music, isn't it?

Live Session
15 April 1987
Ebony Showcase Theatre, Los Angeles

The Thrill Is Gone   *B.B. King And Friends* video

Guitar: Eric Clapton
Guitar/vocals: B.B. King
Drums: Phil Collins
Harmonica: Paul Butterfield
Horns: B.B. King Band
Bass: ——

Why I Sing The Blues   *B.B. King And Friends* video
Let The Good Times Roll   *B.B. King And Friends* video
Lead Me Home   *B.B. King And Friends* video

Guitar: Eric Clapton
Guitar/vocals: B.B. King
Guitar: Stevie Ray Vaughn
Guitar/vocals: Albert King
Drums: Phil Collins
Harmonica: Paul Butterfield
Piano/vocals: Dr John
Vocals: Etta James
              Gladys Knight
              Chaka Khan
              Billy Ocean
Horns: B.B. King Band
Bass: ——
Drums: ——

Guitar used: Eric Clapton Signature Fender Stratocaster

Producer: ——
Engineer: ——

ERIC CLAPTON: *It was a tribute to B.B. and they had a lot of other people there such as Chaka Khan, Gladys Knight, Etta James, Albert King, Stevie Ray Vaughn, Paul Butterfield, Dr John and myself and Phil Collins. I would have liked to get more involved, but we flew in from somewhere to do it in an afternoon.*

It was slotted in between two dates and we really didn't have time to do much more. Sometimes those things come off a little light. And for me, it felt a little light, because we walked in on it and walked out before it was finished so we were not in at the ground floor. I didn't feel ready for it. Maybe it comes off better – I am not sure.

Live Session
26 April 1987
Civic Center, Providence, Rhode Island

Live Session
27 April 1987
Madison Square Garden, New York

Crossroads	*Unissued*
White Room	*Unissued*
I Shot The Sheriff	*Unissued*
Hung Up On Your Love	*Unissued*
Wonderful Tonight	*Unissued*
Miss You	*Unissued*
Same Old Blues	*Unissued*

Tearing Us Apart   *Unissued*
Holy Mother   *Unissued*
Badge   *Unissued*
Let It Rain   *Unissued*
Cocaine   *Unissued*
Layla   *Unissued*
Further On Up The Road   *Unissued*
Sunshine Of Your Love   *Unissued*

Guitar/vocals: Eric Clapton
Drums: Phil Collins
Bass: Nathan East
Keyboards/backing vocals: Greg Phillinganes
Guitar/vocals: Robert Cray (Further On Up The Road)

Guitar used: Eric Clapton Signature Fender Stratocaster

Producer: Mike Ponczek
Engineer: Mike Ponczek

These were the last two shows to be recorded for the proposed double live album/CD. It was never released, as two studio compilations were released which covered pretty much the same material (THE CREAM OF ERIC CLAPTON and CROSSROADS). To release a further compilation of the same tracks in the live format would have been a bad commercial move.

Cancelled live album 1987

Crossroads (Royal Albert Hall, 12 January 1987)
White Room (Birmingham, NEC, 15 July 1986)
I Shot The Sheriff (Royal Albert Hall, 12 January 1987)
Hung Up On Your Love (Royal Albert Hall, 12 January 1987)
Wonderful Tonight (Providence, Civic Centre, 26 April 1987)
Miss You (Royal Albert Hall, 10 January 1987)
Same Old Blues (Birmingham NEC, 15 July 1986)
Tearing Us Apart (Royal Albert Hall, 12 January 1987)
Holy Mother (Birmingham, NEC, 15 July 1986)
Badge (Madison Square Garden, 27 April 1987)
Let It Rain (Madison Square Garden, 27 April 1987)
Cocaine (Montreux, 10 July 1986)
Layla (Royal Albert Hall, 12 January 1987)
Further On Up The Road (Birmingham, NEC, 15 July 1986)
Sunshine Of Your Love (Montreux, 10 July 1986)

For personnel details, check individual concert dates

Studio Session for George Harrison
May 1987
FPSHOT (Friar Park Studios, Henley-on-Thames, Oxon)

Cloud Nine   CLOUD NINE
That's What It Takes   CLOUD NINE
Devil's Radio   CLOUD NINE
Wreck Of The Hesperus   CLOUD NINE

Guitar: Eric Clapton
Guitar/vocals: George Harrison
Guitars/bass/keyboards: Jeff Lynne
Piano: Elton John
       Gary Wright
Drums: Ringo Starr
       Jim Keltner
Percussion: Ray Cooper
Saxes: Jim Horn

Guitar used: Sunburst Fender Stratocaster belonging to George

Producers: Jeff Lynne, George Harrison
Engineer: Richard Dodd

GEORGE HARRISON: *When he comes over to play on my songs, he doesn't bring an amplifier or a guitar, he says, 'Oh, you've got a goot Strat.' He knows I've got one because he gave it to me!!! He plugs in, and just his vibrato and everything ... he makes that guitar sound like Eric.*

Live Session for Prince's Trust
6 June 1987
Wembley Arena, London

Running In The Family (Mark King and Mike Lindup)   PRINCE'S TRUST CONCERT 1987
If I Was (Midge Ure)   PRINCE'S TRUST CONCERT 1987
Wonderful Tonight (Eric Clapton)   PRINCE'S TRUST CONCERT 1987
Behind The Mask (Eric Clapton)   PRINCE'S TRUST CONCERT 1987
Stand By Me (Ben E. King)   PRINCE'S TRUST CONCERT 1987
You've Lost That Loving Feeling (Phil Collins and Paul Young)   PRINCE'S TRUST CONCERT 1987
Through The Barricades (Tony Hadley and Gary Kemp)   PRINCE'S TRUST CONCERT 1987
Saturday Night's Alright For Fighting (Elton John)   PRINCE'S TRUST CONCERT 1987

While My Guitar Gently Weeps
(George Harrison)   PRINCE'S TRUST CONCERT 1987
It's The Same Old Song (Phil
Collins and Paul Young)   PRINCE'S TRUST CONCERT 1987
I Can't Help Myself (Phil
Collins and Paul Young)   PRINCE'S TRUST CONCERT 1987
Reach Out I'll Be There (Phil
Collins and Paul Young)   PRINCE'S TRUST CONCERT 1987
Everyone   PRINCE'S TRUST CONCERT 1987
With A Little Help From
My Friends   PRINCE'S TRUST CONCERT 1987

Guitar/Vocals: Eric Clapton
Bass/vocals: Mark King
Piano/vocals: Elton John
Keyboards: Mike Lindup
       Jools Holland
Percussion: Ray Cooper
Drums/vocals: Phil Collins
Drums: Mark Brzezecki
Sax: Mel Collins
Horns: The Phantom Horns
Vocals: Tony Hadley
       Paul Young
       Ringo Starr
       Ben E. King
Backing vocals: Jimmy Helms
       George Chandler

Guitar used: Eric Clapton Signature Fender Stratocaster

Producer: Midge Ure
Engineer: Doug Hopkins
Recorded by: The Rak Mobile

Live Session
18 June 1987
Wembley Stadium, London

Tearing Us Apart   LIVE IN EUROPE

Guitar/vocals: Eric Clapton
Vocals: Tina Turner
Drums: Jack Bruno
Sax: Deric Dyer
Bass/vocals: Bob Feit
Keyboards/vocals: Ollie Marland
Guitar/vocals: John Miles
       James Ralston
Percussion: Steve Scales
Guitar: Laurie Wisefield

Guitar used: Eric Clapton Signature Fender Stratocaster

Producer: John Hudson
Engineer: Mike Ging
Recorded by: Manor Mobile

Live Session
4 July 1987
Pinewood Studios, Elstree

I Shot The Sheriff   *Alright Now* video

Guitar/vocals: Eric Clapton
Rest: Island All Stars

Guitar used: Eric Clapton Signature Fender Stratocaster

Producer: ——
Engineer: ——

Studio Session
August–September 1987
Power Station Studios, New York

After Midnight   A side/CROSSROADS

Guitar/vocals: Eric Clapton
Keyboards: Alan Clark
Bass: Nathan East
Drums: Andy Newmark

Guitar used: Eric Clapton Signature Fender Stratocaster

Producers: Peter McHugh, Jim Harris
Engineer: Justin Neibank

The new version of 'After Midnight' was controversial since it was the soundtrack for an American beer commercial. As Eric was a practising alcoholic at the time, it seemed somewhat inappropriate. However, the music is what should have counted.

Live Session
6 October 1987
Ronnie Scott's Club, Soho, London

Key To The Highway   TV broadcast
Stormy Monday   TV broadcast
Worried Life Blues   TV broadcast
Jam   TV broadcast

Guitar/vocals: Eric Clapton
       Buddy Guy
Bass: Greg Rzab
Drums: Gerry Porter
Piano: Chris Stainton

Guitar used: Eric Clapton Signature Fender Stratocaster

Producer: Chris Hunt
Engineer: ——

ERIC CLAPTON: *They showed some of it on TV, late hours. I watched some of that and was very disappointed with the sound mix because you can hardly hear Buddy. And I thought that was sad.*

Although Eric and Buddy played for around two hours, only four numbers were filmed. The rest of the time Eric and Buddy played for the pleasure of the fans while the camera crew changed films. It's a shame that the entire show wasn't recorded, as it was one of the best jams that these two have had. When Buddy's on form, no one can touch him, and that afternoon was certainly one of those occasions.

Dingwalls, London, 1987

Hammersmith Odeon, London, 1988

SCREAMING THE BLUES

1988–1989

Studio Session for *Buster* soundtrack
25 March 1988
Townhouse Studios, London

The Robbery   BUSTER

Guitar: Eric Clapton
Synthesizers: Anne Dudley

Guitar used: Eric Clapton Signature Fender Stratocaster

Producer: Anne Dudley
Engineer: ——

ERIC CLAPTON: *I just played guitar. It was part of the score. The actual robbery scene, which is quite early on in the film was where Anne Dudley, who was the lady who wrote the music, wanted some guitar playing. I was just playing a part that she had already written down for a guitar. It is not very long, but it is quite effective.*

Studio Session for Buckwheat Zydeco
March 1988
Studio not known

Why Does Love Got To Be So Sad   TAKING IT HOME

Guitar: Eric Clapton
Vocals/accordion/Hammond B-3 organ/melodica: Buckwheat
  Zydeco
Bass: Lee Allen Zeno
Guitar: Melvin Veazie
        Robert James Ahearn
Drums: Herman 'Rat' Brown
Rubboard: Patrick Landry
Baritone sax/tenor sax: Dennis Taylor
Trumpet: Calvin Landry
Alto sax: Anthony Butler

Guitar used: Eric Clapton Signature Fender Stratocaster

Producer: Rob Fraboni
Engineer: Rob Fraboni

ERIC CLAPTON: *He wasn't there when I did it. This session came about through a mutual friend, Rob Fraboni, who produced* NO REASON TO CRY. *He is just a dear old friend of mine and when I was in New York late 1987 he introduced me, and in fact I went to see Buckwheat play. I got up and jammed with him and one thing led to another.*

Buckwheat was offered some material. He chose 'Why Does Love Got To Be So Sad', *the Dominos' song. When Rob came to England earlier this year, he brought over the tape with him. I played on the thing, two takes. And I played it just like I did on the Dominos' album.*

Studio Session for *Homeboy* soundtrack
23–29 April 1988
Townhouse Studios, London and Olympic
Sound Studios, Barnes, London

Travelling East	HOMEBOY
Johnny	HOMEBOY
Bridge	HOMEBOY
Dixie	HOMEBOY
Ruby's Loft	HOMEBOY
Country Bikin'	HOMEBOY
Bike Ride	HOMEBOY
Ruby	HOMEBOY
Party	HOMEBOY
Training	HOMEBOY
Final Fight	HOMEBOY
Chase	HOMEBOY
Dixie 2	HOMEBOY
Homeboy	HOMEBOY

Guitar: Eric Clapton
Keyboards: Michael Kamen
Drums: Steve Ferrone
Bass: Nathan East

Guitar used: Eric Clapton Signature Fender Stratocaster

Producer: Frazer Kennedy
Engineers: Steve Chase, Jeremy Wheatley, Ben Kape, Lorraine
  Francis

ERIC CLAPTON: *I worked in collaboration with Michael Kamen initially, but then Michael had to move on to another project and I took over on my own. I played dobro on one track – I don't play it very often. It's funny, because I'd forgotten how unique that sound is. And when you play it for other people they go crazy. You really have to work at it for three to four weeks without touching anything else to get back to your good state of playing.*

Studio Session for *Peace In Our Time* soundtrack
7–21 May 1988
Townhouse Studios, London

Title music	*Unissued*
Various incidental pieces	*Unissued*

Guitar: Eric Clapton

Guitar used: Eric Clapton Signature Fender Stratocaster

Producer: ——
Engineer: ——

ERIC CLAPTON: *I just did some film music for a TV documentary about the beginning of the Second World War, because it's the fiftieth year of the Munich Agreement with Hitler and Chamberlain, and a Czechoslavakian company have made a documentary about it and they asked me to do the music and I was a bit lost, when I first thought about it . . . And when I saw the footage, which is archive black and white material, I just wrote a very simple kind of blues progression and got some string players in and set it to a kind of philharmonic setting and it still works, which is an example of the fact that I always think from a blues point of view and try to frame it in different ways to make it palatable.*

Live Session for Prince's Trust
6 June 1988
Royal Albert Hall, London

Behind The Mask	KING BISCUIT CD only
Cocaine	KING BISCUIT CD only
Money For Nothing	KING BISCUIT CD only
I Don't Want To Go On With You Like That	KING BISCUIT CD only
Layla	KING BISCUIT CD only

Guitar/vocals: Eric Clapton
               Mark Knopfler
Piano/vocals: Elton John
Bass: Nathan East
Drums: Steve Ferrone
Drums: Phil Collins
Backing vocals: Tessa Niles
                Katie Kissoon

With A Little Help From My Friends	KING BISCUIT CD only

As above plus:
Guitar: Brian May
        Midge Ure
Vocals: Joe Cocker
        T'Pau
        Wet Wet Wet
        Bee Gees

Guitar used: Eric Clapton Signature Fender Stratocaster

Producer: ——
Engineer: ——

Live Session for *Free Nelson Mandela*
11 June 1988
Wembley Stadium, London

Walk Of Life	TV/radio broadcast
Sultans of Swing	TV/radio broadcast
Romeo And Juliet	TV/radio broadcast
Money For Nothing	TV/radio broadcast
Brothers In Arms	TV/radio broadcast
Wonderful Tonight	TV/radio broadcast
Solid Rock	TV/radio broadcast

Guitar/vocals: Eric Clapton
               Mark Knopfler
Bass: John Illsley
Drums: Terry Williams
Keyboards: Alan Clark
           Guy Fletcher
Sax: Chris White

ARTISTS AGAINST APARTHEID AAA
IN SUPPORT OF
THE ANTI APARTHEID MOVEMENT
INVITE YOU TO

NELSON MANDELA

70th Birthday Tribute

CHRISSIE HYNDE
DIRE STRAITS
EURYTHMICS
GEORGE MICHAEL
HUGH MASEKELA
JESSYE NORMAN
MAXI PRIEST
MIDGE URE
MIRIAM MAKEBA
PHIL COLLINS
SIMPLE MINDS
SLY AND ROBBIE
UB 40
WHITNEY HOUSTON
AND MANY MORE

HOSTS
**BILLY CONNOLLY   HARRY BELAFONTE
WHOOPI GOLDBERG**

WEMBLEY STADIUM
SATURDAY JUNE 11th

SUBJECT TO LICENCE
TICKETS £25 (LIMITED TO 4 PER PERSONS)   DOORS OPEN 11.00 AM

PERSONAL CALLERS
AVAILABLE FROM
WEMBLEY BOX OFFICE (01-902 1234/01-903 8444)
AND TOWER RECORDS, PICCADILLY CIRCUS.

THE PROMOTER RESERVES THE RIGHT TO CHANGE
THE COMPOSITION OF THE PROGRAMME.

PRODUCED BY ELEPHANT HOUSE PRODUCTIONS
LTD. IN ASSOCIATION WITH MARSHALL ARTS LTD.
FOR FREEDOM PRODUCTIONS LTD.

CREDIT CARDS
USE YOUR CREDIT CARD TO PURCHASE TICKETS BY
TELEPHONE.
CALL 031-226 2295
(BOOKING FEE OF £1.00 PER TICKET).
CALL 061-273 3775
(BOOKING FEE OF £1.00 PER TICKET).
CALL 01-902 1234
(BOOKING FEE OF £2.00 PER TRANSACTION).
CALL 01-748 1414
(BOOKING FEE OF £1.50 PER TICKET).

24 HOUR INFORMATION LINE 01-387 0937.

Studio Session for Davina McCall
15–25 June 1988
Townhouse Studios, London

The Very Last Time	*Unissued*
I'm Too Good For You	*Unissued*
Sticky Situation	*Unissued*

Guitar: Eric Clapton
Vocals: Davina McCall
Bass: ——
Drums: ——
Keyboards: ——

Guitar used: Eric Clapton Signature Fender Stratocaster

Producers: Eric Clapton, Rob Fraboni

Studio Session for Gail Anne Dorsey
July 1988
The Smokehouse Studios, London

Wasted Country	THE CORPORATE WORLD

Guitar: Eric Clapton
Vocals: Gail Anne Dorsey
Bass/acoustic guitar/keyboards: Nathan East
Drums: Steve Ferrone
Guitar: Andy Gill
Keyboards: Mickey Gallagher
Backing vocals: Tessa Niles
                Katie Kissoon

Guitar used: Eric Clapton Signature Fender Stratocaster

Producer: Nathan East
Engineer: ——

Studio Session for Jim Capaldi
July 1988
Backyard Studios, Surrey

You Are The One	SOME COME RUNNING

Guitar: Eric Clapton
Bass: Peter Vale
Vocals/drums: Jim Capaldi
Vocals: Stevie Winwood
Guitar: Mike Waters

Oh Lord Why Lord	SOME COME RUNNING

Guitar: Eric Clapton
        George Harrison

Vocals/drums: Jim Capaldi
Keyboards: Chris Parren
Bass: Rosko Gee

Guitar used: Eric Clapton Signature Fender Stratocaster

Producer: Jim Capaldi
Engineer: Andy MacPherson

ERIC CLAPTON: *I played on two tracks. In fact I played on more, but I think two tracks are going to be released. I drove over to a studio he was using in Marlow and just over-dubbed it in no time at all. It's a very good sounding record.*

Live Session
2 November 1988
Tokyo Dome, Tokyo

Crossroads	Radio broadcast
White Room	Radio broadcast
I Shot The Sheriff	Radio broadcast
Lay Down Sally	Radio broadcast
Wonderful Tonight	Radio broadcast
Tearing Us Apart	Radio broadcast
Can't Find My Way Home	Not broadcast
After Midnight	Not broadcast
Money For Nothing	Radio broadcast
Candle In The Wind	Radio broadcast
I Guess That's Why They Call It The Blues	Radio broadcast
I Don't Wanna Go On With You Like That	Radio broadcast
I'm Still Standing	Not broadcast
Daniel	Radio broadcast
Cocaine	Radio broadcast
Layla	Radio broadcast
Solid Rock	Radio broadcast
Saturday Night's Alright For Fighting	Radio broadcast
Sunshine Of Your Love	Radio broadcast

Guitar/vocals: Eric Clapton
        Mark Knopfler
Piano/vocals: Elton John (Candle In The Wind onwards)
Bass: Nathan East
Keyboards: Alan Clark
Drums: Steve Ferrone
Percussion: Ray Cooper
Backing vocals: Tessa Niles
        Katie Kissoon

Guitar used: Eric Clapton Signature Fender Stratocaster

Studio Session for Carole King
December 1988
Skyline Studios, New York

City Streets   CITY STREETS

Guitar: Eric Clapton
Vocals/synthesizers: Carole King
Guitar: Rudy Guess
Bass: Wayne Pedzwater
Drums: Steve Ferrone
Tambourine: Jimmy Bralower
Tenor sax: Michael Brecker

Ain't That The Way   CITY STREETS

Guitar: Eric Clapton
Vocals/piano/organ: Carole King
Bass: Wayne Pedzwater
Drums: Steve Ferrone
Percussion: Sammy Figueroa

Guitar used: Eric Clapton Signature Fender Stratocaster

Producers: Carole King, Rudy Guess
Engineer: James Farber

Eric's next session would have been fascinating – the James Bond theme tune, for use in a Bond movie! However, due to various legal problems it was not to be, and the resultant doomed recording was stored in the vaults for good.

Studio Session for *Licence To Kill*
7 February 1989
Townhouse Studios, London

James Bond Theme   *Unissued*

Guitar: Eric Clapton
        Vic Flick
Percussion: Ray Cooper
Drums: Steve Ferrone
Orchestration: Michael Kamen

Guitar used: Eric Clapton Signature Fender Stratocaster

Producer: Michael Kamen
Engineer: ——

Royal Albert Hall, London, 1989

Studio Session for JOURNEYMAN
March–April 1989
Power Station Studios and Skyline Studios, New York

No Alibis	JOURNEYMAN
Old Love	JOURNEYMAN
Hound Dog	JOURNEYMAN
Before You Accuse Me	JOURNEYMAN
Pretending	JOURNEYMAN
Breaking Point	JOURNEYMAN
Hard Times	JOURNEYMAN
Lead Me On	JOURNEYMAN
Anything For Your Love	JOURNEYMAN
Run So Far	JOURNEYMAN
Running On Faith (electric version)	JOURNEYMAN
Running On Faith (dobro version)	*Unissued*
Higher Power	*Unissued*
Murdoch's Men	*Unissued*
Forever	*Unissued*
Don't Turn Your Back	*Unissued*
Something About You	*Unissued*
That Kind Of Woman	NOBODY'S CHILD

Guitar/vocals: Eric Clapton
Bass/backing vocals: Nathan East
Keyboards: Greg Phillinganes
Drums: Steve Ferrone
      Jim Keltner
Keyboards: Alan Clark
Guitar/harmony vocals/backing vocals: Jerry Williams
Synthesizers: Jeff Bova
Backing vocals: Chaka Khan
Keyboards: Robbie Kondor
Piano: Richard Tee
Congas: Carol Steele
Guitar: John Tropea
Sax: David Sanborn
Backing vocals: Vaneese Thomas
          Tawatha Agee
Acoustic guitar/vocals: Cecil Womack
Vocals: Linda Womack
Bass: Darryl Jones
Guitar/harmony vocals: George Harrison (Run So Far, That Kind Of Woman)
Guitar: Robert Cray (Before You Accuse Me, Old Love, Hound Dog, Anything For Your Love)

Guitar used: Eric Clapton Signature Fender Stratocaster

Producer: Russ Titelman
Engineer: ———

ERIC CLAPTON: *I had a subconscious feeling that we didn't want this album to be filled with too many similar tracks. We could have made a pure R & B album, or a pure blues album, or just a straight rock album because we had enough material to make it that way. I'm like that – I will deliberately choose a lot of opposites, if I'm given complete control, which my producer Russ Titelmen gave to me.*

Studio Session for *Lethal Weapon 2*
April 1989
Power Station Studios, New York

Knockin' On Heaven's Door	LETHAL WEAPON 2
Riggs	LETHAL WEAPON 2
The Embassy	LETHAL WEAPON 2
Riggs And Roger	LETHAL WEAPON 2
Leo	LETHAL WEAPON 2
Goodnight Rika	LETHAL WEAPON 2
The Stilt House	LETHAL WEAPON 2
The Shipyard/Knockin' On Heaven's Door	LETHAL WEAPON 2

Guitar: Eric Clapton
Alto sax: David Sanborn
Kurzweil: Michael Kamen
Keyboards: .Greg Phillinganes
Bass: Tom Barney
Drums: Sonny Emory
Trumpet: Lew Soloff (Leo)
Vocals: Randy Crawford (Knockin' On Heaven's Door)

Guitar used: Eric Clapton Signature Fender Stratocaster

Producer: Michael Kamen
Engineer: Stephen McLaughlin

Studio Session for Zucchero
April 1989
Power Station Studios, New York

Wonderful World	ZUCCHERO

Guitar: Eric Clapton
Vocals: Zucchero
Guitar/keyboards: Corrado Rustici
Bass: Polo Jones
Drums: Giorgio Francis
Keyboards: David Sancious
Percussion: Rosario Jermano

Guitar used: Eric Clapton Signature Fender Stratocaster

Producer: Corrado Rustici
Engineer: ——

Studio Session for Cyndi Lauper
April 1989
Hit Factory, New York

Insecurious   A NIGHT TO REMEMBER

Guitar: Eric Clapton
Vocals: Cyndi Lauper
Drums: Steve Ferrone
Bass: ——
Keyboards: Jeff Bova
Percussion: Carole Steele

Guitar used: Eric Clapton Signature Fender Stratocaster

Producer: Cyndi Lauper
Engineer: E.T. Thorngren

ERIC CLAPTON: *Cindy Lauper asked me to play my part exactly like I did on 'White Room'. That angered me. What about the music I'm making now? How did I play that then? I didn't remember how I played on 'White Room' because that was so long ago! And I didn't want to have to listen to the original recordings just to find out how to play that session! But such an experience is good for my ego, because it knocks me right down and I have to be a working musician just to get the job done.*

Studio Session for Elton John/Bernie Taupin tribute
May 1989
Power Station Studios, New York

The Border Song   TWO ROOMS

Guitar/vocals: Eric Clapton
Piano: Greg Phillinganes
Synth horns: Jeff Bova
Synthesizer: Alan Clark
                Robbie Kondor
Bass: Daryl Jones
Drums: Steve Ferrone
Tambourine: Carol Steele
Tenor sax: Michael Brecker
Alto sax: George Young
Baritone sax: Ronnie Cuber

Trumpet: Alan Rubin
Trombone: Dave Bargeron
Choir: Reverend Timothy Wright Washington Temple Concert
    Choir

Guitar used: Eric Clapton Signature Fender Stratocaster

Producers: Eric Clapton, Truman Stiles
Engineer: Dave O'Donnell

Live Session
31 May 1989
The Armoury, New York

I Hear You Knockin'   TV broadcast

Guitar/vocals: Eric Clapton
                Keith Richards
                Dave Edmunds
Guitar: Jeff Healey
        Vernon Reid
        Waddy Wachtel
Sax: Bobby Keys
    Clarence Clemens
Drums: Steve Jordan
Bass: Charley Drayton
Keyboards: Ivan Neville
Vocals: Sarah Dash
        Tina Turner

Guitar used: Eric Clapton Signature Fender Stratocaster

Producer: ——
Engineer: ——

Studio Session for JOURNEYMAN
June 1989
Townhouse Studios, London

Bad Love   JOURNEYMAN

Guitar/vocals: Eric Clapton
Guitar: Phil Palmer
Drums/harmony vocals/backing vocals: Phil Collins
Keyboards: Alan Clark
Bass: Pino Palladino
Backing vocals: Tessa Niles
                Katie Kissoon

Guitar used: Eric Clapton Signature Fender Stratocaster

Producer: Russ Titelman
Engineer: ——

ERIC CLAPTON: *Warner Brothers wanted another 'Layla'. I thought, well if you sit down and write a song in a formulated way, it's not so hard. You think, 'What was Layla comprised of? A fiery intro modulated into the first verse, and a chorus with a riff around it.' I had this stuff in my head, so I just juggled it around, and Mick Jones came in to help tidy up. He was the one who said, 'You should put a "Badge" middle in there.' So we did that. Although it sounds like a cold way of doing it, it actually took on its own life.*

Studio Session for Phil Collins
June 1989
Townhouse Studios, London

I Wish It Would Rain   BUT SERIOUSLY

Guitar: Eric Clapton
Drums/keyboards/vocals/tambourine: Phil Collins
Bass: Pino Palladino

Guitar used: Eric Clapton Signature Fender Stratocaster

Producers: Phil Collins, Hugh Padgham
Engineer: ——

Studio Session for Brendan Crocker
August 1989
Matrix Studios, London

This Kind Of Life
          BRENDAN CROKER AND THE FIVE O'CLOCK SHADOWS

Vocals: Eric Clapton
Vocals/acoustic guitar: Brendan Croker
Bass: Marcus Cliffe
Drums: Steve Goulding
Percussion: Preston Heyman

Producer: John Porter
Engineer: Kenney Jones

The reason Eric only sings on this session is because he had injured his hand while playing cricket.

Live Session for Zucchero
28 September 1989
Da Campo Boario, Rome

Wonderful World   Italian TV broadcast

Guitar/vocals: Eric Clapton
Vocals: Zucchero
Guitar: Corrado Rustici
Bass: Polo Jones
Drums: Giorgio Francis
Keyboards: David Sancious
Percussion: Rosario Jermano
Backing vocals: Lisa Hunt

Guitar used: Eric Clapton Signature Fender Stratocaster

Producer: ——
Engineer: ——

Live Session for David Sanborn
25 October 1989
Rockefeller Center Television Studios, New York

Hard Times   TV broadcast
Old Love   TV broadcast
Before You Accuse Me (two takes)   TV broadcast
Instrumental jam   TV broadcast

Guitar/vocals: Eric Clapton
Guitar: Robert Cray (Old Love onwards)
Keyboards: Greg Phillinganes
Sax: David Sanborn
Rest: Night Time house band

Guitar used: Eric Clapton Signature Fender Stratocaster (7-Up green)

Producer: ——
Engineer: ——

Live Session
28 October 1989
BBC Television Studios, Shepherds Bush, London

Standin' Around Cryin'   *Saturday Matters* TV show

Acoustic guitar/vocals: Eric Clapton
Acoustic guitar: Pete Townshend

Guitar used: Martin acoustic

Producer: ——
Engineer: ——

Live Session for Parents For Safe Food
18 November 1989
Royal Albert Hall, London

Edge Of Darkness   *Unissued*

Guitar: Eric Clapton
Drums: Andrew Newmark
Percussion: Ray Cooper

Orchestra: Organic Symphony Orchestra
Conductor: Carl Davis

Guitar used: Eric Clapton Signature Fender Stratocaster

Producer: ——
Engineer: ——

Studio Session for film *Communion*
8–9 December 1989
Townhouse Studios, London

Title music   *Unissued*
Incidental music   *Unissued*

Guitar: Eric Clapton
Keyboards/synthesizers: Alan Clark

Guitar used: Eric Clapton Signature Fender Stratocaster

Producer: ——
Engineer: ——

Live Session for The Rolling Stones
19 December 1989
Convention Center, Atlantic City, New Jersey

Little Red Rooster   FLASHPOINT
Boogie Chillin'   *Unissued*

Guitar: Eric Clapton
        Keith Richards
        Ronnie Wood
Guitar/vocals: John Lee Hooker (Boogie Chillin')
Bass: Bill Wyman
Drums: Charlie Watts
Vocals/harmonica: Mick Jagger
Keyboards/piano/Hammond organ: Chuck Leavell
Keyboards: Matt Clifford

Guitar used: Eric Clapton Signature Series Fender Stratocaster

Producers: Chris Kimsey And The Glimmer Twins
Engineers: Richard Sullivan, Spencer May

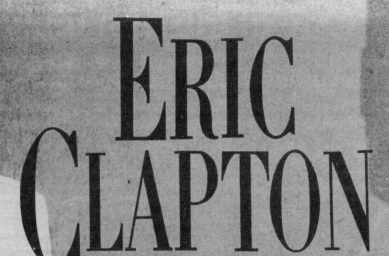

HARVEY GOLDSMITH BY ARRANGEMENT WITH ROGER FORRESTER PRESENTS

ERIC CLAPTON

RECORD BREAKING 18 NIGHTS

THE ROYAL ALBERT HALL

JAN 18, 19, 20, 22, 23, 24, 26, 27, 28, 30, 31, FEB 1
WITH HIS BAND

FEB 3, 4, 5
AN EVENING OF THE BLUES WITH SPECIAL GUESTS

FEB 8, 9, 10
AN EVENING WITH
THE NATIONAL PHILHARMONIC ORCHESTRA
WITH MICHAEL KAMEN

TICKETS: £17.50, £15.00, £13.50

From R.A.H. Box Office. Tel: 01-589 8212 or 01-589 9465 and usual agents
Credit Card Hotlines (subject to booking fee) 01-240 7200/01-379 4444/01-741 8989

NEW ALBUM "JOURNEYMAN" – OUT NOVEMBER ON RECORDS

NOT THE PROMS!

1990–1992

Eric recorded several shows for another proposed double live album. As the shows took on four different line-ups, the title was to be FOUR FACES OF ERIC CLAPTON. It was given a release date and a catalogue number. A single, 'Wonderful Tonight', from the 24 January show was planned, as was a live video also titled *Four Faces of Eric Clapton*. Eric decided the performances were not as good as they might have been and the album was scrapped, although most of it survived for a release in 1991 as 24 NIGHTS.

Live Session (four-piece)
24 January 1990
Royal Albert Hall, London

Pretending	USA Radio broadcast
Running On Faith	USA Radio broadcast/24 NIGHTS
Breaking Point	*Unissued*
I Shot The Sheriff	USA Radio broadcast
White Room	USA Radio broadcast/24 NIGHTS
Can't Find My Way Home	*Unissued*
Bad Love	USA Radio broadcast
Lay Down Sally	USA Radio broadcast
Before You Accuse Me	USA Radio broadcast
No Alibis	USA Radio broadcast
Old Love	USA Radio broadcast
Tearing Us Apart	USA Radio broadcast
Wonderful Tonight	USA Radio broadcast
Cocaine	USA Radio broadcast
Layla	USA Radio broadcast
Knockin' On Heaven's Door	*Unissued*
Crossroads	USA Radio broadcast
Sunshine Of Your Love	USA Radio broadcast/24 NIGHTS

Guitar/vocals: Eric Clapton
Bass: Nathan East
Drums: Steve Ferrone

Keyboards: Greg Phillinganes
Tambourine/vocals: Phil Collins (Knockin' On Heaven's Door, Crossroads, Sunshine Of Your Love)

Guitars played: Eric Clapton Signature Fender Stratocaster, Chet Atkins acoustic

Producer: Russ Titelman
Engineer: ——

Live Session (13-piece)
1 February 1990
Royal Albert Hall, London

Pretending	*Unissued*
Running On Faith	*Unissued*
Breaking Point	*Unissued*
I Shot The Sheriff	*Unissued*
White Room	*Unissued*
Can't Find My Way Home	*Unissued*
Bad Love	*Unissued*
Lay Down Sally	*Unissued*
Before You Accuse Me	*Unissued*
No Alibis	*Unissued*
Old Love	*Unissued*
Tearing Us Apart	*Unissued*
Wonderful Tonight	*Unissued*
Cocaine	*Unissued*
Layla	*Unissued*
Crossroads	*Unissued*
Sunshine Of Your Love	*Unissued*

Guitar/vocals: Eric Clapton
Bass: Nathan East
Drums: Steve Ferrone
Keyboards: Greg Phillinganes
          Alan Clark
Guitar: Phil Palmer
Percussion: Ray Cooper
Backing vocals: Katie Kissoon
               Tessa Niles

Horns: Ronnie Cuber
           Randy Brecker
           Louis Marini
           Alan Rubin

Guitars used: Eric Clapton Signature Fender Stratocaster, Chet
  Atkins acoustic

Producer: Russ Titelman
Engineer: ——

Live Session (blues band)
3 February 1990
Royal Albert Hall, London

Full show broadcast live on BBC Radio 1

Key To The Highway	Radio broadcast
Worried Life Blues	Radio broadcast
All Your Love	Radio broadcast
Have You Ever Loved A Woman	Radio broadcast
Standing Around Crying/	
Long Distance Call	Radio broadcast
Johnnie's Boogie	Radio broadcast
Going Down Slow	Radio broadcast
You Belong To Me	Radio broadcast
Cry For Me	Radio broadcast
Howling For My Baby	Radio broadcast
Same Thing	Radio broadcast
Money (That's What I Want)	Radio broadcast
Five Long Years	Radio broadcast
Everything's Gonna Be Alright	Radio broadcast
Something On Your Mind	Radio broadcast
My Time After A While	Radio broadcast
Sweet Home Chicago	Radio broadcast
Hoochie Coochie Man	Radio broadcast
Wee Wee Baby	Radio broadcast

Guitar/vocals: Eric Clapton
                Robert Cray (Going Down Slow onwards)
                Buddy Guy (Money onwards)
Keyboards: Johnnie Johnson
Drums: Jamie Oldaker
Bass: Robert Cousins

Guitar used: Eric Clapton Signature Fender Stratocaster

Producer: BBC
Engineer: ——
Recorded by: BBC Mobile Recording Unit

Live Session (blues band)
5 February 1990
Royal Albert Hall, London

Key To The Highway	*Unissued*
Worried Life Blues	24 NIGHTS
Watch Yourself	24 NIGHTS
Have You Ever Loved A Woman	24 NIGHTS
Johnnie's Boogie	*Unissued*
Standing Around Crying/Long Distance Call	*Unissued*
Going Down Slow	*Unissued*
You Belong To Me	*Unissued*
Cry For Me	*Unissued*
Howling For My Baby	*Unissued*
Same Thing	*Unissued*
Money (That's What I Want)	*Unissued*
Five Long Years	*Unissued*
Something On Your Mind	*Unissued*
Everything's Gonna Be Alright	*Unissued*
Sweet Home Chicago	*Unissued*
My Time After A While	*Unissued*
Wee Wee Baby	*Unissued*

Guitar/vocals: Eric Clapton
                Robert Cray
                Buddy Guy
Keyboards: Johnnie Johnson
Drums: Jamie Oldaker
Bass: Robert Cousins

Guitar used: Eric Clapton Signature Fender Stratocaster

Producer: Russ Titelman
Engineer: ——

Live Session (orchestra)
9–10 February 1990
Royal Albert Hall, London

Full show on 10 February broadcast live on BBC Radio 1

Crossroads	*Unissued*
Bell Bottom Blues	24 NIGHTS
Lay Down Sally	*Unissued*
Holy Mother	*Unissued*
I Shot The Sheriff	*Unissued*
Hard Times	24 NIGHTS
Can't Find My Way Home	*Unissued*
Edge Of Darkness	*Unissued*
Old Love	*Unissued*
Wonderful Tonight	*Unissued*
White Room	*Unissued*

Concerto For Electric Guitar   *Unissued*
Layla   *Unissued*
Sunshine Of Your Love   *Unissued*

Guitar/vocals: Eric Clapton
Bass: Nathan East
Drums: Steve Ferrone
Keyboards: Greg Phillinganes
        Alan Clark
Percussion: Ray Cooper
Guitar: Phil Palmer
Backing vocals: Tessa Niles
        Katie Kissoon
Orchestra: National Philharmonic

Guitar used: Eric Clapton Signature Fender Stratocaster

Producers: Russ Titelman (9th), BBC (10th)
Engineer: ——

Studio Session for Michael Kamen
March 1990
Sarm West Studios, London

Sandra   CONCERTO FOR SAXOPHONE AND ORCHESTRA

Guitar: Eric Clapton
Oboes/keyboards: Michael Kamen
Guitar: Elliot Randall
Bass: Pino Palladino
Acoustic guitar: Terry Reed
Drums: Gary Wallace
Percussion: Ray Cooper
Alto sax: David Sanborn

Guitar used: Eric Clapton Signature Fender Stratocaster

Producers: Michael Kamen, Stephen McLaughlin
Engineer: John McClure

Live Session for *Saturday Night Live*
24 March 1990
Saturday Night Live television show, New York

No Alibis   TV broadcast
Pretending   TV broadcast
Wonderful Tonight   TV broadcast

Guitar/vocals: Eric Clapton
Bass: Nathan East
Drums: Steve Ferrone
Keyboards: Greg Phillinganes
        Alan Clark
Guitar: Phil Palmer

Percussion: Ray Cooper
Backing vocals: Tessa Niles
        Katie Kissoon

Guitars used: Eric Clapton Signature Fender Stratocaster,
   Gibson Les Paul

Producer: ——
Engineer: ——

Live Session for Elvis Awards
6 June 1990
The Armoury, New York

Before You Accuse Me   TV broadcast

Guitar/vocals: Eric Clapton
Guitar: Phil Palmer
Bass: Nathan East
Drums: Steve Ferrone
Keyboards: Greg Phillinganes
        Alan Clark
Percussion: Ray Cooper
Backing vocals: Tessa Niles
        Katie Kissoon

Sweet Home Chicago   TV broadcast

Band as above plus:
Guitar/vocals: Buddy Guy
Guitar: Lou Reed
      Bo Diddley
      Richie Sambora
      Dave Stewart
      Neil Schon

Guitar used: Eric Clapton Signature Fender Stratocaster

Producer: ——
Engineer: ——

Live Session for Nordoff Robins
30 June 1990
Knebworth, Hertfordshire

Full show broadcast on BBC Radio 1

Pretending   *Unissued*
Before You Accuse Me   *Unissued*
Old Love   *Unissued*
Tearing Us Apart   *Unissued*
Solid Rock   *Unissued*
Think I Love You Too Much   KNEBWORTH

Money For Nothing	KNEBWORTH
Sacrifice	*Unissued*
Sad Songs	KNEBWORTH
Saturday Night's Alright	KNEBWORTH
Sunshine Of Your Love	KNEBWORTH

Guitar/vocals: Eric Clapton
　　　　　Mark Knopfler (Solid Rock onwards)
Guitar: Phil Palmer
Keyboards: Elton John (Sacrifice onwards)
　　　　　Greg Phillinganes
　　　　　Alan Clark
　　　　　Guy Fletcher (Solid Rock, Think I Love You Too
　　　　　　Much, Money For Nothing)
Bass: Nathan East
Drums: Steve Ferrone
Percussion: Ray Cooper
Backing vocals: Tessa Niles
　　　　　Katie Kissoon
Bass: John Illsey (Solid Rock, Think I Love You Too Much,
　　Money For Nothing)

Guitar used: Eric Clapton Signature Fender Stratocaster

Producers: Chris Kimsey, Steve Smith
Engineer: ——
Recorded by: Advision Mobile

Studio Session for Honda Cars Japan
September 1990
Electric Lady Studios, New York

Bad Love	Japanese TV ad backing

Guitar: Eric Clapton

Guitar used: 'Blackie' Fender Stratocaster

Producer: ——
Engineer: ——

Live Session
29 September 1990
Estadio Nacional, Santiago, Chile

Live Session
5 October 1990
Estadio River Plate, Buenos Aires, Argentina

Live Session
7 October 1990
Praca da Apoteose, Rio de Janeiro, Brazil

Pretending	*Unissued*
No Alibis	*Unissued*
Running On Faith	*Unissued*
I Shot The Sheriff	*Unissued*
White Room	*Unissued*
Can't Find My Way Home	*Unissued*
Bad Love	*Unissued*
Before You Accuse Me	*Unissued*
Old Love	*Unissued*
Badge	*Unissued*
Wonderful Tonight	*Unissued*
Cocaine	*Unissued*
Layla	*Unissued*
Crossroads	*Unissued*
Sunshine Of Your Love	*Unissued*

Guitar/vocals: Eric Clapton
Guitar: Phil Palmer
Bass: Nathan East
Drums: Steve Ferrone
Keyboards: Greg Phillinganes
Percussion: Ray Cooper
Backing vocals: Tessa Niles
　　　　　Katie Kissoon

Guitar used: Eric Clapton Signature Fender Stratocaster

Producer: ——
Engineer: ——

Studio Session for Lamont Dozier
December 1990
The Hit Factory, New York

That Ain't Me	INSIDE SEDUCTION
Hold On Tight	*Unissued*

Guitar: Eric Clapton
Keyboards/vocals: Lamont Dozier
Drums: Phil Collins
Programmer/keyboards: Ryo Okumoto
Sax: David Boroff

Guitar used: Eric Clapton Signature Fender Stratocaster

Producers: Lamont Dozier, Phil Collins
Engineer: Reginald Dozier

ERIC CLAPTON: *I don't think people realize how good a singer he is. It's very easy to work with Lamont because he writes such straightforward material.*

Live Session (four-piece)
10 February 1991
Royal Albert Hall, London

Pretending	*Unissued*
No Alibis	*Unissued*
Running On Faith	*Unissued*
I Shot The Sheriff	*Unissued*
White Room	*Unissued*
Can't Find My Way Home	*Unissued*
Bad Love	*Unissued*
Before You Accuse Me	*Unissued*
Old Love	*Unissued*
Badge	24 NIGHTS
Wonderful Tonight	*Unissued*
Cocaine	*Unissued*
Layla	*Unissued*
Crossroads	*Unissued*
Sunshine Of Your Love	*Unissued*

Guitar/vocals: Eric Clapton
Bass: Nathan East
Keyboards: Greg Phillinganes
Drums: Steve Ferrone

Guitars used: Eric Clapton Signature Fender Stratocaster, Chet Atkins acoustic

Producer: Russ Titelman
Engineer: John Harris

Live Session (nine-piece)
17–18 February 1991
Royal Albert Hall, London

Full show on 17 February broadcast live on BBC Radio 1

Pretending	24 NIGHTS
No Alibis	CD single
Running On Faith	*Unissued*
I Shot The Sheriff	CD single
White Room	*Unissued*
Can't Find My Way Home	*Unissued*
Bad Love	24 NIGHTS
Before You Accuse Me	*Unissued*
Old Love	24 NIGHTS
Tearing Us Apart	*Unissued*
Wonderful Tonight	24 NIGHTS
Cocaine	CD single
Layla	*Unissued*
Crossroads	*Unissued*
Sunshine Of Your Love	*Unissued*

Guitar/vocals: Eric Clapton
Guitar: Phil Palmer
Bass: Nathan East
Drums: Steve Ferrone
Keyboards: Greg Phillinganes
            Chuck Leavell
Percussion: Ray Cooper
Backing vocals: Tessa Niles
                Katie Kissoon

Guitars used: Eric Clapton Signature Fender Stratocaster, Chet Atkins acoustic

Producers: BBC (17th), Russ Titelman (18th)
Engineers: ⸺ (17th), John Harris (18th)

Live Session (blues band)
25 and 28 February 1991
Royal Albert Hall, London

Full show on 25 February broadcast live on BBC Radio 1

Watch Yourself	*Unissued*
Hoodoo Man	24 NIGHTS
Hideaway	*Unissued*
Standin' Around Crying	*Unissued*
All Your Love	*Unissued*
Have You Ever Loved A Woman	*Unissued*
Long Distance Call (25th only)	Radio broadcast
It's My Life Baby	*Unissued*
Key To The Highway	*Unissued*
Wee Wee Baby	*Unissued*
Tanqueray	*Unissued*
Johnnie's Boogie	*Unissued*
Tired Man	*Unissued*
Mother-In-Law Blues	*Unissued*
Black Cat Bone	*Unissued*
I Feel So Glad	*Unissued*
Reconsider Baby	*Unissued*
Stranger Blues	*Unissued*
Hoochie Coochie Man	*Unissued*
Little By Little	*Unissued*
My Time After Awhile	*Unissued*
Sweet Home Chicago	*Unissued*

Royal Albert Hall, London, 7 March 1991

Guitar/vocals: Eric Clapton
 Jimmie Vaughan
 Albert Collins (Tired Man onwards)
 Robert Cray (I Feel So Glad onwards)
 Buddy Guy (Hoochie Choochie Man onwards)
Piano/vocals: Johnnie Johnson
Keyboards: Chuck Leavell
 Greg Phillinganes
Drums: Jamie Oldaker
Bass: Joey Spampinato
Harmonica: Jerry Portnoy

Guitar used: Eric Clapton Signature Fender Stratocaster

Producers: BBC (25th), Russ Titelman (28th)
Engineers: —— (25th), John Harris (28th)

Live Session (orchestra)
8 March 1991
Royal Albert Hall, London

Crossroads	*Unissued*
Bell Bottom Blues	*Unissued*
Holy Mother	*Unissued*
I Shot The Sheriff	*Unissued*
Hard Times	*Unissued*
Can't Find My Way Home	*Unissued*
Edge Of Darkness	24 NIGHTS
Old Love	*Unissued*
Wonderful Tonight	*Unissued*
White Room	*Unissued*
Concerto For Electric Guitar	*Unissued*
Layla	*Unissued*
Sunshine Of Your Love	*Unissued*

Same line-up as nine-piece, plus the National Philharmonic
 Orchestra

Producer: Russ Titelman
Engineer: John Harris

RUSS TITELMAN: *We set up a control room under the stage (our little cave) with two 48-track digital machines to document this amazing event. The main difference to other live recordings is that we had the mic pre-amps onstage — so the musicians went direct into the machine, bypassing any extraneous electronics. About half of what is on* 24 NIGHTS *was recorded this way. The rest of the album was recorded by Steve Chase and expertly mixed by Alex Haas.*

Studio Session for Buddy Guy
March 1991
Battery Studios, London

Early In The Morning   DAMN RIGHT I'VE GOT THE BLUES

Guitar: Eric Clapton
Guitar/vocals: Buddy Guy
Guitar: Jeff Beck
Drums: Richie Hayward
Piano: Pete Wingfield
Bass: Greg Rzab
Organ: Mick Weaver
Guitar: Neil Hubbard
Horns: Memphis Horns

Guitar used: Eric Clapton Signature Fender Stratocaster

Producer: John Porter
Engineer: Tony Platt

Studio Session for Johnnie Johnson
March 1991
Nomis Studios, London

Creek Mud	JOHNNIE B BAD
Blues #572	JOHNNIE B BAD

Guitar: Eric Clapton
Piano: Johnnie Johnson
Guitar: Steve Ferguson
Bass: Joey Spampinato
Drums: Tom Ardolino

Guitar used: Eric Clapton Signature Fender Stratocaster

Producer: Terry Adams
Engineer: Ted Mayton

Studio Session for Richie Sambora
March 1991
Studio not known

Mr Bluesman   STRANGER IN THIS TOWN

Guitar: Eric Clapton
Guitar/vocals: Richie Sambora
Keyboards: David Bryan
Bass: Tony Levin
Drums: Tico Torres

Guitar used: Eric Clapton Signature Fender Stratocaster

Producers: Neil Dorfsman, Richie Sambora
Engineer: ——

RICHIE SAMBORA: *I had written this song for the album called 'Mr Bluesman', which is about me and him. It's about a young boy aspiring to be a guitar player. And I wrote him a letter and sent a demo and said that this song is essentially about you and me, or you and Robert Johnson, who you looked up to, or some kid who's just picked up guitar because of me, you know what I'm saying?*

Studio Session for *Rush* soundtrack
September 1991
The Village Recorder, Los Angeles

Double Trouble	*Unissued*
Tracks And Lines	RUSH
Realization	RUSH
Kristen And Jim	RUSH
Preludin Fugue	RUSH
Cold Turkey	RUSH
Will Gaines	RUSH

Guitar: Eric Clapton
Keyboards: Randy Kerber
        Greg Phillinganes
Piano/organ: Chuck Leavell
Synthesizer: Robbie Kondor
Bass: Nathan East
     Tim Drummond
Drums: Steve Ferrone
Percussion: Lenny Castro

Hoochie Coochie Man	*Unissued*
Don't Know Which Way To Go	RUSH

Guitar: Eric Clapton
Guitar/vocals: Buddy Guy
Piano: Chuck Leavell
Organ: Greg Phillinganes
Bass: Nathan East
Drums: Steve Ferrone

Help Me Up	RUSH

Guitar/vocals: Eric Clapton
Organ: Randy Kerber
Piano: Greg Phillinganes
Bass: Nathan East
Drums: Steve Ferrone
Percussion: Lenny Castro
Backing vocals: Bill Champlin
             Vaneese Thomas
             Jenni Muldaur
             Lani Groves

Tears In Heaven	A side/RUSH

Guitar/dobro/vocals: Eric Clapton
Synthesizer: Randy Kerber
Pedal steel: Jaydee Maness
Bass: Nathan East
Celtic harp: Gayle Levant
Percussion: Lenny Castro
Drum machine: Jimmy Bralower

Guitars used: Eric Clapton Signature Fender Stratocaster,
    dobro, gut string acoustic

Producer: Russ Titelman
Engineer: Ed Cherney, Jeff DeMorris

ERIC CLAPTON: *For* RUSH *I've been playing very, very quietly, so if I hit a note and hold it with vibrato you can hear it just sizzling against the fret. But not very loud. You have to strain to hear it. And I love that. It's different from the big, big sound people are more used to.*

Studio Session
October 1991
The Village Recorder, Los Angeles

Circus Has Left Town	*Unissued*
Lonely Stranger	*Unissued*
My Father's Eyes	*Unissued*
Signe	*Unissued*

Guitar/vocals: Eric Clapton

Guitar used: ——

Producer: ——
Engineer: ——

ERIC CLAPTON: *There are already six songs which I've started recording in Los Angeles. The songs are about my son. I've three on tape and there are three more. And every day I start to work on other ones. It's happening all the time. I'm writing continually because I need to. This is the way I repair myself, recover from the tragedy.*

Studio Session for David Sanborn
November 1991
Power Station, New York

Full House	UPFRONT

Guitar: Eric Clapton
Alto sax: David Sanborn
Bass/keyboards/bass clarinet: Marcus Miller
Drums: Steve Jordan
Hammond B-3 organ: Ricky Peterson
Rhythm guitar: Chris Bruce
                  William 'Spaceman' Patterson
Congas: Don Alias
Tenor sax: John Purcell
Trumpet: Randy Brecker
Trombone: Dave Bargeron

Guitar used: Eric Clapton Signature Fender Stratocaster

Producer: Marcus Miller
Engineer: Joe Ferla

Live Session for George Harrison
10–12 December 1991
Osaka Castle Hall, Osaka, Japan

Live Session for George Harrison
14, 15 and 17 December 1991
Tokyo Dome Stadium, Tokyo

I Want To Tell You	LIVE IN JAPAN
Old Brown Shoe	LIVE IN JAPAN
Taxman	LIVE IN JAPAN
Give Me Love	LIVE IN JAPAN
If I Needed Someone	LIVE IN JAPAN
Something	LIVE IN JAPAN
What Is Life	LIVE IN JAPAN
Dark Horse	LIVE IN JAPAN
Piggies	LIVE IN JAPAN
Pretending	*Unissued*
Old Love	*Unissued*
Badge	*Unissued*
Wonderful Tonight	*Unissued*
Got My Mind Set On You	LIVE IN JAPAN
Cloud Nine	LIVE IN JAPAN
Here Comes The Sun	LIVE IN JAPAN
My Sweet Lord	LIVE IN JAPAN
All Those Years Ago	LIVE IN JAPAN
Cheer Down	LIVE IN JAPAN

Devil's Radio	LIVE IN JAPAN
Isn't It A Pity	LIVE IN JAPAN
While My Guitar Gently Weeps	LIVE IN JAPAN
Roll Over Beethoven	LIVE IN JAPAN

Guitar/vocals: Eric Clapton
                  George Harrison
                  Andy Fairweather Low
Bass: Nathan East
Drums: Steve Ferrone
Keyboards: Greg Phillinganes
                       Chuck Leavell
Percussion: Ray Cooper
Backing vocals: Tessa Niles
                      Katie Kissoon

Guitar used: Eric Clapton Signature Fender Stratocaster

Producers: Spike and Nelson Wilbury
Engineer: John Harris

Eric started 1992 with a special all-acoustic show which was filmed and recorded by MTV for their *Unplugged* series. This was quite a historic occasion as it was the first time that Eric had performed such a show, although he had played the occasional acoustic set as an introduction to his concerts in the mid-seventies. One of the many highlights was the impromtu version of Fresh Cream's 'Rollin' And Tumblin', which had the crowd on their feet, stomping and clapping.

Live Session for MTV's *Unplugged*
16 January 1992
Bray Studios, Berkshire

Signe	UNPLUGGED
Before You Accuse Me	UNPLUGGED
Hey Hey	UNPLUGGED
Tears In Heaven	Not broadcast/*unissued*
Circus Has Left Town	TV broadcast only
Lonely Stranger	UNPLUGGED
Nobody Knows You When You're Down And Out	UNPLUGGED
Layla	A side/UNPLUGGED
Signe 2	Not broadcast/*unissued*
My Father's Eyes	Not broadcast/*unissued*
Running On Faith	UNPLUGGED
Walking Blues	Not broadcast/*unissued*

```
M.T.V. - UNPLUGGED

TRIANGLE      INSTRUMENTAL -
(TACET)       BEFORE YOU ACCUSE ME,
(TACET)       HEY - HEY -
CONGAS        TEARS IN HEAVEN -
SHAKER        CIRCUS HAS LEFT TOWN -
CONGAS        LONELY STRANGER -
TAMB          NOBODY KNOWS YOU -
TAMB          LAYLA -
(CONGAS)
CONGAS        MY FATHERS EYES -
TAMB.         RUNNING ON FAITH
(TACET)       WALKING BLUES
TAMB          ALBERTA.
TAMB.         SAN FRANCISCO BAY BLUES
```

The actual running list used by the musicians during the recording for UNPLUGGED

Alberta	UNPLUGGED
San Francisco Bay Blues	Not broadcast/*unissued*
Malted Milk	Not broadcast/*unissued*
Signe 3	Not broadcast/*unissued*
Tears In Heaven 2	UNPLUGGED
My Father's Eyes 2	Not broadcast/*unissued*
Rollin' And Tumblin'	Part TV broadcast/UNPLUGGED
Running on Faith	Not broadcast/*unissued*
Walking Blues 2	UNPLUGGED
San Francisco Bay Blues 2	UNPLUGGED
Malted Milk 2	UNPLUGGED
Worried Life Blues	Not broadcast/*unissued*
Old Love	TV broadcast/UNPLUGGED

Guitars/vocals: Eric Clapton
Guitars: Andy Fairweather Low
Bass: Nathan East
Drums: Steve Ferrone
Percussion: Ray Cooper
Piano: Chuck Leavell
Backing vocals: Katie Kissoon
               Tessa Niles

Guitars used: Martin acoustic, Dobro, gut string acoustic, 12-string acoustic

Producer: Alexi Coletti
Recorded by: Russ Titelman, James Barton, Steve Boyer

Producer: ——
Engineer: ——

Live Session for Sue Lawley
January 1992
Eric's Chelsea house, London

Tears In Heaven	TV broadcast

Gut string guitar: Eric Clapton

Producer: ——
Engineer: ——

Studio Session for Elton John
March–April 1992
Townhouse Studios, London

Runaway Train	THE ONE

Guitar/vocals: Eric Clapton
Keyboards/vocals: Elton John
Bass: Pino Palladino
Drums: Ollie Romo
Guitar: Davey Johnstone
Keyboards: Guy Babylon
Backing vocals: Jonice Jamison
               Carole Fredericks
               Beckie Bell

Guitar used: Eric Clapton Signature Fender Stratocaster

Producer: Chris Thomas
Engineer: Andy Bradfield

Studio Session for *Lethal Weapon 3*
March–April 1992
Power Station, New York

It's Probably Me	LETHAL WEAPON 3

Guitar: Eric Clapton
Bass/vocals: Sting
Sax: David Sanborn
Keyboards: Michael Kamen
Percussion: Don Alias
Drums: Steve Gadd

Grab	LETHAL WEAPON 3
Riggs And Rog	LETHAL WEAPON 3
Roger's Boat	LETHAL WEAPON 3
Armour Piercing Bullets	LETHAL WEAPON 3
God Judges Us By Our Scars	LETHAL WEAPON 3
Lorna – A Quiet Evening By The Fire	LETHAL WEAPON 3

Guitar: Eric Clapton
Sax: David Sanborn
Orchestra: The Greater New York Alumni Orchestra

Guitars used: Eric Clapton Signature Fender Stratocaster, gut string acoustic

Producers: Michael Kamen, Stephen McLaughlin, Christopher Brooks

Engineers: Andy Warwick, Vince Caro, Doug McKean, Howard Bargoff, William Easystone, Mark Johnston

At the 1992 MTV Awards, Eric received the best video award for the hit single 'Tears In Heaven' and, together with his band, played a live version of it.

Live Session for MTV Awards
9 September 1992
Pauley Pavilion, Los Angeles

Tears In Heaven	TV broadcast

Guitar/vocals: Eric Clapton
Guitar: Andy Fairweather-Low
Bass: Nathan East
Drums: Steve Ferrone
Percussion: Ray Cooper
Piano: Chuck Leavell
Backing vocals: Katie Kissoon
 Gina Foster

Producer: ——
Engineer: ——

Live Session to celebrate Bob Dylan's 30 years as a recording artist
16 October 1992
Madison Square Garden, New York

Love Minus Zero	TV/radio broadcast
Don't Think Twice	TV/radio broadcast

Vocals/guitar: Eric Clapton
Guitar: Steve Cropper
 G.E. Smith
Bass: Duck Dunn
Organ: Booker T
Drums: Jim Keltner

My Back Pages	TV/radio broadcast

As above plus
Guitar/vocals: Bob Dylan
Guitar: Tom Petty
 George Harrison

Knockin' On Heaven's Door	TV/radio broadcast

As above plus
Vocals/guitar: Bob Dylan
Guitar: Ron Wood
 George Harrison
 Neil Young
 Roger McGuinn
 Pat Clancy

Vocals: Sinead O'Connor
 Johnny Cash
 Willie Nelson
 Chrissie Hynde
 Kris Kristofferson
 Richie Havens
 Tracy Chapman

STOP PRESS

Just as this book was going to press came the news
of the live session for Cream's induction into the 8th Rock and Roll Hall of Fame
on 12 January 1993 at the Crown Plaza Hotel, Los Angeles. The line-up was unchanged
from that in their heyday, with Eric Clapton on guitar and vocals, Jack Bruce on bass and vocals
and Ginger Baker on drums. They performed, as part of a TV broadcast, versions of
'Sunshine Of Your Love', 'Politician' and 'Born Under A Bad Sign'.

2 ALBUMS FEATURING THE FULL LENGTH VERSION OF THE HIT SINGLE 'LAYLA'

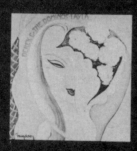 

Derek and the Dominos.
Layla and other assorted love songs
Double Album

Eric Clapton.
History of Eric Clapton
Double Album
Also available on Musicassette

Also available
Eric Clapton
Also available on Musicassette

Discography

The Yardbirds

SINGLES

I Wish You Would/A Certain Girl
Columbia DB7283 released June 1964

Good Morning Little Schoolgirl/I Ain't Got You
Columbia DB7391 released October 1964

For Your Love/Got To Hurry
Columbia DB7499 released February 1965

ALBUMS

Five Live Yardbirds
Columbia 33SX 1677 released February 1965
CD version Charly 182

Sonny Boy Williamson And The Yardbirds
Fontana TL 5277 released January 1966

Remember . . . The Yardbirds
Regal Starline SRS 5069 released June 1971

Shapes Of Things
Charly BOX 104 released November 1984
CD version Decal LIK BOX 1

John Mayall's Blues Breakers

SINGLES

I'm Your Witchdoctor/Telephone Blues
Immediate IM012 released October 1965

Lonely Years/Bernard Jenkins
Purdah 3502 released August 1966

Parchment Farm/Key To Love
Decca F12490 released September 1966

ALBUMS

Blues Breakers With Eric Clapton
Decca SKL4804 released July 1966
Available on CD

Raw Blues
Decca Ace Of Clubs SLC1220 released January 1967

Looking Back
Decca SKL5010 released September 1969
Available on CD

Back To The Roots
Polydor 2425 020 released June 1971

Primal Solos
Decca TAB66 released 1983
Available on CD

Archives To Eighties (revised versions of songs originally recorded as **Back To The Roots** album of 1971)
Polydor 837127 released 1988
Available on CD

Cream

SINGLES

Wrapping Paper/Cat's Squirrel
Reaction 591007 released October 1966

I Feel Free/N.S.U.
Reaction 591011 released December 1966

Strange Brew/Tales Of Brave Ulysses
Reaction 591015 released June 1967

Anyone For Tennis/Pressed Rat And Warthog
Polydor 56258 released May 1968

Sunshine Of Your Love/Swlabr
Polydor 56286 released September 1968

White Room/Those Were The Days
Polydor 56286 released January 1969

Badge/What A Bringdown
Polydor 56315 released April 1969

ALBUMS

Fresh Cream
Reaction 593001 mono 594001 stereo released
December 1966
Available on CD

Disraeli Gears
Reaction 593003 mono 594003 stereo released
November 1967
Available on CD

Wheels Of Fire
Polydor 583031 released August 1968
Available on CD

Goodbye Cream
Polydor 583053 released March 1969
Available on CD

Best Of Cream
Polydor 583060 released November 1969
Available on CD (Japan only)

Live Cream
Polydor 2383016 released June 1970
Available on CD

Live Cream Vol. 2
Polydor 2383119 released July 1972
Available on CD

Blind Faith

SINGLE

Instrumental jam
Island promo released June 1969

ALBUM

Blind Faith
Polydor 583059 released August 1969
Available on CD (UK version has two bonus tracks
from the abortive Rick Grech solo album sessions
and are not Blind Faith out-takes as the sleeve
would have you believe)

Delaney And Bonnie

SINGLE

Comin' Home/Groupie (Superstar)
Atlantic 584308 released December 1969

ALBUM

On Tour
Atlantic 2400013 released June 1970
Available on CD

Plastic Ono Band

SINGLE

Cold Turkey/Don't Worry Kyoko
Apple 1001 released October 1969

ALBUMS

Live Peace In Toronto
Apple 1003 released December 1969

Sometime In New York City
Apple PCSP716 released September 1972
Available on CD

Eric Clapton

SINGLE

After Midnight/Easy Now
Polydor 2383021 released October 1970

ALBUMS

Eric Clapton
Polydor 3383021 released August 1970
Available on CD

History Of Eric Clapton
Polydor 2659012 released July 1972
Available on CD (Japan only)

Rainbow Concert
RSO 2394116 released September 1973
Available on CD

Derek And The Dominos

SINGLE

Tell The Truth/Roll It Over
Polydor 2058057 released September 1970
withdrawn September 1970

Layla/Bell Bottom Blues
Polydor 2058130 released July 1972

Why Does Love Got To Be So Sad (live)/**Presence
Of The Lord** (live)
RSO 2090104 relased April 1973

ERIC CLAPTON
CROSSROADS

ALBUMS

Layla And Other Assorted Love Songs
Polydor 2625005 released December 1970
Available on CD as original as well as a special 20th
Anniversary edition box set containing three CDs
with various jams and unreleased out-takes.

In Concert
RSO 2659020 released March 1973
Available on CD

Eric Clapton And His Band

SINGLES

I Shot The Sheriff/Give Me Strength
RSO 2090132 released July 1974

Willie And The Hand Jive/Mainline Florida
RSO 2090139 released October 1974 in limited
edition picture sleeve with instructions on how to
do the hand jive!

Swing Low Sweet Chariot/Pretty Blue Eyes
RSO 2090158 released May 1975

Knockin' On Heaven's Door/Someone Like You
RSO 2090166 released August 1975

Hello Old Friend/All Our Pastimes
RSO 2090208 released October 1976

Carnival/Hungry
RSO 2090222 released February 1977

Lay Down Sally/Cocaine
RSO 2090264 released November 1977

Wonderful Tonight/Peaches And Diesel
RSO 2090275 released March 1978

Promises/Watch Out For Lucy
RSO 21 released October 1978

If I Don't Be There By Morning/Tulsa Time
RSO 24 released March 1979 in picture sleeve

I Can't Stand It/Black Rose
RSO 74 released February 1981

Another Ticket/Rita Mae
RSO 75 released April 1981 in picture sleeve

Layla/Wonderful Tonight (live)
RSO 87 released February 1982 in picture sleeve
RSOX 87 12in released February 1982

I Shot The Sheriff/Cocaine
RSO 88 released May 1982 in picture sleeve
RSOX 88 released May 1982 with bonus live version

of **Knockin' On Heaven's Door** from the December
1979 Budokan shows in Japan

I've Got A Rock And Roll Heart/Man In Love
Duck W9780 released January 1983 in picture
sleeve
Duck W9780T 12in with bonus **Everybody Oughta
Make A Change**

The Shape You're In/Crosscut Saw
Duck W9701 released April 1983 in picture sleeve
Duck W9701T 12in with bonus **Pretty Girl**
Duck W9701P picture disc

Slow Down Linda/Crazy Country Hop
Duck W9651 released May 1983 in picture sleeve
Duck W9651T 12in with bonus live version of **The
Shape You're In** was planned but withdrawn before
release

Wonderful Tonight/Cocaine
RSO 98 released April 1984 in picture sleeve

You Don't Know Like I Know/Knock On Wood
Duck 7-29113 released November 1984 in Australia
only

Edge of Darkness/Shoot Out
BBC RESL178 released January 1985

Forever Man/Too Bad
Duck W9069 released March 1985
Duck W9069T 12in with bonus **Something's
Happening**

She's Waiting/Jailbait
Duck W8954 released June 1985

Behind The Mask/Grand Illusion
Duck W8461 released January 1987
Duck W8461T 12in with bonus **Wanna Make Love
To You**
Duck W8461F 7in double pack with bonus live
versions of **Crossroads** and **White Room** from 15
July 1986 NEC show

It's In The Way That You Use It/Bad Influence
Duck W8397 released March 1987
Duck W8397T 12in with bonus **Same Old Blues** and
Pretty Girl

Tearing Us Apart/Hold On
Duck W8299 released June 1987
Duck W8299T 12in with bonus live version of **Run**
from 15 July 1986 NEC show

Wonderful Tonight/Layla
Polydor POSP881 released August 1987
Polydor POSPX881 12in with bonus **I Shot The**

Sheriff and a live version of **Wonderful Tonight** from the Budokan 1979 show
Polydor POCD881 CD single with bonus **I Shot The Sheriff** and **Swing Low Sweet Chariot**

Holy Mother/Tangled In Love
Duck W8141 released November 1987
Duck W8141T 12in with bonus **Forever Man** and **Behind The Mask**

After Midnight (1988 re-recorded version)**/I Can't Stand It**
Polydor PO8 released July 1988
Polydor PZ8 12in with bonus **Whatcha Gonna Do**
Polydor PZCD8 CD single with bonus **Whatcha Gonna Do** and an unreleased live version of **Sunshine Of Your Love** by Cream from 7 March 1968 at San Francisco's Winterland

Bad Love/Before You Accuse Me
Duck W2644 released November 1989
Duck W2644T 12in with bonus live versions of **Badge** and **Let It Rain** from 15 July 1986 NEC show
Duck W2644CD CD single with same bonus tracks as 12in
Duck W2644B box set single with exclusive live version of **I Shot The Sheriff** from 15 July 1986 NEC show and a family tree

No Alibis/Running On Faith
Duck W9981 released March 1990
Duck W9981T 12in with bonus live version of **Behind The Mask** from 15 July 1986 NEC show
Duck W9981CD CD single with same bonus tracks as 12in
Duck W9981B box set single with guitar badge and photos

Pretending/Hard Times
Duck W9970 released May 1990
Duck W9970T 12in with bonus **Knock On Wood**
Duck W9970CD CD single with bonus **Behind The Sun**

Wonderful Tonight (live)**/Edge of Darkness** (live)
Duck W0069 released October 1991
Duck W0069CD CD single with bonus live version of **Layla Intro** and **Cocaine** from the big band Royal Albert Hall 1991 shows
Duck W0069CDX special limited collectors' CD single containing two exclusive live versions of **I Shot The Sheriff** and **No Alibis** from the big band Royal Albert Hall 1991 shows

Tears In Heaven/White Room (live)
Duck W0081 released January 1992
Duck W0081T 12in with bonus **Tracks And Lines** and live version of **Bad Love**
Duck W0081CD CD single with same bonus tracks as 12in

Layla (live)**/Tears In Heaven** (live)
Duck W0134 released September 1992
Available on CD with MTV interview

ALBUMS

461 Ocean Boulevard
RSO 2479118 released August 1974
Available on CD

There's One In Every Crowd
RSO 2479132 released April 1975
Available on CD

EC Was Here
RSO 2394160 released August 1975
Available on CD with bonus full version of **Driftin' Blues**

No Reason To Cry
RSO 2394160 released August 1976
Available on CD with bonus track **Last Night**

Slowhand
RSO 2479201 released November 1977
Available on CD

Backless
RSO 2479221 released November 1978
Available on CD with bonus full version of **Early In The Morning**

Just One Night
RSO 2479240 released May 1980
Available on CD

Another Ticket
RSO 2479285 released February 1981
Available on CD

Time Pieces – Best of Eric Clapton
RSO RSD5010 released March 1982
Available on CD

Money And Cigarettes
Duck W3773 released February 1983
Available on CD

Time Pieces Volume 2 – Live In The Seventies
RSO RSD5022 released May 1983
Available on CD

Behind The Sun
Duck W925166-1 released March 1985
Available on CD

Edge Of Darkness
BBC 12RSL178 released November 1985
Available on CD

August
Duck WX71 released October 1986
Available on CD with bonus **Grand Illusion**

Lethal Weapon Soundtrack
Warner released 1987

The Cream of Eric Clapton
Polydor ECTV1 released September 1987
Available on CD

Crossroads
Polydor ROAD1 released April 1988
Available on CD

Homeboy Soundtrack
Virgin released November 1988
Available on CD

Lethal Weapon 2 Soundtrack
Warner released September 1988
Available on CD

Journeyman
Duck WX322 released November 1989
Available on CD

24 Nights
Duck WX373 released December 1991
Available on CD
Also available in a limited edition box featuring the double CD set with bonus tracks **No Alibis, I Shot The Sheriff** and **Layla Introduction**. Also contained in this set is a scrapbook including drawings by Peter Blake as well as rare back-stage photographs with items of memorabilia pasted in by hand, a commentary written by Derek Taylor, a printed envelope containing copies of Eric's guitar picks, a button badge, a laminated back-stage pass and a guitar string. All this is available in a hand-made buckram solander box with gilt tooling and the book is autographed by Eric and Peter Blake. A must for dedicated fans and anybody who enjoys beautiful books. Available from Genesis Publications in Guildford, Surrey.

Rush Soundtrack
Duck released January 1992
Available on CD

Lethal Weapon 3
Warner released June 1992
Available on CD

Unplugged
Duck WX480 released August 1992
Available on CD

ERIC CLAPTON — GUEST SESSIONS

Ashton Gardner And Dyke

ALBUM
The Worst Of A, G And D
EMI released February 1971

John Astley

ALBUM
Everyone Loves The Pilot
Atlantic released June 1987
Available on CD

The Band

ALBUM
The Last Waltz
Warner released April 1978
Available on CD

The Beatles (White Album)

ALBUM
The Beatles
Apple released November 1968
Available on CD

Marc Benno

ALBUM
Lost In Austin
A&M released June 1979
Available on CD (Japan only)

Chuck Berry

ALBUM
Hail Hail Rock 'N' Roll
MCA released October 1987
Available on CD

Stephen Bishop

ALBUMS
Careless
ABC released December 1976
Available on CD (Japan only)

Red Cab To Manhattan
Warner released October 1980
Available on CD (Japan only)

Bowling In Paris
Atlantic released September 1989
Available on CD

Leona Boyd

ALBUM
Persona
CBS released August 1986
Available on CD

Paul Brady

ALBUM
Back To The Centre
Mercury released March 1986
Available on CD

Gary Brooker

SINGLES
Leave The Candle/Chasing The Chop
Chrysalis released April 1981

A side **Home Lovin'**
Eric does not play on B side; Mercury
released March 1981

ALBUMS
Lead Me To The Water
Mercury released March 1982
Available on CD

Echoes In The Night
Mercury released September 1985
Available on CD

Jack Bruce

ALBUM
Willpower
Polygram released January 1989
Available on CD

Buckwheat Zydeco

ALBUM
Taking It Home
Island released August 1988
Available on CD

The Bunburys

SINGLE
Fight
Arista released January 1988

ALBUM
Bunbury Tails
Polydor released October 1992
Available on CD

Jim Capaldi

ALBUM
Some Come Running
Island released December 1988
Available on CD

Joe Cocker

ALBUM
Stingray
A&M released June 1976
Available on CD

Phil Collins

ALBUMS
Face Value
Virgin released February 1981
Available on CD

But Seriously
Virgin released November 1989
Available on CD

The Crickets

ALBUM
Rockin' 50's Rock 'N' Roll
CBS released February 1971

Brendan Croker

ALBUM
Brendan Crocker And The Five O'Clock Shadows
Silvertone released December 1989
Available on CD

King Curtis

SINGLE
Teasin'
Atlantic released July 1970
Available on **History of Eric Clapton** CD (Japan only)

Roger Daltrey

ALBUM
One Of The Boys
Polydor released May 1977

Rick Danko

ALBUM
Rick Danko
Arista released January 1978
Available on CD

Jesse Ed Davis

ALBUM
Jesse Davis
Atlantic released April 1971
Available on CD (Japan and Germany only)

James Luther Dickinson

ALBUM
Dixie Fried
Atlantic released February 1972

Dr John

ALBUMS
Sun Moon And Herbs
Atlantic released November 1971
Available on CD (Japan only)

Hollywood Be Thy Name
United Artists released December 1975
Available on CD

Gail Anne Dorsey

ALBUM
The Corporate World
WEA released October 1988
Available on CD

Danny Douma

ALBUM
Night Eyes
Warner released August 1979

Lamont Dozier

ALBUM
Inside Seduction
Atlantic released August 1991
Available on CD

Champion Jack Dupree

ALBUM
From New Orleans To Chicago
Decca released April 1966
Available on CD

Bob Dylan

ALBUMS
Desire
CBS released December 1975
Available on CD

Hearts Of Fire
CBS released October 1987
Available on CD

Down In The Groove
CBS released June 1988
Available on CD

Aretha Franklin

ALBUM
Lady Soul
Atlantic released March 1968
Available on CD

Kinky Friedman

ALBUM
Lasso From El Paso
Epic released November 1976

Bob Geldof

SINGLE
A side **Love Like A Rocket**
Eric does not play on B side; Mercury

ALBUM
Deep In The Heart Of Nowhere
Mercury released November 1986
Available on CD

Buddy Guy

ALBUM
Damn Right I've Got The Blues
Silvertone released July 1991
Available on CD

Buddy Guy And Junior Wells

ALBUM
Play The Blues
Atlantic released July 1971
Available on CD

George Harrison

ALBUMS
Wonderwall Music
Apple released November 1968
Available on CD

All Things Must Pass
Apple released November 1970
Available on CD

The Concert For Bangladesh
Apple released January 1972
Available on CD

George Harrison
Dark Horse released February 1979
Available on CD

Cloud Nine
Dark Horse released November 1987
Available on CD
Live In Japan released August 1992
Available on CD

Corey Hart

ALBUM
First Offence
EMI released June 1984
Available on CD

Howlin' Wolf

ALBUMS
The London Howlin' Wolf Sessions
Rolling Stones Records released August 1971
Available on CD

London Revisited
Chess released October 1974 (USA only)

Elton John

ALBUM
The One
Rocket released June 1992
Available on CD

Johnnie Johnson

ALBUM
Johnnie B Bad
Elektra released September 1991
Available on CD

Michael Kamen

ALBUM
Concerto For Saxophone And Orchestra
Warner released September 1990
Available on CD

Jonathan Kelly

SINGLE
Don't You Believe It
Parlophone released June 1970

Bobby Keys

ALBUM
Bobby Keys
Warner released July 1972

Carole King

ALBUM
City Streets
Capitol released April 1988
Available on CD

Freddie King

ALBUMS
Burglar
RSO released November 1974
Available on CD

1934–1976
RSO released October 1977
Available on CD

Alexis Korner

ALBUM
The Party Album
Interchord released March 1980 (Germany only)
Available on CD (Castle Communications)

Corky Laing

ALBUM
Makin' It On The Street
Elektra released May 1977

Ronnie Lane

ALBUM
See Me
RCA released July 1980

Ronnie Lane and Pete Townshend

ALBUM
Rough Mix
Polydor released September 1977
Available on CD

Cyndi Lauper

ALBUM
A Night To Remember
CBS released November 1989
Available on CD

Jackie Lomax

SINGLES
Sour Milk Sea/The Eagle Laughs At You
released February 1969; Apple
Available on **Is This What You Want?** CD

A side **New Day**
Eric does not play on B side; Apple
released May 1969
Available on **Is This What You Want?** CD

ALBUM
Is This What You Want?
Apple released March 1969
Available on CD

Arthur Louis

SINGLES
Knockin' On Heaven's Door/Plum
Plum released August 1975

Knockin' On Heaven's Door/The Dealer
Island released June 1978

Still It Feels Good/Come On And Love Me
Mainstreet released July 1981

ALBUMS
First Album
Polydor released August 1975 (Japan only)

Knockin' On Heaven's Door
PRT released July 1988
Available on CD

John Martyn

ALBUM
Glorious Fool
WEA released October 1981

Christine McVie

ALBUM
Christine McVie
Warner released January 1984
Available on CD (Japan only)

Yoko Ono

ALBUM
Fly
Apple released December 1971

Eric Clapton with Jimmy Page and various artists

ALBUM
Blues Anytime Vols 1,2,3,4
Immediate released December 1967
Available on CD

Shawn Phillips

ALBUM
Contribution
A&M released January 1970

The Powerhouse

ALBUM
What's Shakin'
Elektra released June 1966

Billy Preston

SINGLE
That's The Way God Planned It Parts 1 and 2
Apple released August 1969

ALBUMS
That's The Way God Planned It
Apple released June 1969
Available on CD

Encouraging Words
Apple released September 1970
Available on CD

Lionel Richie

ALBUM
Dancing On The Ceiling
Motown released August 1986
Available on CD

The Rolling Stones

ALBUM
Flashpoint
Rolling Stones Records released December 1990
Available on CD

Leon Russell

ALBUMS
Leon Russell
A&M released May 1970
Available on CD

Leon Russell And The Shelter People
Shelter released June 1971
Available on CD

Richie Sambora

ALBUM
Stranger In This Town
Phonogram released August 1991
Available on CD

David Sanborn

ALBUM
Upfront
Elektra released March 1992
Available on CD

Otis Spann

SINGLE
B side **Stirs Me Up**
Decca

ALBUM
The Blues Of Otis Spann
Decca released November 1964
Available on CD as **Cracked Spanner Head**

Vivian Stanshall

SINGLE
Labio-Dental Fricative/Paper Round
Liberty released February 1970

Ringo Starr

ALBUM
Rotogravure
Polydor released October 1976

Old Wave
Bellaphon released June 1983 (Germany, Canada and Brazil only)

Stephen Stills

ALBUMS
Stephen Stills
Atlantic released November 1970
Available on CD

Stephen Stills 2
Atlantic released July 1971
Available on CD

Sting

ALBUM
Nothing Like The Sun
A&M released October 1987
Available on CD

Doris Troy

SINGLES
A side **Ain't That Cute**
Eric does not play on B side; Apple
released February 1970

B side **Get Back**
Eric does not play on A side; Apple
released August 1970
Available on **Doris Troy** CD

ALBUM
Doris Troy
Apple released September 1970
Available on CD

Tina Turner

SINGLE
What You See Is What You Get
Capitol 12 in version only released March 1987

ALBUM
Live in Europe
Capitol released March 1988
Available on CD

Martha Velez

ALBUM
Fiends And Angels
London released June 1969
Available on CD

Roger Waters

ALBUM
The Pros and Cons of Hitch-Hiking
Harvest released May 1984
Available on CD

Bobby Whitlock

ALBUM
Bobby Whitlock
CBS released July 1971

Raw Velvet
CBS released December 1972

The Who

ALBUM
Tommy The Movie
RSO released July 1978
Available on CD (Japan only)

Zucchero

ALBUM
Zucchero
London released November 1989
Available on CD

Various Artists

ALBUMS
Anthology of British Blues Vols 1 & 2 (reissue of
'Blues Anytime')
Immediate released November 1968

Music From Free Creek
Charisma released May 1973

White Mansions
A&M released May 1978
Available on CD

Secret Policeman's Other Ball – The Music
Springtime released March 1982
Available on CD

Prince's Trust 10th Birthday Party
A&M released October 1986
Available on CD

Prince's Trust Concert 1987
A&M released August 1987
Available on CD

Prince's Trust Concert 1988
King Biscuit Flower Hour double promo CD
released November 1988 to radio stations in
America

Buster
Virgin released October 1988
Available on CD

Knebworth
Polydor released August 1990
Available on CD

Nobody's Child
Warner released November 1990
Available on CD

Two Rooms
Mercury released October 1991
Available on CD

VIDEOGRAPHY

Farewell Cream (Royal Albert Hall 1968)
Channel 5

Sweet Toronto (Plastic Ono Band live in Toronto 1969)
Parkfield

Supershow (Staines 1969)
Virgin

Superstars in Concert (live Blind Faith footage from Hyde Park 1969)
Telstar video

Concert For Bangladesh (George Harrison's charity concert 1971)
Warner

The Last Waltz (The Band's farewell concert 1976)
Warner

Old Grey Whistle Test (live 1977)
BBC video

Alexis Korner's Eat A Little Rhythm and Blues (Pinewood Studios 1978)
BBC Video

ARMS – The Complete Concert (Royal Albert Hall 1983)
Channel 5

Live 1985 (Hartford, Connecticut 1985)
Channel 5

A Rockabilly Session, Carl Perkins and Friends (Limehouse Studios 1985)
Virgin

Water (Handmade Films)
Eric appears alongside George Harrison and Ringo Starr in Billy Connelly's backing group. However, they do not actually play on the soundtrack.

The Eric Clapton Concert (Birmingham 1986)
Radio Vision

Prince's Trust Birthday (Wembley Arena 1986)
Video Gems

Hail! Hail! Rock 'N' Roll (Chuck Berry's 60th birthday concert 1986)
CIC

B.B. King and Friends (LA 1987)
Video Collection

Prince's Trust Rock Gala 1987 (Wembley Arena 1987)
PMV

Alright Now – Island Records 25th Anniversary (Pinewood 1987)
Island Video

Prince's Trust Rock Gala 1988 (Royal Albert Hall 1988)
Video Collection

Knebworth (June 1990)
Castle Music

Eric Clapton (Knebworth June 1990-unreleased version of Sunshine Of Your Love)
Castle Music

24 Nights (Royal Albert Hall 1990-1991)
Warner

Unplugged (Bray Studios 1991)
Warner

Tommy (Ken Russell's film of Who epic)
RSO

The Cream Of Eric Clapton (Compilation)
Polygram

Eric Clapton – The Man And His Music (History)
Video Collection

Cream-Strange Brew (Retrospective)
Warner

Yardbirds (Retrospective)
Warner

BOOTLEGS

ERIC CLAPTON: *I don't have an issue on this particular one. I can remember one night playing one of the best concerts of my life, looking down in the front row and seeing a guy with a mike taping. I had the choice of calling someone from security and saying, 'Look there's a bootlegger!' but then I thought that it would ruin one of the best concerts I've ever done. The record companies would always be against the situation though, because otherwise musicians couldn't make a living. If bootleggers ruled the world we wouldn't make a living.*

Bootleg recordings have been with us since 1969 when some enterprising folks in America produced an amazing recording of The Rolling Stones in full flight at their Oakland Coliseum show. At first it was harmless – fans producing limited editions for other fans – but soon more unscrupulous types took over, realizing the massive profit potential. Over the years, bootlegs have come and gone, most of poor quality and in cheap packaging.

Bootleg CDs have now taken over from vinyl and generally offer the listener a better quality than before, although it is the minority rather than the majority which do so. Most of these are now produced by Italian companies and the artist actually receives a royalty cheque deposited in their name in an Italian bank! I list below some of the better bootleg CDs of Eric that are available on the Continent at the time of researching this book.

Eric Clapton's Cream (BBC Sessions 1967-1968)

Live Cream Vol. 3 (Oakland Coliseum 1968)

Creamer (Various live US 1968)

Cream and Blind Faith Steppin' Stones (LA 1968 and Gothenburg 1969) double CD

Blind Faith Morgan Rehearsals (Studio rehearsal 1969) double CD

Domino Theory (Fillmore East 1970) double CD

The Unsurpassed Eric Clapton (The Delaney mix of first solo album 1970)

Blues Power (Live in Providence, Rhode Island 1974)

The Legendary LA Forum Show (Los Angeles 1975) double CD

One Night in Dallas (Dallas 1976)

The Night of the Kings (ARMS Royal Albert Hall 1983) double CD

The Blue Sheriff (Bremen 1983)

The Pros and Cons of Hitch-Hiking Performed Live (Birmingham NEC 1984) double CD

Reziprocol Affection (Richmond 1985)

Georgia Blues (Various live 1986–1987)

Same Old Blues (New York 1987) double CD

A Wednesday Night at the Tokyo Dome (Japan 1988) double CD

On Tour (Royal Albert Hall 1987) double CD

Blues Night (Royal Albert Hall 1990) Japanese double CD

Bad Love (Royal Albert Hall 1990) Japanese double CD

London At Night (Royal Albert Hall 1990) double CD

4th Night (Harrison/Clapton Japan 1991) double CD

Blues Night (Royal Albert Hall 1991) double CD

My Blues (*Unplugged* with unreleased acoustic material 1991)

Another Page (Brighton 1992) double CD

Live At The Royal Albert Hall (12 February 1992) double CD

Eric in 1980

INDEX OF SONG TITLES

This index includes the titles of all songs recorded by Eric Clapton as singles or individual tracks of albums. Throughout the index the use of the definite and indefinite articles as the first word of a title has been avoided.

* indicates that a song is included in a medley
** indicates a reprise

INDEX OF SONG TITLES